UNDERSTANDING PARENT BLAME
Institutional Failure and
Complex Trauma

Edited by
Luke Clements and Ana Laura Aiello

First published in Great Britain in 2025 by

Policy Press, an imprint of
Bristol University Press
University of Bristol
1–9 Old Park Hill
Bristol
BS2 8BB
UK
t: +44 (0)117 374 6645
e: bup-info@bristol.ac.uk

Details of international sales and distribution partners are available at policy.bristoluniversitypress.co.uk

© Bristol University Press 2025

British Library Cataloguing in Publication Data
A catalogue record for this book is available from the British Library

ISBN 978-1-4473-7522-7 hardcover
ISBN 978-1-4473-7523-4 paperback
ISBN 978-1-4473-7524-1 ePub
ISBN 978-1-4473-7525-8 ePdf

The right of Luke Clements and Ana Laura Aiello to be identified as editors of this work has been asserted by them in accordance with the Copyright, Designs and Patents Act 1988.

All rights reserved: no part of this publication may be reproduced, stored in a retrieval system, or transmitted in any form or by any means, electronic, mechanical, photocopying, recording, or otherwise without the prior permission of Bristol University Press.

Every reasonable effort has been made to obtain permission to reproduce copyrighted material. If, however, anyone knows of an oversight, please contact the publisher.

The statements and opinions contained within this publication are solely those of the editors and contributors and not of the University of Bristol or Bristol University Press. The University of Bristol and Bristol University Press disclaim responsibility for any injury to persons or property resulting from any material published in this publication.

Bristol University Press and Policy Press work to counter discrimination on grounds of gender, race, disability, age and sexuality.

Cover design: Andrew Corbett
Front cover image: Stocksy/Mahalo Studio

Contents

Notes on contributors		iv
1	Introduction *Luke Clements and Ana Laura Aiello*	1
2	Recurring themes: parent blame and systems-generated trauma *Luke Clements and Ana Laura Aiello*	6
3	Parent blame and complex trauma *Peter Baker, Linda Hume and Vivien Cooper*	25
4	Parent blame in education: working together to find solutions to school attendance difficulties *Louise Parker Engels*	37
5	That woman! *Amy Payne (pseudonym)*	50
6	Fabricated or induced illness: the controversial history, missing evidence base and iatrogenic harm *Andy Bilson, Alessandro Talia, Taliah Drayak, Mary Margaret (pseudonym), Sarah Smith (pseudonym) and Michelle Spence*	76
7	Managing the data: allegations that parents are fabricating or inducing their child's illness *Luke Clements, Ana Laura Aiello and Derek Tilley*	98
8	Child protection and the experiences of autistic parents accused of fabricated or induced illness *Cathleen Long, Rachel Gavin and Esther Whitney*	123
9	A sibling perspective on fabricated or induced illness *Kaydence Drayak*	142
10	Parent blame and the NHS *Amy (pseudonym)*	153
11	Forging an Alliance *Lucy Fullard*	165
12	Conclusions: The way forward *Luke Clements, Ana Laura Aiello, Louise Arnold and Lucy Fullard*	174
Index		186

Notes on contributors

Dr Ana Laura Aiello is the Cerebra Postdoctoral Researcher at the University of Leeds, School of Law. She studied law and human rights in Argentina, Spain and in the UK (obtaining her PhD at Leeds University). She has worked for a number of international NGOs (including Amnesty International, Disability Rights International and CHANGE) and at universities in Argentina, Spain and the UK. She has a sister with learning disabilities and experience of co-working with disabled people in an accessible and inclusive way.

Amy (pseudonym) has a disabled son and an exhaustive experience of navigating the NHS system while advocating for him.

Louise Arnold is a former Director of the Parent and Carer Alliance, one of the most influential Independent Parent Carer Groups in England.

Dr Peter Baker is Senior Lecturer in Intellectual Disability at the Tizard Centre, University of Kent. He worked as a Consultant Clinical Psychologist for the NHS in Sussex for over 20 years, where he had leadership responsibilities for learning disability psychology services in East Sussex and Brighton and Hove. He lectures at the Tizard Centre on the Masters ABA/PBS course and is widely published in the area of challenging behaviour and intellectual disability. He is currently involved in funded research concerning staff support systems and family trauma.

Andy Bilson is Emeritus Professor in the School of Social Work, Care and Community University of Central Lancashire, adjunct Professor at the University of Western Australia and visiting researcher at the University of Cambridge. Andy has written highly influential papers in this field, including 'Referrals and child protection in England: one in five children referred to children's services and one in nineteen investigated before the age of five' (2016) *The British Journal of Social Work*, 47(3): 793-811.

Luke Clements is the Cerebra Professor of Law and Social Justice at the University of Leeds, School of Law.

Vivien Cooper OBE is the parent of a young man with severe learning disabilities and Founder and CEO of the Challenging Behaviour Foundation.

Kaydence Drayak is a young adult whose sister was temporarily removed from her parents due to a false FII accusation. She is an inspiring advocate, who formerly served as a Member of the Scottish Youth Parliament for Orkney. She has also worked as a peer researcher for the End Child Poverty Coalition and Youth Voices.

Taliah Drayak is a carer and experienced mother of eight children. She has also been the subject of an FII investigation and suffered the temporary removal of one of her daughters. She works as an author and volunteers with several charities focused on families and children. She is passionate that children's rights are of utmost importance, and that every child deserves not only to have equality, but also to be enabled to achieve their dreams.

Louise Parker Engels co-founded Define Fine, a team of professionals and parents with lived experience of school attendance difficulties. They are unique as a school attendance support-focused organisation, as in addition to their online group parent peer support, they offer direct one-to-one support and case management (free) to parent carers. They are a 'not for profit' and work alongside other charitable organisations across SEND and mental health who share their values and ethos. They also provide CPD training to local authorities and health and education professionals. Their training fees for this work, as well as grants and donations, fund their peer support.

Lucy Fullard is a Director of the Parent and Carer Alliance, one of the most influential Independent Parent Carer Groups in England. The Parent and Carer Alliance offers independent practical and emotional support for parents and carers. They have created a welcoming and safe community of families and are a source of reliable, factual, information from both national and local sources, as well as provide peer support. They inform and empower families through training and social events. They gather the lived experiences of families about their difficulties and use this information to lobby all relevant parties, to ensure that positive changes are made.

Rachel Gavin is an independent social worker working with neurodivergent children, young people and adults. Rachel is an expert witness and provides specialist assessments and reports for adults and children with complex needs for Special Educational Needs and Disability Tribunals, Judicial Review and the Court of Protection and Family Court. Rachel and her two colleagues have been recognised for the British Association of Social Workers (BASW) 'Amazing Social Worker 2022' award and the Social Care Wales Leadership and Management award 2023.

Linda Hume is a registered nurse (learning disability) and is Co-production and Engagement Lead at the Challenging Behaviour Foundation.

Cathleen Long is an independent social worker who regularly gives expert evidence in High Court proceedings. She is the lead author of (among other things) the 2022 *Practice Guidance for Social Workers on Fabricated or Induced Illness (FII) and Other Perplexing Presentations*, published by the British Association of Social Work and Social Workers.

Mary Margaret (pseudonym) is the parent of a disabled child.

Amy Payne (pseudonym) is a mum whose daughter was the victim of peer-on-peer abuse and the trauma was then compounded by the failure of the school and the Education Authority to put in place appropriate safeguarding policies, which resulted in High Court proceedings and ongoing inaction/blaming by the authority. See resulting #MeTooSchoolUK website at https://www.metooschool.org.uk/.

Sarah Smith (pseudonym) is the parent of a disabled child. She has experience of misidentification of FII and endured the harm that false allegations of this kind can bring.

Michelle Spence (pseudonym) is the parent of a disabled child and has been accused of FII.

Alessandro Talia is a Wellcome Research Associate at the Department of Public Health and Primary Care of the University of Cambridge. He conducts research on mental health in adults and young people with social work involvement.

Derek Tilley is Senior Development Officer within Cerebra's Legal Rights team. He has had a long interest in supporting parents with disabled children access their legal entitlements.

Esther Whitney is an autistic mother, and an award-winning artist, who endured a prolonged and extremely challenging Family Court battle, to secure the return of her baby, after she was received into the care of the local authority when she was just seven weeks old.

1

Introduction

Luke Clements and Ana Laura Aiello

As parents, we know that 'parenting and blame' are fellow travellers: we are accustomed to blame ourselves, and our children – for good measure – are wont to blame us too. This is part and parcel of family life and is not the focus of this work.

What has driven every contributor to this book is their deep concern for what happens when state institutions develop policies and foster practices that, by default, blame parents too. This book challenges the incremental normalisation of behaviours of this kind. It seeks to identify how such practices have developed and to convey the devastating impact that they have on families.

A primary responsibility of any state is to support family life. It is a fundamental promise states have made on numerous occasions to numerous bodies: a promise to show respect for the private and family lives of all their citizens. In the case of the UK, it is an international promise made on 8 March 1951 when it ratified the European Convention on Human Rights and one that was embedded into domestic law on 2 October 2000, when the Human Rights Act 1998 came into force.

In the context of this book, parent blame arises in situations where there is a failure by a public body to provide a level of support that a responsive state should provide for a child (and/or their family) and the default organisational response of the public body is to blame the child's parents for this failure.

The majority of the contributions to this book relate to the experiences of families with disabled children, and in relation to which the phrase 'parent carer blame' is used.

Parent blame is not a new phenomenon, but media references to 'parent blame' appear to be increasing significantly – essentially as a term used by parents to describe their encounters with social welfare agencies. The phenomenon occurs in relation to a spectrum of support failures by public bodies: in terms of failing to provide adequate social care support for disabled children; in terms of failing to provide appropriate education for children who are 'not fine' in their school; in terms of the organisational responses of healthcare providers, where parents consider a diagnosis or treatment plan inappropriate; in situations where there is a failure to provide adequate measures to protect a child from abuse in public settings – and in many other contexts.

This book aims to explore the nature and causes of this phenomenon, and its prevalence, impact and potential pathways for reform. Research suggests that in the last two decades, there has been a significant increase in conflict between families and social welfare institutions. These conflicts often involve practitioners directly blaming parents for their child's difficulties: accusations that cause significant distress/trauma to families. Many of the book's contributors seek to analyse the reasons for this increasing conflict and to better understand why the resulting harm experienced by families is, so often, disregarded. This book is, therefore, of particular relevance to public policy debates concerning 'families': their support needs, their precarity and the increasing extent to which states are intervening in their 'private and family lives'.

This edited collection contains contributions from parents and young people who have experienced the trauma of being caught up in the process of blame. In addition, there are contributions from key researchers as well as practitioners/activists who have written on this issue. All the chapters are either written by family members who have experienced the direct consequences of parent blame or by authors who work closely with such families and seek to ensure that their voices are heard in everything that they publish.

The grouping and sequencing of the substantive chapters in this book is primarily determined by the social welfare agency responsible for the parent blame: from social care, to education and then healthcare – and concluding with a chapter concerning the challenges encountered by a parent carer in developing an independent support group.

Brief summaries of the book's chapters are as follows:

Chapter 2 ('Recurring themes: parent blame and systems-generated trauma', by Luke Clements and Ana Laura Aiello) establishes the context of parent carer blame. It draws on research that sought to establish the causes, prevalence and impact of parent carer blame practices in English Children's Services departments.

Chapter 3 ('Parent blame and complex trauma', by Peter Baker, Linda Hume and Vivien Cooper) draws on qualitative research that explored the personal experience of families with relatives who have an intellectual disability requiring support and services from 'the system'. The research identified (among much else) the harm that resulted from their 'encounters with the system': the legal duties not being met; the parents being left unsupported; and the families losing trust due to a history of being overpromised. The chapter concludes with a consideration as to what can be done to change the system.

Chapter 4 ('Parent blame in education: working together to find solutions to school attendance difficulties', by Louise Parker Engels) showcases the work developed by the organisation Define Fine to support parent carers whose children and/or young people are facing school attendance difficulties. It identifies the essential need for multi-agency understanding, proper guidance and training – and for practitioners to be curious, kind and supportive in any effective programme to address school non-attendance concerns.

Chapter 5 ('That woman!', by Amy Payne) describes what happened when a mother reached out to local and national government to ensure that other children would not suffer the same human rights breaches endured by her daughter in the wake of being raped by a student at her school. The response of the authorities revealed a deep antipathy to the mother for correctly identifying systemic risks to children and an apparent indifference to breaches of the Human Rights Act 1998.

Chapter 6 ('Fabricated or induced illness: the controversial history, missing evidence base and iatrogenic harm', by Andy Bilson, Alessandro Talia, Taliah Drayak, Mary Margaret, Sarah Smith and Michelle Spence) is co-produced with parents who were wrongly identified as having fabricated or induced illness (FII). It provides a brief history of the development of FII through to its current form in 2021 guidance. It shows how the definition has widened, increasing the risk of misidentification and how earlier cautionary warnings concerning the harm caused by misidentification have been abandoned. It describes a literature search that has highlighted the lack of evidence for the concept and the harm caused by misidentification. Finally, it demonstrates how the flawed approach to the identification of FII results in serious harm to children who have rare, undiagnosed or hard-to-diagnose illnesses and to their families.

Chapter 7 ('Managing the data: allegations that parents are fabricating or inducing their child's illness', by Luke Clements, Ana Laura Aiello and Derek Tilley) addresses a specific concern of parents whose health and social care records continue to flag up the fact that they had been suspected of FII, even when allegations of this kind have been shown to be unsubstantiated. The chapter describes the difficulties that families have in getting such data erased from health and social care records and the harm that this causes. It analyses the underpinning statutory provisions, critiques the relevant guidance published by the Information Commissioner's Office and NHS England and identifies flaws within the health and social care data management systems: systems that can trigger inappropriate and distressing safeguarding alerts.

Chapter 8 ('Child protection and the experiences of autistic parents accused of fabricated or induced illness', by Cathleen Long, Rachel Gavin and

Esther Whitney) considers the high proportion of autistic parents in the UK who are being accused of FII and how decisions taken by children's services authorities to remove their children are often taken without a thorough, evidence-based evaluation of the 'bigger picture'. The authors analyse how autistic parents, particularly mothers, experience significant discrimination and injustice as a result of their words and actions being misattributed as alerting signs for FII. Using case examples and professional insights, they demonstrate how the current system, unintentionally, creates significant trauma for autistic children and autistic parents due to a lack of understanding of their lived experiences and differences.

Chapter 9 ('A sibling perspective on fabricated or induced illness', by Kaydence Drayak) offers a rare insight from the perspective of a sibling whose family was the subject of a traumatising FII investigation. It describes how siblings are, all too frequently, the 'unacknowledged collateral damage' that results from child protection interventions, and how they can feel totally invisible in the process: how their needs and insights – and their feelings of uncertainty, fear, pain and isolation – can be ignored. It details the damage that results from ill-judged interventions, how siblings' trust of professionals can be irreparably damaged and how their own sense of identity/world view is impacted.

Chapter 10 ('Parent blame and the NHS', by Amy) provides a personal insight into one mother's experience of parental blame both within the context of (and as a result of) having challenged health professionals regarding failings of care for her son. It highlights the multi-layered processes involved in parental advocacy when things go wrong, and the precarious position that parents can find themselves in when navigating systems that are fundamentally set up to deflect and deny professional accountability. The chapter describes what it feels like to experience parental blame and the overall implications this has had for the author. It concludes by reflecting on what needs to change to prevent 'parent blaming' and hence, the damaging consequences attributed to it.

Chapter 11 ('Forging an Alliance', by Lucy Fullard) describes the evolution of the Parent and Carer Alliance (an organisation supporting parent carers). It describes how a personal experience provided the impetus for the creation of the Alliance: a traumatic experience characterised by a misdiagnosis of a disabled child's complex needs and parent blaming. It charts the many challenges that the Alliance has encountered and reflects on the crucial elements which have led to its growth (it now has 1,500 members). In this context, it gives particular emphasis to the importance of independence: of not having local authority funding and in consequence, of being able to challenge those in power without fear or favour.

Chapter 12 ('Conclusions: The way forward' by Luke Clements, Ana Laura Aiello, Louise Arnold and Lucy Fullard) summarises the key themes that have emerged from the substantive chapters of this edited work and points to the actions that need to be taken to change the culture and the practices that foster parent blame.

2

Recurring themes: parent blame and systems-generated trauma

Luke Clements and Ana Laura Aiello

> … child protection must be 'risk sensible'. There is no option of being risk averse since there is no absolutely safe option. In reality, risk averse practice usually entails displacing the risk onto someone else. Even if every child who was considered or suspected to be suffering harm was removed from their birth family, that would only incur different risks.
> The Munro Review, 2011, para 3.18

> … we have to make sure, if there is any evidence, any inkling, any iota of harm to any child, that the child is taken away immediately.
> Nadhim Zahawi, Parliamentary debate, December 2021

Introduction

This chapter reflects on research we have undertaken concerning the nature and consequences of 'parent carer blame' (Clements and Aiello, 2021) – referred to in this chapter as the '2021 research'. As we note in Chapter 1, parent carer blame arises in situations where there is a failure by a public body to provide a level of support that a responsive state should provide for a disabled child (and/or their family) and the default organisational response of the public body is to blame the child's parents for this failure.

The 2021 research is socio-legal in nature and part of a wider programme – the Legal Entitlements & Problem-Solving (LEaP) project. The programme is funded by the disabled children's research charity Cerebra and involves a close collaboration between the School of Law at the University of Leeds and the charity's in-house research team. The team listens to families and helps them get the knowledge they need to access health and social care, and other support services. Through this continuous contact with families, the LEaP project is able to identify common legal problems that prevent them from gaining access to care and support services. The purpose of the research is to develop innovative ways of resolving such problems at 'root' – so that (ideally) they cease to be encountered by individual families.

Throughout the research programme, we have continued to receive reports from families concerning their negative interactions with children's services authorities. Not untypically, these come from parents who have approached their local authority for help in order to address the additional barriers they encounter as a result of their child's impairment – only to find that (from the outset) they are treated in a manner that suggests to them that they are considered to be neglectful and/or abusive parents. These are interactions that convey the strong impression that the default position for children's services departments in such cases is to locate the problems families face in parental failings and not in the lack of support that they should provide to these families.

Many of these families described their interactions with children's services as humiliating, intimidating and, indeed, traumatising. For such families, the 'assessment' process was commonly experienced as the most unpleasant, with social workers working to an inflexible script: one that, for example, required them to inspect the children's bedrooms and required them to speak to the child alone – an assessment process that has been described as 'a technocratic, adversarial mode of working' (Hood et al, 2020, p 100).

Legal background and context

Until 5 July 1948, disability was, in the UK, seen as a family affair. The Poor Relief Act of 1601 had survived for almost 350 years and with it an obligation that family members 'relieve and maintain' their poor relations 'upon pain that every one of them shall forfeit twenty shillings for every month which they shall fail therein'.

The post-World War II Beveridgean reforms abolished the Poor Law (National Assistance Act 1948, section 1) and shifted legal responsibility for the provision of care and support for disabled people to the state. But, of course, cultural perceptions and discrimination endure. The giving of Royal Assent to an Act may take seconds, but it takes a great deal longer to reverse the normalising impact of three-and-a-half centuries of state sanctions.

For all its radicalism, the 1948 Act retained a medical focus: that disabled people were 'handicapped' by virtue of their impairment (section 29(1)) – a phrasing that persists to this day in relation to disabled children (Children Act 1989, section 17(10)). Michael Oliver's landmark critique of this model had not been published (Oliver, 1983) and, in 1948, the idea that disabled people (and by association, unpaid carers) should be protected from adverse discrimination (or were indeed 'rights holders') was not in the consciousness of social policy activists – let alone in the consciousness of the legislature or the general public.

The relevant provisions of the 1948 Act secured the rights of disabled people to social care support services from the cradle to the grave. A separate (and equally ground-breaking) Act – the Children Act 1948 – addressed the support needs of children 'deprived of normal home life with their own parents': in current terminology, 'looked after children' (Lynch, 2019).

The next 25 years saw a strengthening of the social care rights of disabled people (children and adults alike) – principally via the Chronically Sick and Disabled Persons Act 1970 and, in parallel, a strengthening of the obligations on local authorities to promote the welfare of children by diminishing their need to be taken into care – principally via the Children and Young Persons Act 1963. It was a period that has been described as the 'high water' mark of family support' (Clapton, 2020, p 92).

1973

On 7 January 1973, a seven-year-old, Maria Colwell, was murdered by her step-father: a killing that resulted in a much-publicised public inquiry (Secretary of State for Social Services, T.G. Field-Fisher, 1974) and a fundamental refocusing of the role of children's social workers. As Parton notes, it was decided that they required 'new skills, new forms of intervention, and new organisational arrangements' to deal with this 'newly discovered problem' of child abuse (Parton, 2006, p 20). Parton (citing Melton, 2005, p 11) argues that the ensuing reforms failed because they sought to apply a simple linear solution to what was a highly complex problem. Instead of understanding the entangled complexity of the system and the causes of abuse, the reforms assumed that all abusive and neglectful parents fell into one of two 'syndromes' – that they were 'either very sick or very evil'.

One of the recurring 'drivers' that has led to today's effective institutionalisation of parent blame policies has been the state's determination to see childcare as a simple linear system to which such simple (generally binary) conceptualisations are then applied.

1973 was a watershed year, not because such homicides and public inquiries had not occurred before this time, but because of the level of media coverage that attended the Maria Colwell Inquiry and almost every child homicide since that time. Parton describes this as a perpetual 'sense of crisis period' (Parton, 2006, p 28) and Clapton as a period of 'Tragedies and Panic' (2020, p 83), where the names of the murdered children became seared in our collective memories: of Jasmine Beckford, Kimberley Carlile, Victoria Climbié, Peter Connolly, Tyra Henry, Arthur Labinjo-Hughes, Daniel Pelka, Sara Sharif and many more. During this period, there were also severe examples of over-reach by social services (for example, in Cleveland and Orkney (Butler-Sloss, 1987; Clyde, 1992)), but on the backdrop to almost every subsequent legislative/policy intervention have been 'illustrations of parental inhumanity' (Behlmer, 1982, p 2) 'parent-blaming' (Clapton, 2020, p 79) and 'child rescue'/'child saving' (from their parents) (Morris et al, 2013; Parton, 2006, p 90).

The net effect of this has been likened to a risk-averse (Munro, 2011, para 3.18) moral panic (Clapton et al, 2012), where the system and the wider public fail to acknowledge the uncertainty and risk that inevitably surrounds child protection (Munro, 2011, para 3.17). The evidence for this is seen in the substantial increase in the numbers of families being investigated by children's services. By 2016, for example, it was estimated that 20 per cent of five-year-olds had been referred to children's services (Bilson and Martin, 2017) and despite the number of referrals remaining constant between 2005 and 2023, the number of children being investigated by children's services more than tripled (Bilson, 2024).

For all the sound and fury of 50 years of resolute state action to address the problem of child abuse, it appears that there has been little substantive impact. A 2012 study (Gilbert et al, 2012) across six countries, including the UK, concluded that there was 'no clear evidence for an overall decrease in child maltreatment despite decades of policies designed to achieve such reductions'. In relation to child homicides (where the parent/step-parent is the suspected perpetrator), these remain very rare (17 in 2023) (ONS, 2023). In 2015, Jütte et al (using police homicide statistics and death certificate data) suggested that the numbers of children dying as a result of homicide or assault were 'in long-term decline', although it appears that the data on child deaths due to deliberately inflicted injuries varies according to its source. Bilson and Munro (2019, p 205) argue that the Child Death Overview Panels data is likely to be a more accurate indicator of the deaths in child protection cases and that this source suggests that 'despite the continued rise in investigations, the number of child deaths recorded ... have changed little since 2010'.

The Children Act 1989

In 1989, the Children Bill, hailed as 'the most comprehensive and far reaching reform of child law ... in living memory' (Mackay, 1988), received Royal Assent. The Bill was subjected to only limited scrutiny (Masson, 1992) not least (and controversially) that it was intended to incorporate the 1948 National Assistance Act's social care obligations to disabled children and, in consequence, that the 1948 Act be amended to apply only to adults (Clements, 2008).

The 1989 Act described the state's child protection and social care duties as owed to 'children in need'. The actual phrasing of section 17(10) is as follows:

For the purposes of this Part a child shall be taken to be in need if—

(a) he is unlikely to achieve or maintain, or to have the opportunity of achieving or maintaining, a reasonable standard of health or development without the provision for him of services by a local authority under this Part;

(b) his health or development is likely to be significantly impaired, or further impaired, without the provision for him of such services; or

(c) he is disabled, and 'family', in relation to such a child, includes any person who has parental responsibility for the child and any other person with whom he has been living.

In effect, the subsection lumps into one definition two very different groups of children: children whose needs arise because of the social barriers they experience by virtue of their impairment and children who are in need because they are considered to be at risk of neglect or abuse due to parental failings. The data on 'child in need' assessments bear this out. In 2024, for example, only 8 per cent of child in need assessments were undertaken because the child was 'disabled', whereas 87 per cent of assessments concerned children suspected of (or actually experiencing) abuse or neglect or acute stress family/dysfunction, or where parents were absent (Department for Education, 2024a).

The 1989 Act adopted the 1948 Act's medical model definition of disability and this, allied to its 'parental responsibility' responsibilisation agenda (Eekelaar, 1991, p 37), obliquely challenged the notion that disability was a complex social phenomenon, for which the state bore responsibility rather than the individual or their family. Of course, today, in glossy, graphics-heavy policy documents, local authorities and the government affirm their commitment to the social model of disability – but virtue-signalling of this kind tends not make it to the coal face where individual assessments and eligibility determinations are hammered out.

The negative consequences of placing 'disabled children' and children at risk of abuse into the same category of 'children in need' were unintended – but with the benefit of hindsight, they should have been obvious. Given the political and local departmental anxieties about adverse publicity in child homicide cases, it was inevitable that when it came to the allocation of scarce resources, children at risk of abuse would be prioritised over disabled children. In practice, that is precisely what has occurred: that the vast majority of disabled children and their families find themselves ineligible for support of any significance, until such time as they fall (or are perceived as being at severe risk of falling) into the child protection regime (Clements and Thompson, 2007, para 2.36).

In the early years of the Children Act 1989, an attempt was made by central government to distinguish between the process that front-line professionals should follow when assessing the needs of a disabled child as opposed to those considered to be at risk of abuse. Notable in this respect was policy and practice guidance issued in 2000 concerning the process by which the needs of disabled children and their families should be assessed (Department of Health, 2000a and Department of Health, 2000b, respectively). However, these years also witnessed several prominent inquiries into child homicides, in particular the 2003 statutory inquiry into the death of Victoria Climbié (Laming, 2003).

In 2010, the Coalition Government commissioned Professor Eileen Munro to conduct an independent review of child protection in England. Munro's final report (Munro, 2011) represents one of the most insightful and important reports of this kind. In large measure, this is due to her interest and expertise in 'systems thinking' (Lane et al, 2016). Using a systems thinking approach Munro identified the reasons why almost all previous inquiry reports had had an unintended negative impact on child protection. In her view:

> Each inquiry adds a few more rules to the book, increases the pressure on staff to comply with procedures, and strengthens the mechanisms for monitoring and inspecting practice so that non-compliance can be detected. Over the years, a combination of national and local reforms and initiatives has led to the heavily bureaucratised system .... Each addition in isolation makes sense but the cumulative effect is to create a work environment full of obstacles to keeping a clear focus on meeting the needs of children. (Munro, 2011, para 1.16)

The Munro Review (as with previous child protection inquiries/reviews) was, in substance, silent concerning the needs of disabled children (Clements and Aiello, 2021, para 2.23).

In the conclusions to her report, Munro recommended 'reducing the degree of central prescription in order to increase the scope for professional exercise of judgment and expertise' (para 8.7). In effect, this was a bonfire of the central government guidance that sought to micromanage the 'children in need' safeguarding process. Ironically chapter 8 of the report contains a section under the heading of 'unintended consequences': ironic, because her recommendation for a reduction in the volume of central government guidance has had a profoundly negative and unintended consequence for disabled children and their families.

In 2013, the English Government followed her recommendation by cancelling a swathe of departmental guidance concerning 'children in need' (HM Government, 2013) – including the 2000 guidance (Department of Health, 2000b) that had been issued concerning the separate process by which disabled children should be assessed.

The 2021 research report (paras 5.55–5.59) considers possible political motivations for the cancellation of the 2000 guidance – including the Government's 'localism drive': the decentralisation of certain resource-dependent/rationing functions (Klein and Maybin, 2012, p 2). The 2013 guidance (para 62) accordingly required that each local authority develop and publish a local protocol for the assessment of 'children in need': a requirement that remains in the current guidance (HM Government, 2023b, para 141).

The 2013 guidance was dominated by concerns of neglect and abuse, and parental failings – and resulted in authorities reviving 'a conceptualisation of the "problem" of disability as located within the individual family – or more particularly the parents' (Clements and Aiello, 2021, para 5.23).

The unforeseen adverse effects of these reforms were most keenly experienced by the parents of disabled children – parents who asked for support and were then subjected to a one-size-fits-all assessment process designed to safeguard neglected/abused children; assessors who, it appeared to families, had little or no training concerning the distinct needs of disabled children and who were required to adhere strictly to their council's tick-box forms – no matter how inappropriate they felt that process to be.

The 2021 research methods

In order to better understand the causes, the prevalence and the impact of such social work practices, a mixed-methods research programme was developed. The research was undertaken in the second half of 2020 and comprised two principal data-gathering methods: (1) searches of 149 English children's services authorities' websites with the aim of locating, and then analysing, their 'local protocols for assessment'; and (2) a survey of parent-carer-led support organisations as to their members' perceptions concerning the nature and impact of assessments that were being carried out in their geographic area.

The 2021 research findings

The findings of the 2021 research were wide ranging and contained considerable detail, but for the purposes of this chapter, three key messages emerged. In each case, these were directly attributable to the inadequacies of the national and local policy frameworks designed to safeguard and promote the welfare of disabled children. These failings:

- created a system that institutionalised parent carer blame into the everyday practices of children's social practitioners;
- meant that disabled children (for whom there was no cogent evidence of neglect or harm) experienced, *prima facie* unlawful discrimination; and
- meant that disabled children and their families were subjected to a one-size-fits-all assessment process and in consequence experienced routine and severe violations of their rights to respect for their private and family lives contrary to Article 8 of the Human Rights Act 1998.

In short, this is a system that institutionalises parent carer blame.

As we have noted above, since the repeal in 2013 of disabled-children-specific assessment guidance, there has been no central government guidance that specifies how this process should operate. The only central government assessment guidance that now exists applies to all 'children in need' and has an overwhelming 'safeguarding' focus – a point made plain in its title, 'Working Together to Safeguard Children' (HM Government, 2023b). The 2013 guidance (and its subsequent iterations) delegated the duty to provide specific guidance (for disabled children and other groups) to individual local authorities. The research was, however, unable to find any local guidance that contained a clear explanation that a different approach should be taken concerning the assessment of the needs of disabled children.

The consequence of this national and local failure was that 'risk' (rather than social care needs) was the primary focus of assessments of disabled children: that the approach was dominated by safeguarding, child protection concerns and in particular the risks posed by children's parents.

> The first thing they ask is [if] the child is in immediate danger. If you say no they close the call down. If you say yes they ask loads of questions about the child's safety, dismiss the child's challenges and say they will call you back which they don't. You call to find out the decision and they say we closed the case.
>
> You cannot get a social services referral unless there are serious child protection needs. Parents can only get an assessment from the early help team but only if the family can prove it's at breaking point. The early help team are not qualified and some have no SEN experience. (Parent carer comments cited in Clements and Aiello, 2021, pp 28 and 30)

A system that discriminates against disabled children

The European Court of Human Rights and the Court of Appeal have held that unlawful discrimination results when (among other things), a person is – 'without an objective and reasonable justification' – treated in the same way as someone whose situation is significantly different (*Thlimmenos v Greece* 2001, para 44; *Burnip v Birmingham City Council* 2012, para 14). Treating disabled children and their families in the same way as those suspected of child neglect/abuse constitutes such an example. In the language of the law, such behaviour is contrary to Article 14 of the European Convention on Human Rights (ECHR) in combination with Article 8 (the right to respect for private and family life, home and correspondence). In the case of many parents of disabled children, the discrimination is not technical: it is experienced as humiliating, intimidating and, indeed, traumatising.

In such circumstances, states are under a positive obligation to take effective action to address this harm: most obviously by ensuring that practices of this kind are prohibited. Sadly, as noted above, the overwhelming evidence of the research study is that in England the central government guidance which mandated and described a distinct disabled children's assessment process (Department of Health, 2000a, paras 1.42–1.43; Department of Health, 2000b, paras 3.10–3.11) has been repealed and replaced by a system that now mandates a 'one-size-fits-all' assessment regime.

A system that unjustifiably interferes with private and family life

The research confirmed that many families with disabled children were being subjected to highly intrusive interferences with the private and family lives: that social workers were routinely entering their 'most intimate spaces': going 'right into the heart of families' inner space – into their bedrooms, bathrooms and kitchens' (Ferguson, 2018).

Action of this kind constitutes a substantial interference with the fundamental right of disabled children and their families to 'respect' for their private and family life, and home. Article 8 of the ECHR requires states to have practical and effective laws and policies to protect this right: in this context, there is a compelling argument that this would include ensuring that there is explicit guidance and social work training – as to when an interference with this right is legitimate and proportionate and when it is not.

Lucy Fullard (Chapter 11) provides a graphic account of such intrusive practice, as did many respondents to the survey of parent-carer-led support organisations – of which the following serves as a not untypical example:

> I felt bullied … suddenly a stranger in our house demanding we answered these questions we had no choice it just was really really horrible … and then she wanted to see [child's] room … and I [asked] why is that relevant to you coming to assess me [for a Parent Carer's Needs Asseement] … and she just said 'oh it's just standard – just what we do' and again I just felt that we can't deny it, because again you'll think what am I hiding. I just felt we were being treated like criminals … it was almost like the police turning up at your door and say we've got a warrant to search your house. (Parent carer response)

Our research found that (regardless of whether there was any evidence to suspect that the child was being neglected or abused) 80 per cent of local authority 'local protocols' for assessment required the assessor to confirm if the 'child's bedroom has been seen' and that almost 90 per cent referred to the need of seeing (or communicating with) the children alone. None of the protocols gave guidance to assessors as to how to determine when it would be/would not be proportionate to behave in this way – and in separate research (Clements and Aiello, 2022) we were unable to find evidence that local authorities had provided their assessors with any human rights or equality training that might have equipped them to make decisions of this kind.

An emerging consensus on the need for fundamental reform

The 2021 research provided strong evidence that the Children's Services assessment and support system for disabled children was in need of major reform. The report noted that there was increasing recognition in official circles that reform was necessary, citing a 2021 Department of Health and Social Care report compiled by the Chief Social Workers for Adults and the Chief Social Worker for Children and Families, that noted:

> Even where the sole reason for contact with children's social care was because of the social care needs of an autistic child, there was a tendency to use the social work assessment as an opportunity to judge parenting capacity through a child protection lens rather than through a lens of social care need. This has long been a complaint of families caring for disabled children.

In March 2021, the English Government commissioned an independent review of the childcare system chaired by Josh MacAlister. An interim report of the review (MacAlister, 2021, para 1.12) echoed the Chief Social Workers' concerns noting that 'a consistent theme in what the review has heard' is that families with disabled children felt 'that they are navigating a system that is set up for child protection, not support'. He went on to make the broader point, namely:

> Despite the prevalence of families struggling to manage in conditions of adversity, the system too often focuses its efforts on investigating and assessing parents without providing real help for the family to deal with the problems they are facing when, often, we can best help children by providing meaningful support to their families. In the last year we have data for, just under 135,000 investigations where a child was suspected of suffering significant harm did not result in a child protection plan – three times as many as just ten years ago … . Each of these investigations is an intrusion into families that in itself can cause additional stress.

A similar observation emerged from the government-commissioned review of the system for supporting children and young people with special educational needs and disabilities (SEND). In its 2022 report (Secretary of State for Education, p 10), it was noted that: 'Some families with disabled children tell us they are put off seeking support from children's social care because of fear they will be blamed for challenges their children face and treated as a safeguarding concern rather than receive the support they need.' In 2023, the Minister for Children recognised the validity of these findings (Claire Coutinho, 2023), stating: 'I note the concern that when parents of disabled children approach their local Children's Services department seeking support, they can be treated in the same way as parents suspected of neglecting or abusing their children.' The Minister went on to confirm that, in the Government's review of the 'Working Together 2018' (HM Government, 2018) guidance, it would consider how it could 'include a stronger focus on support for disabled children' and 'look again at assessment processes'. The Minister separately asked that the Law Commission undertake a review of children's social care disability legislation – a step recommended in the final report of the independent review of the childcare system (MacAlister, 2022, p 60).

Despite compelling evidence that local authority assessment and care planning protocols discriminate against disabled children, the Government opted for procrastination, merely undertaking to 'consider implementing a bespoke assessment protocol' for disabled children (HM Government, 2023a, p 47), but only after it had the 'emerging evidence' from a pilot programme (Department for Education, 2024b) which is scheduled to run until March 2025 and the 'findings of the Law Commission Review' of social care legislation for disabled children: a process that is likely to take considerably longer.

Intentions to address severe discrimination need to be expressed in the language of 'urgency', and not characterised as 'one-day maybe' aspirations. This need is all the pressing given that the Government's consultation response (HM Government, 2023a, p 47) accepted that: 'A significant number of respondents, of which many are parents or carers, requested a bespoke assessment better tailored to the needs of disabled children and their families. Parents reported experience of previous assessments to have been stressful and upsetting and felt such assessments did not reflect their distinctive needs.'

Justifying a one-size-fits-all assessments process

Set against this high-level acceptance of a need for reform, there were, however, a number of senior professionals we encountered in the 2021 research, who believed that the one-size-fits-all assessment process was justified. Not infrequently, this view was rationalised by reference to research concerning the extent to which disabled children are at risk of abuse.

There is research evidence that suggests that disabled children are more likely to be abused than their 'non-disabled' peers (Jones et al, 2012). The findings are, however, replete with caveats and reservations about their applicability in this complex field. More disabled children grow up in poverty than their non-disabled peers and the data suggests that poor children are also at higher risk of abuse (Parton, 2006, p 30) but only in states with high inequalities. The inescapable conclusion appears to be that social context also creates the conditions for abuse.

In a 2012 meta-analysis of the relevant research (Jones et al, 2012), only two of the study sample were UK-based. The analysis concluded that there was a vital need for methodologically rigorous research, but that on the evidence available, disabled children were between three and four times more at risk of abuse than non-disabled children. The researchers were, however, at pains to explain that the data did not identify from where the abuse originated – namely, whether it was internal (family generated) or external (bullying/hate crimes/institutional abuse, etc). In this latter respect, they referred to issues such as societal stigma, discrimination, negative traditional beliefs, ignorance within communities, lack of social support for carers, communication difficulties and problems within institutional settings (including hospitals). The study also noted that some of the data did not account for reverse causation (namely, that the disability arose/resulted from prior abuse).

Of particular concern about the use of the multi-layered abuse statistics to validate severe intrusions into the private and family life of disabled people and their families is the implication that stereotyping can be used to justify such human rights interferences. Intrusive action based on stereotyping is wrong and when action of this kind targets protected statuses – such as disability – it constitutes *prima facie* unlawful discrimination (*European Roma Rights Centre v Immigration Officer at Prague Airport* 2003).

Stereotyping, parent blaming and incautious thinking allows the social contexts of abuse to be overlooked. Firmin (2017) describes how, in cases of child-on-child abuse and gang-related crime, safeguarding bodies have also started with a 'parental deficits' approach to their investigations: of judging parents unable to control or protect their child and assuming that this can be resolved by a parenting class to teach them to be a better parent. In Firmin's opinion, 'contextless assessments' of this kind epitomise the failure of such bodies to 'look beyond the front doors' of families and appreciate the contextual risks that confront young people – in the stairwells of their flats, the bus terminuses, the online spaces, the housing estates and parks, and the school toilets. Her research demonstrates how even when a child was relatively safe with their caregivers but at risk of significant harm in extra-familial settings, statutory interventions 'focused on the home and not the environments that posed a risk'.

Discussion: what needs to be done

The research findings discussed in this chapter identify a dysfunctional social care assessment system – a system that adversely discriminates against disabled children and their families: one that causes them disproportionate harm and one that fails to do what Parliament has decreed – namely, to safeguard and promote their welfare.

Although, as Cathleen Long et al (Chapter 8) demonstrate, parent carer blame is not a new phenomenon, it could be argued that the causes of the specific problem identified in our 2021 research stem from the Children Act's overly simplistic approach to the concept of a 'child in need'. All children are in need and a responsive state should not (in its practices) arbitrarily restrict its role to those who are disabled or at risk of neglect or abuse. That the 1989 Act sought to do this betrays (as others have argued) its neoliberal 'small state, responsibilisation' agenda. Conjoining two quite distinct categories of need into one definition has also had profoundly negative consequences for disabled children and their families.

In simple legal terms, this problem could be addressed by a clear demarcation of the duties to safeguard the needs of children at risk of neglect or abuse from the duty to promote the welfare of all children (including disabled children). Such an approach would require distinct disabled children assessment guidance, distinct assessment forms and a workforce with a profound understanding of the social causes of disadvantage, as well as of human rights and equality principles. Our research suggests that these essential ingredients for reform are not to be found at the 'coal face' where families interact with social care professionals.

Our research also suggests that there are no 'quick fixes'. Superficially, it might be thought that developing 'disabled children' specific guidance might bring about a radical new approach in this field, especially if the guidance was accompanied by a major roll-out of training as to how it should be used, and the human rights and equality principles it encompasses. As part of our research programme, we have supported parent carer groups to craft guidance of this kind (Clements and Aiello, 2023), and developing a training programme to accompany its roll-out would appear to be relatively straightforward. However, our research suggests that bringing about a fundamental change in organisational cultures and practice requires more than this.

What we have learned is that many social care practitioners would welcome such organisational and practice change and that training and discussion programmes of this kind are often highly valued. Problematically, however, the day after such events, they return to their offices where they are then required to fill out the same assessment forms that ask the same questions (about inspecting bedrooms and interviewing children alone, etc). In practice it is the routine use of these forms that communicates the real organisational priorities of their department and these daily PC routines rapidly erase any inspirational 'buzz' that the practitioner may have experienced from the training. As one colleague researching effective change mechanisms stated: 'if you want to change the system, change the computer programme'. White et al (2010, p 422) have referred to this as 'the totalizing dominance of the inspectorial *Weltanschauung* ... [that] ... privileges the secondary work of record keeping and adherence to formal procedure over the primary professional task, providing both an incorrigible explanation for failure and a glibly plausible paradigm for reform'.

During our research, we have worked with an independent parent carer support group that has developed such a template questionnaire (Parent and Carer Alliance, 2024); one that requires assessors to make positive and supportive statements to the parent; one with a primary focus on social care needs rather than risks; and one that aligns, so far as is possible, with the assessment process for disabled adults.

Simple as it might appear to be, the introduction of such a disabled-child-specific assessment tool would be a significant challenge for any single children's services authority – the problem being that, at present, the single assessment form is also designed to capture all manner of demographic and general performance data required by (for example) the Department for Education (DfE) and Ofsted. In reality, this means that, for effective implementation, the DfE would need to take responsibility for the integration of any new assessment tool within current IT systems. That said, there is evidence that one aspect of this problem could be addressed by having two forms: one that allows practitioners to focus on the social care needs of a disabled child and their family; and the other being used to capture the general and performance indicator data. This approach has been trialled in relation to adult social care assessments and the local authority concerned asserts that it has been a success (Community Care, 2023).

Reform of the kind discussed above could immeasurably improve the sense of professional self-worth of many practitioners and go a long way to changing the dreadful experiences of so many families who approach their children's services department for support. Changing the 'top-down' managerialism and the organisational culture it engenders, by empowering front-line workers with new guidance and training, assessment tools and the power to exercise their discretion would go a long way to curtailing the 'parent blaming' that our research has identified as endemic within English children's services. It will be a challenging multi-stranded task, but these changes are all achievable.

White et al (2010) analysed the effectiveness of the first major IT reform in Children's Services (known as 'ICS' – Integrated Children's System). Although they concluded that this had not been a great success, they remained of the view that if properly implemented such system reforms could be positive. They highlighted the importance of user participation in the design of these systems and the optimisation of local autonomy – and suggested that this was not rocket science: that the 'principles of effective design praxis are not the carefully guarded secret knowledge of an hermitic priesthood, they are well known'.

References

Behlmer, G.K. (1982) *Child Abuse and Moral Reform in England, 1870–1908*, Stanford, CA: Stanford University Press.

Bilson, A. (2024) 'Trends in parent and carer blame: patterns of service for children with a disability or mental illness referred to children's social care'. https://doi.org/10.31235/osf.io/vj3q8

Bilson, A. and Munro, E.H. (2019) 'Adoption and child protection trends for children aged under five in England: increasing investigations and hidden separation of children from their parents', *Children and Youth Services Review*, 96(3): 204–11.

Bilson, A. and Martin, K.E.C. (2017) 'Referrals and child protection in England: one in five children referred to Children's Services and one in nineteen investigated before the age of five', *British Journal of Social Work*, 47(3): 793–811.

Burnip v Birmingham City Council [2012] EWCA Civ 629.

Butler-Sloss, E. (1987) *Report of the Inquiry into Child Abuse in Cleveland (Cm 412)*, London: HMSO.

Children Act 1948. Available from: https://www.education-uk.org/documents/acts/1948-children-act.html#:~:text=An%20Act%20to%20make%20further,take%20care%20of%20them%2C%20and [accessed 24 February 2025].

Children Act 1989. Available from: https://www.legislation.gov.uk/ukpga/1989/41/contents [accessed 24 February 2025].

Children and Young Persons Act 1963. Available from: https://www.legislation.gov.uk/ukpga/1963/37 / [accessed 24 February 2025].

Chronically Sick and Disabled Persons Act 1970. Available from: https://www.legislation.gov.uk/ukpga/1970/44/contents [accessed 24 February 2025].

Claire Coutinho MP Minister for Children, Families and Wellbeing, letter 13 March 2023 to Jesse Norman MP.

Clapton, G., Cree, V.E. and Smith, M. (2012) 'Moral panics and social work: towards a sceptical view of UK child protection', *Critical Social Policy*, 33(2): 197–217.

Clapton, G. (2020) 'Child protection anxieties and the formation of UK child welfare and protection practices', in L. Tsaliki and D. Chronaki (eds) *Discourses of Anxiety over Childhood and Youth across Cultures*, Cham, Switzerland: Springer International Publishing.

Clements, L. (2008) 'Respite or short breaks care and disabled children', *Seen and Heard*, 18(4): 23–31.

Clements, L. and Thompson, P. (2007) *Community Care and the Law*, 4th edn, London: Legal Action Group.

Clements, L. and Aiello, A.L. (2021) *Institutionalising Parent Carer Blame: The Experiences of Families with Disabled Children in Their Interactions with English Local Authority Children's Services Departments*, Cerebra, University of Leeds.

Clements, L. and Aiello, A.L. (2022) *Challenging Parent Carer Blame: Interim Implementation Research Report 1: Disability and Human Rights Training and Guidance for Disabled Children's Assessors*, Cerebra, University of Leeds.

Clements, L. and Aiello, A.L. (2023) *Draft Guidance: Assessing the Needs of Disabled Children and their Families*, University of Leeds.

Clyde, J. (1992) *The Report of the Inquiry into the Removal of Children from Orkney in February 1991*, House of Commons, Edinburgh: HMSO.

Community Care (2023) 'How one council is giving social workers the autonomy to empower adults'. Available from: https://www.communitycare.co.uk/2023/09/21/how-one-council-is-cutting-bureaucracy-to-give-social-workers-more-professional-autonomy-to-empower-the-adults-they-support-eza/ [accessed 17 July 2024].

Department for Education (2024a) 'Children in need', 31 October. Available from: https://explore-education-statistics.service.gov.uk/find-statistics/children-in-need [accessed 12 November 2024].

Department for Education (2024b) Policy paper: families first for children (FFC) pathfinder programme and family networks pilot (FNP). Available from: https://www.gov.uk/government/publications/families-first-for-children-ffc-pathfinder-programme/families-first-for-children-ffc-pathfinder-programme-and-family-networks-pilot-fnp [accessed 28 December 2024].

Department of Health (2000a) *Framework for the Assessment of Children in Need and Their Families*, London: The Stationery Office.

Department of Health (2000b) *Assessing Children in Need and Their Families: Practice Guidance*, London: The Stationery Office.

Eekelaar, J. (1991) 'Parental responsibility: State of nature or nature of the state?', *Journal of Social Welfare and Family Law*, 13(1): 37–50. https://doi.org/10.1080/09649069108413929

European Roma Rights Centre and Others v The Immigration Officer at Prague Airport & the Secretary of State for the Home Department, and The United Nations' High Commissioner for Refugees [2003] EWCA Civ 666.

Ferguson, H. (2018) 'Making home visits: creativity and the embodied practices of home visiting in social work and child protection', *Qualitative Social Work*, 17(1): 65–80 at 67.

Field-Fisher, T.G. (1974) *Report of the Committee of Inquiry into the Care and Supervision Provided in Relation to Maria Colwell*, London: HMSO.

Firmin, C. (2017) 'Contextual risk, individualised responses: an assessment of safeguarding responses to nine cases of peer-on-peer abuse', *Child Abuse Review*, 27(1): 42–57.

Gilbert, R., Fluke, J., O'Donnell, M., Gonzalez-Izquierdo, A., Brownell, M., Gulliver, P. et al (2012) 'Child maltreatment: variation in trends and policies in six developed countries', *The Lancet*, 379(9817): 758–72.

HM Government (2013) *Working Together to Safeguard Children: A Guide to Inter-Agency Working to Safeguard and Promote the Welfare of Children*.

HM Government (2018) *Working Together to Safeguard Children: A Guide to Inter-Agency Working to Safeguard and Promote the Welfare of Children*.

HM Government (2023a) *Changes to Statutory Guidance: Working Together to Safeguard Children Government Consultation Response*.

HM Government (2023b) *Working Together to Safeguard Children: A Guide to Inter-Agency Working to Safeguard and Promote the Welfare of Children*.

Hood, R., Goldacre, A., Gorin, S., Bywaters, P. and Webb, C. (2020) *Identifying and Understanding the Link between System Conditions and Welfare Inequalities in Children's Social Care Services*, London: Nuffield Foundation.

Human Rights Act 1998. Available from: https://www.legislation.gov.uk/ukpga/1998/42/contents [accessed 26 February 2025].

Jones, L., Bellis, M.A., Wood, S., Hughes, K., McCoy, E., Eckley, L. et al (2012) 'Prevalence and risk of violence against children with disabilities: a systematic review and meta-analysis of observational studies', *The Lancet*, 380(9845): 899–907.

Jütte, S., Bentley, H., Tallis, D., Mayes, J., Jetha, N., O'Hagan, O. et al (2015) *How Safe Are Our Children? The Most Comprehensive Overview of Child Protection in the UK*, London: NSPCC.

Klein, M. and Maybin, J. (2012) *Thinking about Rationing*, London: The King's Fund.

Lane, D.C., Munro, E. and Husemann, E. (2016) 'Blending systems thinking approaches for organisational analysis: reviewing child protection in England', *European Journal of Operational Research*, 251(2): 613–23.

Lord Laming (2003) *The Victoria Climbié Inquiry Report of an Inquiry (Cm 5730)*, Secretary of State for Health and Secretary of State for the Home Department.

Lynch, G. (2019) 'Pathways to the 1946 Curtis Report and the post-war reconstruction of children's out-of-home care', *Contemporary British History*, 34(1): 22–43.

Mackay, L.C. (1988) Hansard 502 HL Debates, col 488 (23 November).

MacAlister, J. (2021) *The Independent Review of Children's Social Care: the Case for Change*. Available from: https://webarchive.nationalarchives.gov.uk/ukgwa/20230308122442/ https://childrenssocialcare.independent-review.uk/case-for-change/ [accessed 26 August 2024].

MacAlister, J. (2022) 'The independent review of children's social care: final report'. Available from: https://assets.publishing.service.gov.uk/media/640a17f28fa8f5560820da4b/Independent_review_of_children_s_social_care_-_Final_report.pdf [accessed 6 August 2024].

Masson, J. (1992) 'Implementing change for children: action at the centre and local reaction', *Journal of Law and Society*, 19(3): 320–38.

Melton, G. (2005) Mandated reporting: a policy without reason. *Child Abuse and Neglect,* 25(1): 9–18.

Morris, K., Featherstone, B. and White, S. (2013) 'We need to think again about how to protect children', *The Guardian*, 22 October. Available from: https://www.theguardian.com/social-care-network/2013/oct/22/think-again-how-protect-children [accessed 6 August 2024].

Munro, E. (2011) *The Munro Review of Child Protection: Final Report. A Child-Centred System (Cm 8062)*, Department for Education, London: Stationery Office.

National Assistance Act 1948. Available from: https://www.legislation.gov.uk/ukpga/Geo6/11-12/29 [accessed 28 February 2025].

Oliver, M. (1983) *Social Work with Disabled People*, Basingstoke: Palgrave Macmillan.

ONS (2023) 'Homicide in England and Wales: year ending March 2023'. Available from: https://www.ons.gov.uk/peoplepopulationandcommunity/crimeandjustice/articles/homicideinenglandandwales/yearendingmarch2023 [accessed 6 August 2024].

Parent and Carer Alliance (2024) 'Needs assessment'. Available from: https://www.parentandcareralliance.org.uk/projects [accessed 20 August 2024].

Parton, N. (2006) *Safeguarding Childhood: Early Intervention and Surveillance in a Late Modern Society*, New York: Palgrave Macmillan.

Poor Relief Act of 1601, 43 Elizabeth c 2, s 7.

Secretary of State for Education (2022) *SEND Review: Right Support, Right Place, Right Time (CP 624)*, HM Government.

The Chief Social Workers for Adults and the Chief Social Worker for Children and Families (2021) *A Spectrum of Opportunity: An Exploratory Study of Social Work Practice with Autistic Young Adults and Families*, Department of Health and Social Care.

Thlimmenos v Greece (2001) 31 EHRR 15; Application No 34369/9731 6 April 2000.

White, S., Wastell, D., Broadhurst, K. and Hall, C. (2010) 'When policy o'erleaps itself: the "tragic tale" of the Integrated Children's System', *Critical Social Policy*, 30(3): 405–29.

Zahawi, N. (2021) Hansard House of Commons Debate, 6 December 2021, vol 705, col 47.

3

Parent blame and complex trauma

Peter Baker, Linda Hume and Vivien Cooper

Introduction

This chapter will explore the concept of trauma in families who have a member with an intellectual and developmental disability (IDD), consider what causes trauma, how it is linked to parent blame and what needs to change to prevent both.

We all expect the education, health and social care system (and the legal system) to be in place to provide support when it is needed. This of course applies equally to families who have a disabled relative, when the need for that system is likely to be greater, and for it to provide a range of support and services across the lifespan.

This 'system' is made up of multiple systems, all of which have their own access rules, eligibility criteria and funding arrangements – and exactly how they are organised and deliver support varies depending on where you live. Organisational complexities, together with financial and capacity constraints, mean the system is required to find ways to manage demand for and delivery of support and services.

Families are required to navigate this complex system to ensure their relative accesses the support and services they need and are entitled to. This is in addition to providing the love and increased care and support their relative needs on a daily basis. In an ideal world, the 'system' would be seamless and coordinated and swing into action when needed. In the real world, words commonly used by families describing their attempts to get support are 'battle' and 'fight'.

Against this backdrop, it is almost inevitable that conflict will arise: on one side, a family trying to get support; and, on the other, people working in a system that has limited and insufficient capacity and high demands. When families are unable to secure the support their relative needs and consequently express their dissatisfaction, frustration or anger, they are easily labelled as 'difficult' – and the blame is securely and conveniently deposited with them.

This chapter will describe work with families to explore the current situation as families interact with the system that is meant to be there to support them and the assumptions that are made, including the additional label of trauma. This work challenges the conclusion that families are difficult and traumatised and therefore in need of therapy – because families have told us that the interactions with the system cause the trauma they experience, and they can identify how and when. If that is the case, the solution must be to change the system and avoid the trauma in the first place, not provide therapy after it has happened.

The psychological wellbeing of families

The increased risk to family members who have a child (and/or adult) with an IDD of having compromised psychological wellbeing has been firmly established, with many studies over the past 60 years consistently finding associations with higher incidence of poor psychological health (including burnout, depression, anxiety, etc) compared to families of typically developing children. Attempts to explain this association have pointed to several factors: These included:

- the 'shattered dream' of the expected child, with Olshansky (1962) coining the term 'Chronic Sorrow' and suggesting parents suffer from an ongoing grieving process for the child they never had;
- the impact of the reality of daily care and resulting restrictions in social and professional activity and associated financial implications (Goudie et al, 2014; Thakuri, 2014);
- the child's behaviour and impairments of adaptive functioning (Ritzema and Sladeczek, 2011);
- social marginalisation, stigmatisation and feelings of isolation and loneliness (Davies and Hall, 2005; Strong, 2018).

While many of these studies refer to children, there is every reason to believe that this may also apply to families who have adult members with a disability – especially given that families play a key role in caregiving for their family member often across the lifespan, as many individuals will continue to live at home into adulthood.

Many of these studies appeared to be based on the premise that the existence of the child with a disability was the cause of the compromised psychological wellbeing, with a clear lack of attention given to other factors that might impact family experiences as precursors of distress, stress, psychological problems and mental health disorders in the parents. Furthermore, there was, and is, a tendency to focus on a perceived or assumed psychopathology of the parents, and on the individual parental responses, rather than the families' experience of care and support and their relationships with services (Baker et al, 2021). Previous studies have also identified challenges with accessing the support and services needed: a study of parents' experiences prior to their child being sent to a 52-week school concluded that their interactions with the system were highly problematic: 'The over-riding sense is of their being isolated, excluded and left to get on with a task which is too difficult or beyond the expertise of qualified professionals' (McGill, 2005).

The policy context

In the UK, our society is based on a belief that people in need of support will receive it. There may be debates about who is in need and what support they receive, but there is an underlying assumption that there is a 'safety net' in place. This is considered a sign of a 'civilised society'. Parents and carers of a person with an IDD have an understandable expectation that a range of professionals who work in 'the system' will provide them with the specialist information and support they need.

It is clearly acknowledged in policy and legislation that families play a crucial role in the provision of direct support for their relatives with learning disabilities, this often being lifelong love, care, and advocacy, and saving the state considerable amounts of money in the process (Petrillo and Bennett, 2023). Repeatedly, in response to numerous consultations over the years, families have described their key expectations and these can be broadly defined in three categories: firstly, to be provided with high quality, accessible and practical information – about rights, support and services – including what is possible, not just what is currently available; secondly, they expect good support and services for their relative to enable them to lead the fulfilling life they want to; and, thirdly, they want to be acknowledged, respected and valued as key partners (Lenehan, 2017; Williamson and Meddings, 2018; CBF, 2021a; CBF, 2021b).

Current policy for people with IDD is rooted in the concept of community care – segregated institutional provision for disabled children and adults is now an approach consigned to the past. This reflects a human rights approach and a move towards personalisation, supporting individuals within their own environment with the tailored support and services they need to achieve a good quality of life, based on core principles of rights, independence, choice and inclusion (Department of Health, 2001, 2009). Concepts such as 'person centred care' and 'individualised service design' feature heavily in best practice guidance (Care Act 2014; ADASS and ADCS, 2015; NICE, 2015, 2018), as do commitments to proactive, preventative and early intervention approaches.

The overarching system for delivering support to meet these policy objectives is in fact made up of multiple subsystems – in theory, these should be interconnected and seamless, but in practice they are often fragmented and uncoordinated. This encompasses universal human rights, the legal frameworks that define mandatory and optional provisions, and the education, health, and social care systems. These systems are further divided into child and adult sectors, each with its own eligibility criteria, which take effect at different ages depending on the system in question. An added complexity is that social care and education geographical boundaries are not always aligned with health boundaries, and each local area may interpret their responsibilities and arrange their support and services differently. Funding arrangements add another layer of complication to negotiate, with tight budgets in different teams in the systems often fiercely protected with perverse incentives to pass on financial responsibility for individuals to other parts of the system. Furthermore, when resources are allocated, this is commonly on a short-term basis, when the support needed by individuals is long term and ongoing. This results in families being involved in a constant merry-go-round of having to reapply for resource.

It is this complicated arena that families unexpectedly find themselves in when they have a member with an IDD. Even though family expectations and policy objectives are broadly aligned, the delivery of support and services is dependent on 'the system' and navigating through it to achieve good outcomes for the family member. Securing support and services to meet your disabled relative's needs requires firstly understanding the complexities of the different systems and what they provide and secondly navigating through those systems. This involves attempting to shape what is offered to meet the person's individual needs – at the same time as providing full-time support for the individual. This can be especially problematic when the individual has complex needs and will not fit neatly into the service options that are already available. There are multiple conflicts of interest and perverse incentives: family carers are often reliant on professionals to explain what is possible, what they have a right to and what the range of potential options might be. However, all too often, families are only presented with what provision the system is prepared to offer and are directed to existing services which their relative may (or may not) fit into. From the systems perspective, this has become common practice, as it is much simpler than developing and commissioning individually tailored support and services around individual need. As one father put it, 'trying to fit a round peg into a square hole simply won't work' – and it can be extremely damaging to the individual.

An added layer of complexity within 'the system' is that it, and staff within it, are subject to almost continual reorganisation and change. Staff changeover is high, there are often posts which are vacant or temporarily filled resulting in a lack of continuity of care, with families having to frequently establish new working relationships with each new professional. Many services have eligibility criteria that must be met, are oversubscribed and operate lengthy waiting lists.

In order to attempt to address some of these problems, multiple process initiatives have been introduced, including Education Health and Care

Plans for disabled children (to attempt to compel the three different systems to work together) and keyworker pilots (to help families navigate through the systems to get the right support), but in spite of these, the route to support and services remains far from straightforward even when these are in place.

Supporting a relative with complex needs brings additional challenges (and rewards) and it is well established that there are additional pressures as a result, as highlighted in the previous section. Navigating through this complex and often impenetrable maze to get the support the person needs can come at a high cost in terms of the psychological wellbeing of family members, especially when they can clearly see that failure to provide the required support is causing harm and leading to additional issues. The emotional demands of navigating through the system have rarely been acknowledged and, as a result, family members can, at best, feel unsupported and at worst blamed.

Trauma in families

The Tizard Centre (University of Kent), Challenging Behaviour Foundation (CBF) and Respond were commissioned in 2020 by NHS England to investigate trauma in the context of families with a member who has IDD. Part of this work was a survey to ascertain the trauma experiences of families in terms of impactful adverse life events relating to their family member and the consequent responses to these events.

Our starting point involved looking at the definitions of trauma to be clear about what we were referring to. The family carers did not feel that any existing definitions accurately reflected their experience and so the following definition was co-produced and used for the survey:

> Trauma is how a person feels when he/she or someone they love is in a situation that could, or does, cause physical or emotional harm. As a result, the person feels helpless or overwhelmed and the world no longer feels like a safe place. They may find it harder to trust people, feel almost permanently on edge or anxious. It may be more difficult for them to concentrate or sleep, and they may have less patience on a daily basis.

An online survey was sent out to family members and despite having a brief three-week window in which to respond, 214 family members told us about their experiences. In addition, they were asked to identify the extent to which these adverse events and responses were acknowledged by external agencies, what support was offered and/or sought and the extent to which this was helpful, and to give their views about what support should be made available to families (Baker et al, 2021). The results of the survey indicated that many of the experiences reported by family carers would appear to be commensurate with Complex Traumatic Stress Disorder (CPTSD), namely, multi-layered and complex, with many experiencing a wide range of impactful events with the associated emotional and personal sequelae. They told us they experienced little to no help, with the additional burden of needing to independently search for their own support, negotiating a way through a system that is meant to be in place to provide support to them. Their experience was that the system not only failed to provide support but also created additional trauma.

> An overwhelming sense of powerlessness. At any moment I can lose everything and everyone I love, no matter how hard I work or try. Impotent rage at a system that works against common sense and basic support needs. Feel like a beggar. At worst times felt like systems wanted us dead as it would be cheaper. Considered driving me and my son off a cliff because of how strong this feeling was over two years with no way out.
>
> Unable to function – panic when the phone rings, panic when the doorbell rings. Can't focus. Can't trust anyone ever. Find it extremely difficult to keep calm with 'professionals' who are utterly ignorant of autism (and most of them are). I overthink everything, relive it every day.
>
> All of these add to trauma for the individual and the family – families feel like everything is a battle and no one will listen. All professionals involved are responsible, yet no one takes any responsibility. The only thing that worked was removing my brother from all parts of the system and professional support and allowing him to have his life back.
>
> It's been a complete nightmare continually fighting with ineffective and sometimes aggressive social workers, care homes and local authorities. I have spent all of the 45 years of my daughter's life needing reluctantly to fight injustices and probably will die doing so. My experience is not acknowledged or respected at all. I get young professionals who think they know better than me giving me advice. MPs tell me that my daughter must write for help if she needs it, not me. CQC won't investigate, safeguarding complaints are not dealt with. The whole system is corrupt.

Although there was evidence of the impactful and traumatic nature of the diagnosis of the family member's disability, this was not identified by families directly as the most prominent source of their trauma. It is likely that this early trauma, although impactful, becomes lost and buried in the firefighting of managing daily accumulating trauma.

The need for a paradigm shift

Despite the apparent alignment of family expectations and policy objectives, the evidence above would suggest that the system is failing both at a micro level, namely, the point where the service contacts the individual and their family, and at the macro systems/organisational/policy level.

At a micro level, we found that the pervasive impact of interacting with services on the family members has resulted in them often reporting having difficulties in trusting professionals. This lack of trust would result in families being cautious or rejecting even the well-intentioned initiatives from professionals. This in turn will be likely to engender a defensive response if the professional is not sensitive to the extent to which the caution or rejection is not based entirely on the current initiative, but rather is heavily influenced by the family's history of previously being let down by services, namely, trauma. The family is then labelled as a problem and this defensive response will then be interpreted as yet further evidence from the family's perspective that professionals cannot be trusted, thus setting up a vicious circle of mistrust and family blame.

At a macro level, there is a need to move away from having a model that frames trauma within a perspective of a set of symptoms. The impact of trauma is treated after the fact and therefore moves the responsibility for change from the system to the family. Families are viewed as the embodiment of a particular medical or social problem. They are not seen as people whose situation is interconnected and embedded in a history of trauma caused by the system that is meant to be supporting, but rather, they are blamed. Changing of professionals' attitudes is less straightforward than rebranding the organisation's policy and training. There is a need to remember that the system is in place to support families – not for the system to design itself for its own benefit or convenience.

There are some initiatives which have been created to raise awareness – for professionals to become more trauma aware, but often these do not include an understanding of trauma from families' perspectives, with the result that the current narrative surrounding training for professionals working with families continues to disparage them. Training course titles aimed at professionals working with families include such reproachful terms as shown in Figure 3.1.

Thus, such training only serves to further marginalise families and the negative consequences of such application of these labels lead to discrimination and exclusion. Opie et al (2023) in their review of people with lived experience or family's involvement in the training of health professionals found that co-production and co-delivery were rarities.

Some of these issues stem from a system focus on a pathological approach referred to above which searches for problems. When professionals focus on difficulties, they tend to perceive families in essentially negative terms;

Figure 3.1: Common words in training course titles

families are seen through the lens of a collection of problems and diagnostic labels, a focus on what is wrong and why families are not able to cope. When services perceive the problem as family pathology, their obvious response is, at best, to focus on ameliorating the trauma by offering therapy or counselling rather than reflecting on and changing the service's role in causing the trauma, and, at worst, to exclude the family from decision-making with regard to their member with an intellectual disability. This perception of families being difficult, or a problem, not only lowers expectations for any positive change; it also creates a systemic failure within services to acknowledge and respect families as experts in their own lives.

Thus, a major shift in the way services to families are structured and delivered is required – for example, a typical response when families ask for support for their child who has a learning disability is to recommend that they attend a parenting course. The implication is that their parenting skills are deficient. We need to move away from this deficit model to a more supportive investment model: we know families provide significant, often lifelong, care, support and advocacy, so it would make sense to invest in them, acknowledging and enhancing their considerable skills, expertise and knowledge and valuing them as essential partners. In addition, the families in our study clearly told us that the provision of therapy was not the answer; indeed, the overwhelming responses were that they found support provided by charitable organisations such as the Challenging Behaviour Foundation (CBF) as the most useful.

What can we do to change the system?

A typical response when an issue is identified is to introduce training. However, the evidence base for this as an effective strategy is lacking (McNeish et al, 2017) and indeed potentially harmful (see previous discussion regarding training content). Any intervention through training must be designed to shift the expectations of professionals. They should be made aware of what families experience, understand the impact and know they will have to earn trust, which will not be immediately or automatically granted. This work has been started by families, and the CBF is working with them in co-delivering coproduced awareness-raising workshops (CBF, 2022).

A system of support that is causing trauma to the people it is meant to be helping will not be resolved by relatively minor adjustments to that system: a paradigm shift is required. This would need significant government action and system-wide reform. It is widely accepted that the social care system needs adequate funding – and this would help prevent people being failed in the first place, which currently causes the trauma. Equipping and enabling the system to deliver the right support in the right place at the right time would break the vicious cycle which sets up the distrust of families and the disheartening of professionals.

While we campaign for that paradigm shift, families have identified actions that individuals working in the current system can take that would make a big difference. A key and essential starting point is to understand family carer experiences of interactions with the system, the impact and trauma this causes and to move away from labelling them as 'difficult', instead seeing them as valued allies and partners.

Conclusion

The final words are from the families who worked with us to co-produce the survey and compile the Broken report (CBF, 2020), taken from their opening statement:

> We are families who have been traumatised by the continual fights with the very services who are supposed to help us make life easier for our disabled family members. Over the years, we keep coming across other families with disabled children who have suffered in the same way as we have and realised that we were not unique in having to constantly fight the system for even the most basic help for looking after our disabled relative. It begins from the point when hopes and

dreams of a life bringing up a child are shattered, often by a professional handing out a diagnosis, and continues forever. We, and our children, are transformed instantly from being human beings into something lower, because of the way we are treated by the state, by professionals and by the general public. Our main problem is not our relative, but the response from others, especially those who have the power to help but seem unwilling to do so. We feel that change is long overdue, that the present system cannot continue to hurt the most vulnerable in our society, because it is inhumane. … We hope that people in the various care professions take the time to listen and, most importantly, to act to bring about major change. Perhaps then, we can lead ordinary lives, like everyone else, instead of ones full of trauma.

References

ADASS and ADCS (2015) *No Wrong Doors: Working Together to Support Young Carers and Their Families: A Template for a Local Memorandum of Understanding between Statutory Directors of Children's and Adult Social Services.*

Baker, P., Cooper, V., Tsang, W., Garnett, I. and Blackman, N. (2021) 'A survey of complex trauma in families who have children and adults who have a learning disability and/or autism', *Advances in Mental Health and Intellectual Disabilities*, 15(5): 222–39.

Care Act 2014, c 23.

CBF (2020) 'Broken: the psychological trauma suffered by family carers of children and adults with a learning disability and/ or autism and the support required', Challenging Behaviour Foundation. Available from: https://www.challengingbehaviour.org.uk/wp-content/uploads/2021/03/brokencbffinalreportstrand1jan21.pdf [accessed 30 August 2024].

CBF (2021a) 'Engaging and listening to families: commissioning support for children, young people or adults with learning disabilities whose behaviour challenges', Challenging Behaviour Foundation. Available from: https://www.challengingbehaviour.org.uk/wp-content/uploads/2021/02/Engaging-and-Listening-to-Families.pdf [accessed 30 August 2024].

CBF (2021b) 'Tea, smiles and empty promises: Winterbourne View, and a decade of failures – a collection of family stories', Challenging Behaviour Foundation. Available from: https://www.challengingbehaviour.org.uk/news/winterbourne-view-10-years-on/ [accessed 30 August 2024].

CBF (2022) 'Workshops – what we offer'. Available from: https://www.challengingbehaviour.org.uk/workshops/workshops-what-we-offer-2/ [accessed 10 March 2024].

Davies, S. and Hall, D. (2005) '"Contact a family": professionals and parents in partnership', *Archives of Disease in Childhood*, 90(10): 1053–7.

Department of Health (2001) *Valuing People. A New Strategy for Learning Disability for the 21st Century: A White Paper (Cm 5086).*

Department of Health (2009) *Valuing People Now: a New Three-Year Strategy for Learning Disabilities: 'Making it Happen for Everyone'*. Available from: https://www.base-uk.org/sites/default/files/%5buser-raw%5d/11-06/valuing_people_now_executive_summary.pdf [accessed 30 August 2024].

Goudie, A., Narcisse, M.-R., Hall, D.E. and Kuo, D.Z. (2014) 'Financial and psychological stressors associated with caring for children with disability', *Families, Systems, & Health*, 32(3): 280–90.

Lenehan, C. (2017) 'These are our children: a review by Dame Christine Lenehan Director, Council for Disabled Children', commissioned by the Department of Health, Council for Disabled Children. Available from: https://assets.publishing.service.gov.uk/government/uploads/system/uploads/attachment_data/file/585376/Lenehan_Review_Report.pdf [accessed 30 August 2024].

McGill, P. (2005) 'Parents whose children with learning disabilities and challenging behaviour attend 52-week residential schools: their perceptions of services received and expectations of the future', *British Journal of Social Work*, 36(4): 597–616.

McNeish, D., Sebba, J., Luke, N. and Rees, A. (2017) *What Have We Learned about Good Social Work Systems and Practice?* Children's Social Care Innovation Programme, Thematic Report 1, Department for Education.

NICE (2015, updated 2020) *Challenging Behaviour and Learning Disabilities: Prevention and Interventions for People with Learning Disabilities Whose Behaviour Challenges*.

NICE (2018, updated 2019) *Learning Disabilities and Behaviour that Challenges: Service Design and Delivery*.

Olshansky, S. (1962) 'Chronic sorrow: a response to having a mentally defective child', *Social Casework*, 43(4): 190–3.

Opie, J.E., McLean, S.A., Vuong, A.T., Pickard, H. and McIntosh, J.E. (2023) 'Training of lived experience workforces: a rapid review of content and outcomes', *Administration and Policy in Mental Health and Mental Health Services Research*, 50(2): 177–211.

Petrillo, M. and Bennett, M. (2023) *Valuing Carers 2021: England and Wales*, London: Carers UK and Department of Health.

Ritzema, A.M. and Sladeczek, I.E. (2011) 'Stress in parents of children with developmental disabilities over time', *Journal of Developmental Disabilities*, 17(2): 21–34.

Strong, W.E. (2018) 'A grounded case study of parental perceptions surrounding formalized special education processes', PhD Dissertation. Available from: https://eric.ed.gov/?q=%2Caction+begins+the&id=ED582706 [accessed 30 August 2024].

Thakuri, B.S. (2014) 'Stress and coping mechanism among the parents of intellectual disable children', *Journal of Advanced Academic Research*, 1(2): 56–63.

Williamson, H. and Meddings, S. (2018) 'Exploring family members' experiences of the Assessment and Treatment Unit supporting their relative', *British Journal of Learning Disabilities*, 46(4): 233–40.

4

Parent blame in education: working together to find solutions to school attendance difficulties

Louise Parker Engels

Introduction

Our Define Fine team, and colleagues within other parenting SEND and mental health lived experience organisations, have worked for many years providing peer support and advocacy for thousands of parent carers struggling to navigate their way through their child or young person's school attendance difficulties. In recent years, we have seen an unprecedented growth in members linked to what is now being described as a 'national absence crisis'.

School attendance data shows that:

> In Autumn term 2022 1,742,722 pupils were persistently absent, missing over 10% of sessions) which equates to 24.2 per cent of all pupils.
> The number of severely absent pupils (missing over 50% of sessions) has soared by 108 per cent since the pandemic. In Autumn 2022, 125,222 pupils were absent more often than they were present (severely absent), 1.7 per cent of the school population. (Centre for Social Justice, 2023)

This crisis has led Dame Rachel de Souza, the Children's Commissioner for England, to ask: 'Where are England's children?' (Children's Commissioner, 2022), while others have referred to the children missing from Britain's classrooms as 'ghost children' – with a Parliamentary Inquiry (House of Commons Education Committee, 2023) and a House of Commons debate (UK Parliament, 2024) calling for 'improving school attendance' to be made a priority. Attendance is finally on the political radar.

Recent reports, debates, research (Not Fine in School, 2018; Connolly et al, 2023) and parental surveys confirm our collective professional and lived experience around school attendance difficulties. What was previously referred to as 'school refusal', or more recently as EBSA (emotionally-based 'school avoidance'), is now being referred to in government guidance under the umbrella of attendance barriers: barriers linked not only to poverty, but (among other things) also to SEND, mental and physical health conditions, and bullying within the school environment.

In 2022, the Children's Commissioner reported that: 'Children have told us that they face a number of additional barriers to attendance, including lack of support around mental health, emotional and care needs, and problems around feeling safe and supported in school' (2022). In 2023, in evidence to the House of Commons Education Committee, the Special Education Consortium identified 'unmet special educational needs' as the main barrier to attendance – and that in consequence pupils were 'internalising' (which resulted in them experiencing 'an increase in anxiety and mental health challenges') and 'externalising behaviours that challenge and the beginning of problems with attendance'. In the Consortium's opinion, this then led to 'poor and at times traumatic experiences in the school environment, increased pressure on home and family life and, ultimately, to further deterioration in attendance, up to the point of non-attendance and placement breakdown' (House of Commons Education Committee, 2023).

Statistically, SEND children are three times as likely to be absent from school, but the figure is likely to be higher when including unauthorised absences and the children who have not yet had their SEND needs identified and acknowledged (Centre for Social Justice, 2023).

There has also been a marked increase in parents home-educating their children and of young people who are not in education or training post 16 (Office for National Statistics, 2024; Whittaker, 2024). It is, however, difficult to find data concerning the characteristics of pupils who are non-attenders, but we have been advised by one local authority (LA) that it estimated that over 85 per cent of non-attenders had SEND.

Unfortunately, rather than assessing and understanding the barriers around school attendance and working together to find solutions, all too often these children and young people are simply described as being 'fine in school'.

It is vital that all are responsive to the early signs. In many cases, it may be no one at school has noticed these difficulties. It is well established, for example, that many autistic pupils mask their sense of alienation and their consequent anxieties when at school (Hull et al, 2018; Cage and Troxell-Whitman, 2019; Pearson and Rose, 2021). It may well be that they do seem fine, but sooner or later it becomes clear to everyone that they are not fine. They were not fine, and by then many are unable to attend.

When professionals continue to insist children are fine, attention (and then blame) is usually turned towards the family, particularly mothers. Many are faced with threats or the reality of safeguarding referrals for neglect or fabricated or induced illness (FII) allegations and/or non-attendance fines or even criminal proceedings.

Before going down those routes, it's important to consider the Department for Education expectations: 'The aim is to ensure that all children with medical conditions, in terms of both physical and mental health, are properly supported in school so that they can play a full and active role in school life, remain healthy and achieve their academic potential' (Department for Education, 2015). This would be a very good working definition of any child or young person being 'fine' in school. Parents and professionals need to work together to ensure they are.

What kind of difficulties affect school attendance?

Children are often unable to explain why school is so hard for them, but some of our Define parents have shared what they have said:

> School is so noisy. Shouting and loud noises make my tummy and head hurt. (E, aged 10, with anxiety and sensory processing difficulties)

> The days are too long, Maths is too hard, My chair is too hard. My Uniform hurts me. (M, aged 9, autistic)

> I already know when I have done something wrong and I am cross with myself. When I get told off it makes it worse and I get told off a lot. (L, aged 12, ADHD)

> I try hard but I can't finish my writing and then I have to stay in at playtime to catch up so I don't run around outside and play with my friends. (M, aged 8, ADHD, dyslexia)

> At school my tummy hurts, and my legs ache and I feel really tired. I just need a little break sometimes and go to the toilet when I need to but they don't let me. (F, aged 9, medical condition)

> School is a big trick to make me write, even science. Writing is the hardest thing for me but there are lots of things I am good at. I don't do them very often though. They make me write more. (G, aged 12, dyslexia)

> I don't like Wednesdays. That's the day my whole class has a brass brand lesson in the hall. It is so loud. (J, aged 10, autistic, sensory processing difficulties)

Do these children sound like they are fine in school? These may not sound significant in isolation, but day-in-day-out experiences such as these can make school intolerable. These may be labelled as 'emotionally-based school avoidance', but for many of these children their avoidance may be more logical than emotional. They are avoiding intolerable situations.

These are children with SEND needs, particularly over represented but not limited to children who are neurodivergent – autistic, ADHD, dyslexic, with sensory processing and/or executive functioning difficulties. They exhibit signs that they are struggling socially, emotionally and may have mental health (John et al, 2021) as well as physical health conditions.

All too often, the failure to meet the child's needs (and the trauma created by the school's 'blaming' response) then contributes to their burn out (NHS Leicestershire Partnership Trust, nd).

Some are already diagnosed, some are on long waiting lists for assessment – up to four years in some areas for the neurodevelopmental pathways, but many haven't yet met the thresholds to be accepted onto any assessment waiting list! We currently have an education and healthcare system that is not working for a significant number of children and young people. They are being let down and harmed, and still their parents are blamed.

Covid lockdown relief

Many children for whom school is 'not fine' are in need of reasonable adjustments: for the school to think and act differently – and most importantly to become inclusive rather than exclusive. An interesting insight into the impact of systems' change of this kind is provided by research that found that for some of these children, lockdown was, for them, a happier time (Soneson et al, 2023).

For certain students, there may also have been fewer 'typical school day' distractions (for example, negative comparisons with other students, school-based anxiety, sensory challenges, concerns about disciplinary action and uniform requirements) allied to the greater emphasis in both schools and wider society on maintaining wellbeing. There were, in addition, increased opportunities during lockdown for flexible and tailored teaching that encouraged different styles of learning and student autonomy over schedule and schoolwork.

This is consistent with our experience. In some cases, processing their experience in smaller classes, remote or blended learning, learning at a different pace, with less bullying and friendship issues, has meant that many have not been able to return to school.

The education system and the lack of flexibility and inclusion, and a lack of timely assessments and professional intervention, means that too many children and young people are slipping into a zone somewhere between mainstream and special school, and missing out on crucial education.

Assumptions, responses or recommendations from schools

Considering the growing evidence around barriers affecting attendance, the most common recommendations and advice from well-meaning school professionals and others are not only not evidence-based, they also often demonstrate a level of parent blame. Some are potentially harmful. Phrases such as:

- S/he is fine at school … just get her/him in!
- It's your parenting. You need to set firmer boundaries.
- Shall I come and collect him/her and show you how to get them in?
- They have learned this from you. You are projecting your worries on to them.
- Make home as uncomfortable as you can.
- Tell them they need to go to school or they won't get a job.
- If it was my child …
- Have you tried a sticker chart or rewards?

Our parent carers report being expected to physically drag their child into school, with children being prised off their parents in reception, restrained and prevented from leaving. Some feel pressured to agree to plans that they suspect aren't suitable, but don't feel they can question. They are aware of the consequences if they do not follow them and become labelled as 'being difficult'.

Are these responses professionally recommended or even effective? Research findings by Green, concerning the effectiveness of recommendations on a particular cohort of children, are consistent with ours: that these are not effective (Green, 2022).

The impact of describing children as fine when they might not be

The lived experience of their child's distress and the battle for support has a detrimental impact on parent carers and the wider family, particularly on mothers, including on their mental and physical health, their ability to work and their relationships. Many report feeling shame, sadness or isolation. They feel judged and blamed by professionals, family and friends, at a time when they are already blaming themselves.

Parents may have their own SEND needs, particularly neurodiverse autistic/ADHD parents – whose communications and complaints may be misinterpreted or misunderstood.

Our parents have reported:

> If I am perceived to be failing to meet a child's needs, it's neglect or abuse, and I face losing my job, my home, and my child. When

a school or LA fail to meet their needs and cause palpable suffering … nothing.

Stress, constant emails and phone calls, complaint writing, job losses × 2, reduced family income, social isolation judgement and isolation from friends and family who don't understand, threats of fines, expectations to attend meetings and engage with everyone who is thrown at us, sleepless nights, worsening health, guilt.

At one point I thought I was going to have a breakdown. Thoroughly unsupported by the school, shamed and blamed.

2 years of hell. I left my job so financially, health everything and I was blamed. It nearly caused a divorce.

Traumatised really and I don't use that word lightly. Traumatised vicariously because of what my daughter experienced but also from my treatment by the school.

The way forward: multi-agency understanding

All agencies across education, health and social care are under pressure due to reduced budgets, changing (often politically led) policies, gaps in staffing and training, and over-stretched demand for services.

All have a duty to safeguard all children from harm and not miss warning signs of neglect and other abuse. As such, it is vital that all are trained to recognise the signs that some children who do not have their needs met at school may be being harmed in schools, by schools, to the point of no longer being able to attend at all. We need multi-agency understanding, training and accountability to understand the wider issues and provide the most appropriate response.

Our parents report:

I let my child be harmed at school. I kept him there longer than I should have done. I let adults at a new school wrestle my son away from me using 'team teach'. It didn't feel right but I didn't know else to do.

We were powerless to stop a head teacher from allowing serious bullying and neglecting his SEND and medical needs. He was in pain every single day and she refused to accept that even let him have his medication. It went on for so long. He wasn't supported. He ended up with School Trauma and may never go back to school.

Why was I seen as the difficult one, the safeguarding risk? I followed advice, I tried and tried, but nothing worked. Our child in need social worker didn't know what an EHCP was but that was what my child needed.

I was accused of FII by a head teacher for taking my children to too many appointments but the notes from a strategy meeting show she was not asked how many appointments nor which ones. They were all NHS appointments consistent with their conditions. Why didn't the doctors or social workers hold her to account? It turned our lives upside down and meant our children didn't get the help they needed. She just carried on with her career.

Our LA education welfare officer interviewed me under caution, but he said he wasn't interested in SEND. It was nothing to do with him. I asked for help with Alternative Provision, but two years later there hasn't been any. I still don't know if they will prosecute me.

Which guidance should be followed?

It is difficult for professionals to keep up with their own professional policies and practices, let alone those of other agencies, but everyone involved in supporting children who are struggling to attend school needs to know key information on which to base their responses and to plan solutions. We need consistency across schools and LAs. The bare minimum of what every family have a right to expect is that practitioners are fully aware of (and follow) the relevant guidance.

The Department for Education (2024a) 'Working Together to Improve School Attendance' statutory guidance outlines the duties of schools, including academies, LAs and all other partners. Interestingly, there is no mention of school refusal or even EBSA, and instead of parent carer blame, it emphasises that schools should 'build strong relationships with families, listen to and understand barriers to attendance and work with families to remove them' (DfE, 2024a). It is very much a support first model, with schools and LAs expected to 'be particularly mindful of pupils absent due to mental or physical health or their special educational needs and/or disabilities, and provide them with additional support'. (DfE 2024a, p 23).

What should we do?

It is vital that all professionals are professionally curious and question beyond assumptions. Are parent carers neglecting their children, fabricating their SEND and health needs, are they refusing to send their children to school which is potentially a criminal offence, or do these families need support? Do these children have needs that are not being met within school?

Define Fine are able to deliver our co-produced continuing professional development (CPD) accredited training, and the regularly updated Define

Fine Attendance Difficulties guide for parent carers and professionals across education, health and social care based on relevant government guidance.

As an appendix to this chapter, I provide a summary for professionals and parent carers to consider.

Professionals who support

We know of professionals who have made a huge difference, as shown below:

> My child's Educational Psychologist listened to her and advocated for her, and explained in an MDT meeting that school, by not authorising her mental health absence is a barrier to her as it shows her school don't believe she is unwell.

> Our early help worker recorded in her notes 'I have no safeguarding concerns' but I need to keep reminding the school of medical and other professional advice and the need to follow plans.

> My son's secondary school SENCO who despite the feeder primary school sharing that my parenting was at fault and that, my child did not have SEND have put in the necessary support in place to enable a successful transition and he can attend and supported us to get an EHCP.

> A local court officer who won't continue to prosecution but will work with the parents and school to ensure a SEND support and/or Health Care Plan is in place and followed to improve the attendance.

> A CAMHS psychiatrist attended an EHCP annual review to confirm that no matter how many visual timetables or interventions school put in place, the autistic child could not be expected to spend their days in loud, busy school environment, nor would they receive a suitable education alone with a TA in a SEND support room.

Understanding the issues and working together

In 2023, the Children's Commissioner for England reported that: 'I have seen clearly that children aren't absent from school because they don't want to learn. On the contrary, they are desperate to learn but everyday thousands of children find themselves without the support that they need to engage in education and attend school' (Office of the Children's Commissioner for England, 2023). Where are Britain's (England's) children and young people? Thousands are waiting for assessments; waiting for acknowledgment of their needs; waiting for support and a suitable, relevant education. Some are now happily and successfully home educating, and they won't be going back into a system that was not suitable and, in many cases, damaging.

Too many children and young people have not received the support they needed when they needed it. For some, support was eventually put in place, but it was too little too late. Some are too traumatised to ever return to school. Many are at various stages of recovery and re-engagement in education through reasonable adjustments, a more tailored curriculum or a different pathway, through medical needs tuition, or hospital school, online learning, nurturing or therapeutic provision, alternative provision based around interests, one-to-one coaches or mentors to meet them where they are and to follow their lead. Some need specialist provision, and some need 'Education Otherwise than at School' (EOTAS) packages, or supported internships. Some will return to education later and others may manage better in a college environment, or through apprenticeships.

Department for Education statistics reveal a strong negative relationship between poor school attendance and GCSE grades (Department for Education, 2024b). This finding and the well-established link between grades and lifetime earnings suggests that a large number of children and young people who are unable to attend school full time, if at all, are likely to be adversely affected throughout their lives (Department for Education, 2014).

Working together requires overcoming assumptions and embracing evidence-based practice to avoid these situations and others. We need to be sure that timely services are commissioned to prevent school distress and the decline in attendance and to support these children and their families in their recovery around school trauma and burnout.

Now more than ever we need professionals with 'professional curiosity', to be brave, to be aware and to have the integrity to do the right thing: to challenge, to be honest, to be kind. To ask questions and to play a role in holding their own organisations, and others, to account. Professionals who need to be properly trained and adequately resourced.

We all need to consider 'what if this child isn't really fine in school?' And if not, then 'what if the school is not fine for the child?'

Without this, the school attendance problem will continue to grow. There will be more missing children.

Define Fine parent peer support for school attendance difficulties

Define Fine is a team of professionals and parents with lived experience of school attendance difficulties. To our knowledge, we are unique as a school attendance support-focused organisation, as in addition to our online group parent peer support, we offer direct one-to-one support and case management at no cost to parent carers. We are a 'not for profit' and we work alongside other charitable organisations across SEND and mental health who share our values and ethos. We also provide CPD training to LAs, and health and education professionals. Our training fees for this work, as well as grants and donations, fund our peer support.

Appendix: School Attendance Difficulties
(Define Fine, nd)
A summary for professionals and parent carers to consider in school non-attendance situations.

- Is the school environment supporting mental and physical health?
- Do they need a referral to CAMHS, paediatricians, OTs, SALT? Are they already on a pathway? Could these appointments be prioritised or expedited if attendance is severely affected? Has the necessary provision been commissioned?
- Have they been assessed by an educational psychologist? Have specialist teaching services been consulted? Are their recommendations being followed?
- Does this child have Special Educational Needs, diagnosed, suspected or not yet diagnosed across the four board areas of need:
  1. cognition and learning
  2. communication and interaction
  3. social, emotional and mental health
  4. physical and sensory
- School and Local Authorities have a duty to identify special educational needs, but they don't need a diagnosis to need support.
- Are children and young people, their parents, school or college and other professionals working together to develop a flexible, tailored, evidence-based action plan, SEND support plan and/or an individual health care plan to remove barriers, provide support and set targets?
- Do they need an assessment for Educational Health and Care Plan (EHCP) or Statement?
- All plans should be shared with all staff and include training and resources. Are they being followed? Do they need to be reviewed?
- Is this a suitable provision for their needs?
- Do they need alternative provision including hospital school or tutors?
- How is attendance being recorded? Schools should only record physical and mental health absences as unauthorised if they have genuine, evidence based reasons to doubt this (there is no sickness or wellness note for children).
- After 15 days of absence for health or other reasons, the LA has a duty to provide an education.

- Are there plans to provide a broad and balanced curriculum?
- Is school responding appropriately to all incidents of bullying?
- Has the family been referred to appropriate, relevant family support, including Parent Carer Peer Support, signposting to the Local Offer and advocacy, and advice services such as SENDiass?
- Some families may benefit from Early Help or social care assessments, but school attendance difficulties are not necessarily safeguarding or parenting issues. It is vital that there is multi-agency understanding of the issues and guidance surrounding these difficulties. Any interventions should be led by professionals who are qualified and experienced in SEND, mental health and attendance difficulties.

References

Cage, E. and Troxell-Whitman, Z. (2019) 'Understanding the reasons, contexts and costs of camouflaging for autistic adults', *Journal of Autism and Developmental Disorders*, 49(5): 1899–911.

Centre for Social Justice (2023) 'School Absence Tracker: a termly analysis of official data relating to absence from schools'. Available from: https://www.centreforsocialjustice.org.uk/wp-content/uploads/2023/05/CSJ-Absence_Tracker.pdf [accessed 26 August 2024].

Children's Commissioner (2022) 'Where are England's children? Interim findings from the Children's Commissioner's Attendance Audit'. Available from: https://assets.childrenscommissioner.gov.uk/wpuploads/2022/03/cco-where-are-englands-children-interim-findings-mar-2022.pdf [accessed 6 August 2024].

Connolly, S., Constable, H.L. and Mullally, S.L. (2023) 'School distress and the school attendance crisis: a story dominated by neurodivergence and unmet need', *Frontiers in Psychiatry*, 14: 1–24.

Define Fine (nd) 'Parent peer support for school attendance difficulties'. Available from: https://www.definefine.org.uk/assets/img/1797862.pdf [accessed 3 April 2024].

Department for Education (2014) *The Economic Value of Key Intermediate Qualifications: Estimating the Returns and Lifetime Productivity Gains to GCSEs, A Levels and Apprenticeships*.

Department for Education (2015) *Supporting Pupils at School with Medical Conditions: Statutory Guidance for Governing Bodies of Maintained Schools and Proprietors of Academies in England*.

Department for Education (2024a) *Working Together to Improve School Attendance Statutory Guidance for Maintained Schools, Academies, Independent Schools and Local Authorities*.

Department for Education (2024b) 'Attendance communications toolkit for schools: March 2024 update'. Available from: https://dfegovukassets.blob.core.windows.net/assets/Attendance%20campaign/Attendance%20campaign%20commuications%20toolkit%20for%20schools.pdf [accessed 19 July 2024].

Green, A. (2022) 'What can we learn from parents and caregivers of school-aged autistic children to inform current Emotionally Based School Attendance (EBSA) intervention approaches in England? A small study written as part submission to my: MEd Special Education Autism (Children) University of Birmingham'. Available from: https://www.pdasociety.org.uk/wp-content/uploads/2022/12/Amelia-Green-A-small-study-to-investigate-what-can-be-learnt-from-parents-about-EBSA-in-autistic-pupils-Distribution-Version-v2-1.pdf [accessed 27 March 2024].

House of Commons Education Committee (2023) *Persistent Absence and Support for Disadvantaged Pupils*, Seventh Report of Session 2022–23, HC 970, London.

Hull, L., Mandy, W., Lai, M.-C., Baron-Cohen, S., Allison, C., Smith, P. et al (2018) 'Development and validation of the camouflaging autistic traits questionnaire (CAT-Q)', *Journal of Autism and Developmental Disorders*, 49(3): 819–33.

John, A., Friedmann, Y., DelPozo-Banos, M., Frizzati, A., Ford, T. and Thapar, A. (2021) 'Association of school absence and exclusion with recorded neurodevelopmental disorders, mental disorders, or self-harm: a nationwide, retrospective, electronic cohort study of children and young people in Wales, UK', *The Lancet Psychiatry*, 9(1): 23–34.

NHS Leicestershire Partnership Trust (nd) 'Understanding the reasons why a child may not want to attend school'. Available from: https://www.leicspart.nhs.uk/autism-space/education/understanding-the-reasons-why-a-child-may-not-want-to-attend-school/ [accessed 19 July 2024].

Not Fine in School (2018) *School Attendance Difficulties: Parent Survey Results*.

Office for National Statistics (2024) 'Young people not in education, employment or training. (NEET), UK: February 2024'. Available from: https://www.ons.gov.uk/employmentandlabourmarket/peoplenotinwork/unemployment/bulletins/youngpeoplenotineducationemploymentortrainingneet/february2024 [accessed 3 April 2024].

Office of the Children's Commissioner for England (PA0148) (2023) 'Written evidence submitted by the Children's Commissioner'. Available from: https://committees.parliament.uk/writtenevidence/118322/html/ [accessed 27 March 2024].

Pearson, A. and Rose, K. (2021) 'A conceptual analysis of autistic masking: understanding the narrative of stigma and the illusion of choice', *Autism in Adulthood*, 3(1): 52–60.

Soneson, E., Puntis, S., Chapman, N., Mansfield, K.L., Jones, P.B. and Fazel, M. (2023) 'Happier during lockdown: a descriptive analysis of self-reported wellbeing in 17,000 UK school students during Covid-19 lockdown', *European Child & Adolescent Psychiatry*, 32(6): 1131–46.

UK Parliament (2024) 'School attendance: volume 744: debated on Tuesday 23 January 2024'. Available from: https://hansard.parliament.uk/Commons/2024-01-23/debates/65CB5417-1B85-4AC9-944B-A199ACFE194E/SchoolAttendance#contribution-262D795C-0CFB-4E74-8692-A9E1A3C5BDD1 [accessed 19 July 2024].

Whittaker, F. (2024) 'Home education: rate of pupils leaving school doubles: poorer areas see some of the biggest rises, as more parents withdraw children because of unmet needs'. Available from: https://schoolsweek.co.uk/rate-of-pupils-leaving-for-home-education-doubles/ [accessed 3 April 2024].

5

That woman!

Amy Payne (pseudonym)

Introduction

Until my mid-40s, I was walking around in a myopic daze, still hanging on to the comforting belief that while flawed, the UK state was essentially reasonable and fair. In such a world, if a well-intentioned citizen pointed out systemic breaches of children's human rights, the state would want to proactively and swiftly step in to prevent harm. In such a world, it was reasonable to expect that the Government believed its own mantra – that 'Every Child Matters', that the state authorities would be responsive to evidence and reasoned arguments and that there would be accountability if mistakes were made and children were harmed.

The scales have fallen from my eyes. I now know that the state is not receptive to parents who raise concerns about the impact on children of the state's actions or inactions. I know this, not only because of my own experiences, but also because I've met so many other parents whose stories mirror my own experience of struggling to be heard when raising the alarm on behalf of children. I would go as far as to say that the state's default position appears to be to ignore parent voices and hope parents go away. When that doesn't work, things can swiftly turn nasty, if the state, as gaslighter in chief, turns its attention on the parent. It turns out that what the state, in its various forms, has done to me over the last few years is not at all unusual.

Trying to point out human rights abuses to various bodies paid to protect children, including the Department for Education, Ofsted, my local authority and my children's school, has been a traumatic experience for me. I have been gaslighted, harassed and vilified. In 2021, my local authority tacitly conceded that its actions and inactions had caused me trauma when it offered to pay for trauma therapy. Ironically, even though I met the trauma therapist for weeks, and our conversations were extremely helpful, she was unable to start trauma therapy because the local authority's behaviours had not changed. The local authority paid around £700 to the therapist, but the gaslighting and vilification continue and have even intensified.

State-induced trauma is common among parents like me who try to raise the alarm about a risk to children. Subjecting parents to trauma is an effective weapon in suppressing the voices of many parents; the price you pay for persisting and repeatedly exposing yourself to gaslighting is high. I've often described my position as similar to being in an abusive relationship.

It shouldn't be that families whose children have been harmed have to endure further distress fighting an unresponsive and at times vindictive state to prevent their children or other children suffering further harm. If you are unfortunate to become aware of state failings which are harming children and you feel moved to speak up for those children, know what you are dealing with. It might help to think of the state as a lazy, petulant, arrogant behemoth which deeply resents criticism and calls to action. It is likely to rise up against anyone foolish enough to keep prodding it for action.

I share my story here in the interest of shining a light on the unresponsiveness of this beast to the suffering of children and in the hope that I can pass on some protective pointers to anyone else contemplating raising a concern with state bodies.

The start

Imagine this: a 15-year-old is arrested by the police on suspicion of raping a girl from his school. He is interviewed, then released on bail. The day after his arrest, the school allows him back into class with the traumatised victim.

Imagine that the victim is your daughter. What would you do?

What the school wanted me to do was to meekly accept their decision not to protect my daughter from contact in school with the accused. The local authority wanted me to accept the decision too – a decision it had endorsed; in a subsequent external inquiry which heavily criticised the handling of the rape disclosure, it was noted that the local authority officer 'saw no reason to separate the children'.

Neither the school nor the local authority understood why I was so exercised by them putting the boy arrested for rape back into class with her. Unbelievably, they did not seem to have any sense that she could be further psychologically harmed by this decision. They wondered out loud what I was expecting them to do; after all, they bleated, the boy suspected by the police of rape was innocent until proven guilty, so what else could they do? They made sure I knew how difficult this was for them. They suggested that if my daughter didn't want to go to classes with him, she could skip classes. It was her GCSE year.

She sat her GCSEs in the same hall as the accused, because they would not set up a separate exam space for him, but at the same time they applied to her exam boards for special consideration on the grounds she had been raped.

As a teacher, I had experienced how the authorities respond to an allegation of sexual assault made by a child against a teacher; years earlier, a colleague had been swept off the premises by the police and was refused entry back into school until the police had concluded their investigations.

It was glaringly obvious that the school and local authority's response to my daughter's rape disclosure was hopelessly inadequate, but it took me a while to work out that it was also unlawful. When I finally joined the legal dots, I realised that the failure to protect my daughter after disclosure was part of a wider national picture which today is still routinely failing hundreds of victims of child-on-child sexual abuse. The Department for Education's (DfE) response to victims of child-on-child sexual violence has been and remains crushingly awful. The effort it has put into 'dealing' with me is a hundredfold the effort it would have required to produce adequate guidance for schools which would protect children's human rights. My story is the story of a state which appears, in practical terms, indifferent to the suffering of child victims of sexual violence.

The background

It appears that about one-third of all cases of sexual abuse of children is committed by other children (Hackett, 2014; McNeish and Scott, 2023). In July 2016, the Women and Equalities Committee (WEC) undertook an Inquiry into Sexual Harassment and Sexual Violence in schools and colleges (House of Commons, Women and Equalities Committee, 2016). The Inquiry found that there was already an 'epidemic' of sexual harassment and sexual violence in our schools. Figures obtained by the BBC from a Freedom of Information (FOI) request were presented at the Inquiry and suggested that there was one rape in school for every school day.

The Inquiry received evidence that, without guidance, schools were floundering in their response to sexual violence between students and making catastrophic errors in their handling of disclosures.

Point 4 of the Conclusions and Recommendations was clear: 'The Government and schools must make tackling sexual harassment and sexual violence an immediate policy priority.' Despite this, over a year later, the DfE had failed to issue any new guidance to schools and colleges and had not even committed to a timetable for producing draft guidance. In subsequent legal exchanges, the Department blamed the delay of over a year on a range of laughable excuses, including :

- Its staff were busy working on 'unrelated matters'.
- The 2017 snap general election (which put Parliament into purdah for just seven weeks).
- The summer holidays, which made convening meetings difficult.

Legal action

In the absence of any meaningful action from the Government, my daughter agreed to be the litigant in judicial review proceedings against the then Secretary of State for Education. The Secretary of State was to be sued for her failure to take action to protect girls in school from sexual harassment and sexual violence and after making a disclosure of sexual violence. My daughter was under 18 at the time, so I was appointed as her 'Litigation Friend' and was party to the correspondence which ensued.

My daughter's legal action was fully funded by the Equality and Human Rights Commission who shared our concern that the Government's failure to act was resulting in widespread harm to girls and widespread breaches by schools of the Equality Act and the Human Rights Act.

The legal action against the Secretary of State for Education started with a pre-pre-action protocol letter. For those unfamiliar with this terminology, this is a legal letter which seeks to avoid the need for judicial review; typically, it identifies a problem and asks the respondent to work, often collaboratively with the litigant, on a remedy. The response from the DfE to the letter demonstrated little urgency, an inability to commit to a timetable for the production of the urgently needed guidance and no intention to engage meaningfully.

We moved swiftly to the next legal stage, which was the issuing of the formal pre-action protocol letter.

The response from the DfE was described by our lawyer as 'aggressive'. It accused the child litigant of making a 'pointless claim' which was both wasting public funds and the DfE's time, stating, among other things:

> 33 It ought to be self-evident that the proposed claim is academic. It was rendered academic when the Department wrote to you [*date*], and the failure to provide any explanation at all about how the use of public funds to bring about a pointless claim could be justified is conspicuous by its absence in your letter. It is a matter of regret to the Secretary of State that this correspondence has posed a distraction to the Department in finalising interim advice and consultation documents.

The whole tone of the response was one of deep irritation and barely disguised contempt. It is, of course, frightening to receive such a response from the state machinery. It takes considerable effort not to be intimidated.

The DfE's response caused another sleepless night. There were so many in those days. The only advantage of the sleepless nights was that I had time to read and digest the correspondence and craft replies, because of course unlike the DfE lawyers and civil servants who were paid to deal with this correspondence during office hours, this was not my day job, and had to be squeezed in around work and looking after a traumatised family. My sleeping has never returned to normal.

The reply to the pre-action protocol was typical of much of the correspondence I received during that period. It had the hallmarks of what Bishop James Jones described, in the context of the authorities' response to the Hillsborough tragedy, as 'the patronising disposition of unaccountable power'. The behemoth resented being held to account, and it showed.

The next day, in my email to my wonderful lawyer, I said:

> The Gov response woke me up in the middle of the night. The letter has clarified to me one thing – that they did not consider interim advice until mid-July, which is interesting as I wrote to [named civil servant] on 9th July and threatened media exposure if no action was taken. It is so clear that they care more about their media image than any child under their care. The only place in the letter where they express any kind of emotion is their 'considerable disappointment' over being contacted by a journalist. If only they had some emotions about children getting hurt.
>
> [...]
>
> I think the reason I'm awake is that I found the response so rude and so patronising and so unapologetic. Not sure why I am surprised.

These paragraphs below were part of our official legal reply to the Government's response:

> As requested by our client, we wish to preface our further representations with the following observation. This is a matter of very great importance to many thousands of schoolgirls facing sexual harassment and violence every day, which is being inadequately dealt with by their schools. The very grave and extremely detrimental impact on them of this failure to act cannot be understated. It is not disputed that schools must take responsibility for their actions. However, this does not obviate the need for the Secretary of State to use her powers to address this failure via guidance, the absence of which has been identified at the highest level over a year ago.
>
> Moreover, our client has not taken the decision to instruct us to threaten legal action lightly. Nor has the EHRC taken the decision to fund the case without careful consideration of the issues raised. It is therefore particularly upsetting to our client and her family for the Department to continue to refuse to take any responsibility or acknowledge any failure on their part for the year's delay in providing adequate guidance. It is also unhelpful for the [Department's] letter to

be written in a tone which suggests our client's concerns are misplaced or somehow unreasonably held.

There were further legal skirmishes, and as a direct result of the pre-action protocol letter, draft guidance was finally produced (six weeks after the letter was sent). The Department had mobilised its efforts to protect the Secretary of State from further highly embarrassing legal action, but had not mobilised its effort to protect children in the fifteen months since a Parliamentary Inquiry shone a spotlight on the problem. I was both delighted that we had the new guidance and sickened that protecting a politician was more motivating than protecting young rape victims.

For the first time, the legal rights of victims of child-on-child sexual assault were explicitly recognised in DfE guidance with both the Equality Act and the Human Rights Act being cited. The draft guidance was consulted upon and the amended version became statutory guidance on 3 September 2018 as Part 5 of Keeping Children Safe in Education (KCSIE) (Department for Education, 2018).

The new guidance was a major breakthrough in the long-standing campaign by the End Violence Against Women (EVAW) Coalition for girls' legal rights to protection from sexual harassment and sexual violence in school and after disclosure. It had been actively campaigning on this issue since 2010, and in September 2016, shortly after the conclusion of the WEC Inquiry, had published a sixteen-page legal briefing (Whitfield et al, 2016). The briefing, 'All day, every day', had been shared with the DfE in September 2016, but to no avail. One of the former directors of EVAW later informed me that in early 2017 she had been at a meeting with a civil servant in the DfE and had asked for his response to the legal issues raised in the briefing. He is reported to have said that no doubt the analysis was correct, but the DfE would not do anything until it was sued. This was probably simply a statement of fact, rather than belligerence, the servant knowing the master for what it was: the lazy behemoth which would act in its own self-interest, not in the interests of those it is publicly funded to protect.

The new guidance was not effective

Sadly, even though the EHRC-funded legal action against the Department produced new and substantial statutory guidance, there was no transformational effect on the mindset of the behemoth. Just enough had been done to protect the Secretary of State from further legal action, but the Department stopped short of ensuring that the guidance had teeth. There was no funding for any kind of training for teachers. All schools are expected to give annual updates to their teachers on significant changes to KCSIE, but in the pressure of school life, this is often minimal and perfunctory.

Teaching friends of mine were not trained on the new guidance and some were unaware of it. A Teacher Tapp survey initiated by MPs Emma Hardy and Jess Phillips revealed how few teachers knew about the guidance, let alone felt confident in following it.

On 26 April 2019, Nadhim Zahawi MP, then a Minister in the DfE, was quoted in the *Times Education Supplement* as follows: 'I, too, am concerned to hear that there are many teachers who are not aware that the department's advice on peer-on-peer abuse exists.' Even teachers who were aware of the new guidance would have struggled to understand the import of the references to the Human Rights Act (HRA) 1998 as most teachers are not qualified lawyers with specialist expertise in human rights. So in consequence a crucial part of the statutory guidance was almost certainly meaningless to even those who had read it.

Under the HRA, it is unlawful for schools and colleges to act in a way that is incompatible with the Convention. The specific Convention rights applying to schools and colleges are:

> Article 3: the right to freedom from inhuman and degrading treatment (an absolute right).
> Article 8: the right to respect for private and family life (a qualified right) includes a duty to protect individuals' physical and psychological integrity.
> Article 14: requires that all of the rights and freedoms set out in the Act must be protected and applied without discrimination.
> Protocol 1, Article 2: protects the right to education.

Since September 2018, the guidance has consistently exhorted schools to have due regard for the HRA, without once, anywhere, explaining to schools how that Act applies to a disclosure of child-on-child sexual violence, including in cases which do not result in a criminal prosecution.

Consequently, many schools and local authorities are still routinely failing to protect victims of child-on-child sexual violence from further contact in school with the accused. To this day, the most common outcome for such victims is that they either have to share the same classroom/lunch hall/school bus/corridors/exam hall with a fellow student they have named as the perpetrator of sexual violence against them or they have to leave their school. When they are forced to leave their school, they are in effect re-victimised by having significant disruption to their education and social infrastructure.

Correspondence after the legal action

Once the new statutory guidance was published, I could see that without training for teachers, nothing much would change on the ground. So,

I wrote to the DfE again, to find out how the DfE intended to ensure that all teachers not only read but also understood the guidance and would know how to protect future victims of sexual assault after disclosure.

Once again, I encountered the lazy behemoth, which replied by email in this casual way: 'As with all changes to statutory guidance, we want to give the advice and guidance a period to bed in.' As usual, there was no timeline attached. As I write this chapter, it is now well over five years since the email. There is abundant anecdotal evidence that schools still do not understand the HRA and the DfE has still failed to provide advice for schools on *how* the HRA applies.

Other cases

In 2018, through journalists, I was put in touch with other parents whose children were being catastrophically failed by the system.

One of those parents was a father whose 13-year-old had been groomed by a 15-year-old double rapist who was attending her school unsupervised. I was both angry and distraught that two years after the WEC Inquiry, and the revelation that there was one rape in school for every school day (House of Commons, Women and Equalities Committee, 2016), we were still allowing boys already charged with rape to mix freely with our children in school without teachers even being made aware.

As these stories emerged, my anger and disgust was starting to brim over. I wrote to the Permanent Secretary at the DfE in late 2018.

> Dear [name]
> Last night I read the DfE annual report and accounts for the last two years.
> I am reeling from the fact that there is not a single mention in either report of the epidemic of sexual harassment and sexual violence in our schools and the need to take action to protect girls.
> I quote below from the Government response to the WEC Inquiry into sexual harassment and sexual violence, which was published two years ago tomorrow.
>
> 3) Sexual harassment and sexual violence is unacceptable. It has serious implications for the mental health and well-being of children and young people. It has the potential to impact their educational attainment as well as harming their ability to develop happy relationships in the future.
> 4) Nobody should suffer discrimination, harassment or bullying because of who they are. We want to see a culture where all children

and young people feel safe and able to meet their potential whatever their sex, ethnicity, nationality, disability, religion or belief, sexual orientation, gender reassignment or background.

In the DfE annual reports you pay lip service to the importance of equality and protecting human rights, but you have still not taken decisive steps to protect girls in school. The recent BBC FOI shows that YOU HAVE MADE NO PROGRESS in the two years since the inquiry. The figures from the FOI clearly show that there is still one rape in school for every school day. Today, while you sit safely in important meetings, a girl will be raped in school. One is weeping this morning because she was raped yesterday. Tomorrow another girl will be raped. And on Friday. Which bit of that do you not care enough about to put tackling sexual violence against girls in school into your departmental priorities list?

Have you even read the legal briefing sent to you in September 2016? https://www.endviolenceagainstwomen.org.uk/new-report-reveals-schools-ignoring-sexual-harassment-can-be-sued-by-girls/

I have spent a large part of the last 18 months taking a case which is now won, which proves that the analysis in that briefing was accurate. The current system will lead repeatedly to breaches of the Human Rights Act and the Equality Act.

Is it fair to ask parents to try to raise the profile of this issue in their spare time, during sleepless nights, when you are paid an enormous amount of money to take responsibility for this?

Today I am speaking for the first time to another distraught parent, whose story mirrors ours. But his story is recent. You have had two and a half years to do something about it. But for some reason you are choosing not to take decisive action to protect girls. I will find out the name of the victim. I will find out how old she is. Would you like the opportunity to meet with the father, and he can tell you face to face why your system is not protecting girls?

I hope you have a safe day at work. But I also hope you spend a large part of today wondering what the name of the next victim will be, and how old she will be.

Yours sincerely

The story of the 15-year-old double rapist broke in the press in June 2019 (Tahir, 2019):

A 13-year-old was raped in the toilets at an academy by a boy who had been moved from another school for raping two pupils, it has been reported.

The girl's dad said the boy had raped his 'naïve' daughter after 'grooming' her even though concerns had been raised about his behaviour.

The girl's dad has hit out at the way the case has been dealt with. The boy was convicted of two rapes, days after the alleged attack on the girl in spring last year.

There was still no reaction from the behemoth. The school was sanctioned, but still no changes were made to the guidance for schools.

In October 2019, the BBC published an article about a case in Essex where a boy who was already convicted of sexual assault was allowed back into school with his victim (West and Issimdar, 2019). Here is an extract of the article:

A 15-year-old boy convicted of sexually assaulting a girl in a classroom has been allowed to stay at the same school as his victim.

The teenager, who cannot be named for legal reasons, was found guilty of two counts of sexual assault and put on the sex offenders register.

The victim said: 'I have to just keep my head down, pretend he's not there, otherwise it makes me panic.'

The boy, who remained at school while awaiting prosecution, was tried at a youth court almost a year after the assault and given a restraining order, and told not to contact or approach his victim.

I was so outraged at the failure of the Essex school to protect the victim's Article 8 rights that I wrote to the then Chief Inspector at Ofsted and the Secretary of State for Education as follows.

Dear [names]

How do any of you sleep at night while this is allowed to go on? How much more evidence do you need before you take action?

You have NO systems in place to ensure that schools understand the new statutory guidance and implement it effectively. There is no doubt after the Education Select Committee accountability hearing 2 weeks ago that the Chief Inspector herself would get it wrong if she was in charge of a school. We have girls' lives being ruined day after day after day and none of you are taking responsibility for it, and yet you keep collecting the salaries which pay you to take responsibility.

Last week I was told of a girl who has killed herself because she wasn't safeguarded after an assault. Yes, she killed herself. She is now dead.

One by one the public will find out about all these children. They all have names. There are hundreds and hundreds of them. It is feeble to blame the schools. The blame lies at the door of the DfE who has known of this problem for years and chooses not to take responsibility for it.

It is time to prevent further tragedies, further breaches of the Human Rights Act and the Equality Act.

I knew there would be no response from any of the other addressees, but I wanted it to be on record that the cost of inaction would be a child's death. I knew that sooner or later a parent would go public and a child would be named.

On 12 June 2021, Semina Halliwell died. She was 12 years old and had reported being raped by an older boy from her school. In a BBC article about the 12-year-old's death, it was clear that the school had failed to protect her properly after her disclosure from further contact with the accused in school. The BBC article (Price, 2021) reported the case as follows:

> School rape culture: 'Her death could have been prevented'
> Semina's Covid bubble crossed over with the boy's one day a week, so on that day Semina started refusing to go to school.
> In June ... Semina tried to take her own life. Four days later she passed away in hospital.
> Rachel (her mother) says despite being really poorly, Semina was still worried about going back to school and seeing the boy again.
> According to the article, her final words to her mother were these: 'I don't want to go back to school. He raped me.'

Cumulative trauma leading to radicalisation

The behemoth remained unmoved by these cases, but for me there was a cumulative traumatic impact. When I heard of Semina's death, I wept. It was an unspeakable tragedy and an unspeakable collective failure from politicians and civil servants. In the mother's words, Semina's death was preventable. I was raging that the behemoth was so unharmed and indifferent to her death.

When I started corresponding with the DfE after my daughter's rape, I held the naïve belief that it would be quick to listen and would want to do something to prevent widespread unlawful practices in schools which were harming children. Despite mounting evidence of institutional indifference to children's rights and wellbeing, I had kept writing. I believe that motivation occupies the space between anger and hope. I was furious with state indifference to the evidence, and refused to give up hope that children would be protected from avoidable harm.

I continued my correspondence with the DfE without a plan, fuelled by ongoing and exhausting outrage, and a stubborn refusal to accept that children's legal rights could continue to be ignored. No doubt there was a vague hope that if I wrote enough times, the Department would take the necessary steps to protect child victims of sexual assault just to get me off its back.

I was becoming increasingly radicalised by the indifference and immovability of the authorities. I felt strongly that I didn't want to live in a society that could willfully trash children's lives.

In a diary entry from that time I wrote: 'We have been asking nicely for change for a long time. But the time for asking nicely is over. It is time to take direct action.'

I thought about how suffragists had morphed into suffragettes. I started to wonder if I might have to 'do an Emily Davison' to get the issue the attention I thought it needed. I thought about hunger striking outside the DfE offices and other stunts. But my family life kept me anchored, and in any case I could not do anything myself without breaching my child's right to anonymity. So, I carried on writing, all the while wondering how other people managed not to worry about the next child who would be raped in school. I simply have never understood how anyone could fail to react to the statistics.

I broadened my range of correspondents and wrote to two members of the Board of Directors at the DfE. Their silence did not deter me; in fact, it inspired an unflattering poem called 'The Silent Ones'. My correspondence to them was passed to a civil servant who wrote a long but bland and pointless response. I replied to the board members as follows:

> Yesterday I received a letter from [civil servant] which I am assuming constitutes your response to the concerns I raised with you in September 2018. There is a fundamental failure in the response to engage with reality and to take responsibility for the widespread failure by schools to protect girls from sexual harassment and sexual assault.
>
> [The civil servant's] letter avoids mentioning the scale of the problem, or the fact that the most recent BBC FOI shows that no progress has been made on this issue since the WEC Inquiry in 2016. There is still one rape in school for every school day.
>
> [The civil servant's] letter, and the documents to which it links, are riddled with phrases such as 'Schools could' or 'Schools should' or 'Effective schools have been shown to' or 'There is an expectation that …'
>
> The point is that frequently, 'Schools don't' and worryingly, 'School don't have to because the inspection regime allows them not to'.
>
> That is when children, mainly girls, get hurt. That is the reality all of us need to deal with. If the safety of our children in school really matters to you, you need to do more than take the easy option of setting out what should or could happen in an ideal world. The new

figures on sexual harassment and sexual violence in schools clearly demonstrate that the DfE has failed to tackle the problem effectively.

You insist that the inspection regime is robust, but our case and other cases clearly show that a school can breach a child's human rights for failing to safeguard them from a rapist and still be given a judgement of 'safeguarding effective'. As I have said many times, to you and to Ofsted, I am very happy to talk you through the details of our case so that finally you would be in a proper position to make an informed judgement on the effectiveness of the inspection regime.

As I have said before, if you were interested, I could also share information about our local situation; I can evidence how our Local Authority is not providing schools with advice or training on the new statutory guidance, how headteachers don't feel equipped to deal with this area, and are desperate for specialist training, how the specialist support services for victims are overwhelmed and not able to meet the needs of victims in a timely fashion. I can introduce you to headteachers, students, the head of our local rape support centre. Why don't you visit us all and find out what is going on in the real world?

Since I first contacted you, there will have been, on average, 67 rapes of children in school. Each victim has a name.

With best wishes for a happy Christmas and a more constructive New Year.

Meeting with senior civil servants

By February 2019, my lobbying had resulted in two senior civil servants agreeing to a day-long meeting with me, teachers, headteachers, survivors and representatives from the third sector. In fairness, [the civil servants] listened attentively, but when a 14-year-old survivor asked why they weren't doing anything to fix the problem, they replied that they didn't have the power to do anything. Incredulous, I asked who did have the power. [One of the civil servant's] said it was the Secretary of State for Education. I asked why he wasn't doing anything. She said that he was 'ideologically opposed to interfering with headteachers' autonomy'.

As a teacher, I know how profoundly untrue this is. The DfE interferes with headteachers' autonomy in any and every area it cares about. It demands data on everything and anything it cares about and holds schools to account on the basis of that data. To date, the DfE is still not collecting data on child-on-child sexual abuse, even though this was recommended in the WEC Inquiry findings in 2016. The sexual assault and rape of children in school is still not a policy priority.

This admission from [the civil servant] was the moment the penny really dropped that the reason for inaction was indifference. I decided to go public.

In early March 2019, my 'open' letter to the Secretary of State was covered in an article in *The Times* (Woolcock, 2019).

Minister doesn't care, says mother of girl kept in class with alleged rapist
… The mother, who cannot be named, said that two education officials had told her that [Secretary of State], education secretary, did not want to interfere with the independence of head teachers …

The DfE's response to *The Times* article and the subsequent correspondence was to close down all further correspondence with me.

Dear XXXX

I am writing in response to your most recent emails to the Secretary of State and Permanent Secretary about the department's work in relation to peer on peer abuse, rape, sexual violence, sexual harassment and the support available for victims and any other pupils.

You have contacted various people within the Department for Education many times outlining your view that the department is not doing enough. A number of officials have replied previously, clearly setting out the department's position. Most recently, I provided a substantive reply on 20 December and followed this up with answers to additional questions on 14 January. In addition, [civil servant] and I met with you on 26 February.

The meeting was extremely useful and I would like to thank you for the time you invested in bringing together a number of people who were prepared to share with us their views and experiences. Thank you again for setting it up.

I want to be very clear that the department is committed to continue working with sector specialists to consider improvements in policy and processes that will support schools and outcomes for victims in such circumstances. This includes both …, Chief Executive Officer of [Regional] Rape & Sexual Abuse Support Centre and …, Co- Director of the End Violence Against Women Coalition who I have been in touch with since we met on 26 February. As we discussed at the meeting, amongst other things, the department is considering teacher training, data collection and updating guidance.

As we progress this work I want to inform you that the department will no longer be responding to letters, emails or telephone calls from you that repeat the points you have already raised with us. There is nothing more we can say on that and we need to focus our activity on working to consider further and to develop policy and processes along with … and …. I hope that you will understand this decision has not been taken lightly. If you write to the Department for Education on any other subject, we will reply as usual.

Yours sincerely
[Civil servant]

This was my reply (bold emphasis from original letter):

Dear [Secretary of State]

Thank you for the letter of 3rd April 2019 written in reply to my letter to you of 4 March.

My letter of 4 March was the subject of an article in The Times and included the following paragraphs:

> Your civil servants blame the failure of your department to take effective action [to protect children before and after sexual assault by peers] on **your ideological position**, which, they claim, means that you do not wish to undermine school leaders' autonomy. That is utterly disingenuous: the Department for Education takes a very proactive approach in many aspects of education and school life. **You happily override school leaders' autonomy in issues which matter to you and you regulate these areas heavily, demanding data and performance improvement.**
>
> The only conclusion I can reach is **the real reason you have failed to take effective action** to protect girls from sexual harassment and sexual violence in schools **is that this issue does not matter enough to you**.

I note that your response of 3rd April confirms that the Department of Education will not be corresponding with me further but does not attempt to challenge my analysis of your position.

I am therefore concluding that I have hit the nail on the head; put simply **protecting girls' vaginas matters less to you than testing nine year olds on their times tables**.

It is a farcical that you continue to claim that 'nothing is more important than keeping children safe'. Actions speak louder than empty words.

The Department of Education and I have been locked into a tedious correspondence for over two years because you persistently refuse to take effective action to ensure that schools tackle sexual harassment and sexual assault. Your laissez-faire approach in this area means that thousands of children and their families have suffered.

I do hope you read this letter from a 13 year old survivor, published in the Times Educational Supplement [Anonymous, 2019]. This case happened 10 months after the Women and Equalities Select Committee

(WEC) concluded their inquiry into Sexual Harassment and Sexual Violence in schools and was preventable.

Over the last two years the Department of Education has repeatedly supplied 'answers' to specific questions but the so-called 'answers' simply do not address the issues raised. Let me give an example. You have been repeatedly asked why you choose not to collect data on the scale, nature and distribution of sexual harassment and sexual assault in schools. In a written 'answer', you claim that the Department looks at figures already available and you quote four websites. None of these identifies the number, or nature of sexual assaults between school peers. Your so-called 'answer' is not an answer. It is evasion of the question.

The fact is that nearly three years on from the WEC Inquiry the statistics on sexual assault in our schools have got worse not better. We know this because of the work the BBC has done on FOIs, not thanks to any work done in your Department. **More than one child a day is raped at school.** Schools continue to fail to safeguard children appropriately after an assault and are still not supervising boys charged or convicted of sexual assault in appropriate ways. Please look at the pain you are causing to parents and children – it is there for you to see @Parents400

Please remember that every day you choose not to take action, another child is raped in school. As I have said before, each child has a name. One day they will tell their stories.

I very much hope that empty words will quickly be replaced with measures which really do protect children.

It has been an education corresponding with your department.

Yours sincerely

2021: Everyone's Invited and the Ofsted review of sexual abuse in schools

In early 2021, 'Everyone's Invited' went viral. This is a website dedicated to changing rape culture in our schools. There are now over 50,000 firsthand testimonies from survivors of sexual harassment and sexual assault by a school peer. The testimonies could not be ignored, not even by the behemoth, and the Prime Minister at the time ordered an urgent review from Ofsted. Weeks later, Ofsted reported what the WEC Inquiry had already revealed five years earlier: that there is an epidemic of child sexual abuse in our schools being perpetrated by children, and schools need guidance and support to know how to prevent it and how to deal with disclosures. Ofsted even raised the specific point I had been raising for five years, as follows:

Ofsted's findings and recommendations:
When it comes to sexual violence, it appears that school and college leaders are increasingly having to make difficult decisions that guidance does not equip them to make. For example, some school and college leaders told us that they are unsure how to proceed when criminal investigations do not lead to a prosecution or conviction. Schools and colleges should not be left to navigate these 'grey areas' without sufficient guidance.

The government should:

- produce clearer guidance for schools and colleges to help them make decisions when there are long-term investigations of harmful sexual behaviour, or when a criminal investigation does not lead to a prosecution or conviction.

The Ofsted report was published on 12 June 2021. Nearly four years on as I complete this chapter, there is no new guidance to help schools navigate these 'grey areas'. If schools understood how the human rights should apply in these situations, this would provide a clear framework for decision making in situations where there is no criminal prosecution or conviction.

New legal action in 2023

After the Ofsted review, I wrote to the Good Law Project to see if they had any interest in campaigning about systemic human rights abuses in schools. They did. I was put in touch with a leading human rights KC and a solicitor from law firm Leigh Day, both of whom worked *pro bono* to pull together another legal challenge against the DfE.

Our new pre-pre-action protocol (PPAP) letter set out the problem and suggested a solution – new guidance – and a willingness to work collaboratively on new guidance. An extract from the PPAP stated:

a. Whilst the relevant articles of the Human Rights Act 1998 (the 'HRA') are detailed within Keeping Children Safe in Education, there is no guidance for schools on how their obligations would apply to cases of sexual violence where there are no criminal proceedings or convictions.
b. Given that cases of sexual violence ought to be referred to a local Multi Agency Safeguarding Hub, the local authorities also require guidance on how obligations under the HRA would apply to them.
c. Most schools do not have suitably trained and skilled staff to take evidence from children who are victims or suspected perpetrators of

sexual violence. Schools therefore need clear guidance on how they fulfil their legal obligations towards victims under Article 3 of the HRA to 'investigate' an allegation of sexual violence and to reach a conclusion on the balance of probabilities. This may require guidance for local authorities on how they assist schools to meet their legal obligations under Article 3. Schools need more guidance to understand the different evidential thresholds which apply to a criminal investigation and to safeguarding decisions and those decisions which a school is legally obliged to make as a result of their Article 3 duties.

The PPAP also contained compelling evidence from third parties, including Rape Crisis England and Wales:

We are deeply concerned to see, over the course of very many years, the widespread and almost total lack of knowledge from school staff, teachers, including designated safeguarding leads, in responding appropriately to sexual violence and abuse between children in their schools, particularly when there is no open police investigation, or when a case has concluded.

These systematic failings span the country; we are currently aware of over 100 live cases where schools have not understood their obligations to safeguard their students, and are therefore in breach of the Human Rights Act. Leaving students without any safeguards against some of the most traumatic and serious offences is nothing short of a dereliction of duty. It could not be clearer that schools are in desperate need of very clear and practical guidance to support teachers and school staff in how to meet their legal duties, and prevent harm to their students. So that guidance is properly adhered to, it should be accompanied by a comprehensive package of high-quality training, ideally provided by organisations with trauma expertise, such as Rape Crisis Centres, who have specialism and can support with the range of issues that arise because of sexual violence and abuse cases in schools. (Evidence from Rape Crisis England, 2023)

In the legal letter, we even quoted Ofsted's finding from its 2021 review of sexual abuse in schools which recommended that schools needed better guidance from Government.

In response to our PPAP letter, the DfE once again focused on me, not the issue. They attempted to invalidate my standing in the eyes of my own lawyer by:

- complaining about the number of emails I had sent to them;
- stating how many times they had already explained to me that they had done enough; and
- invoking a four-year-old policy of not communicating with me.

All the new and up-to-date third-party evidence in our legal letter was ignored. The DfE's effort went into counting the number of emails I had sent, and finding the dates these were sent, and quoting from its correspondence with me prior to March 2019 in which it claimed it had done enough.

It was an extraordinary response, not least because the account given to my lawyer of my misdemeanours was not even accurate, and totally missed the rather large point that I was also party to the successful legal action which led to the creation of Part 5 of KCSIE. The way the response was phrased (see paragraph 5 cited below) suggests that anyone who writes to the DfE at all is somehow a shady character who cannot be trusted and that any self-respecting lawyer would not represent such a character.

When a state body responds in this way – focusing on the messenger rather than the message – it diverts its energy from the issue, but it also (as the state must know full well) diverts and diminishes the energy of the campaigner.

Was the inaccurate presentation of the past a deliberate attempt to smear me, or was it carelessness?

I do not believe any of this was accidental – it is out of the 'handbook', which may not be in print, but appears to be well understood within the Department.

Ironically, the quotation from my 2017 correspondence in paragraph 6 shows how consistent my question has been all this time.

Response to Pre-Pre-Action Protocol

Before addressing the issues raised in your letter, we feel that it is important that your offices are fully aware of the Department's historical engagement with your client and that there is presently a policy in place not to correspond with your client.

Background and context
5. According to the Department's records, XXXX started to engage with the Department in XXXX. This correspondence related to the sex and relationship education (SRE) offered by her daughter's school which, in XXXX's opinion, was contrary to the DfE's guidelines in this area. A later letter in XXXX called for the Department's statutory guidance, Keeping children safe in education ('KCSIE') to better cover peer-on-peer abuse.
6. In early 2017, the Department received a separate series of correspondence. These letters and emails made reference to 'gaps' in safeguarding legislation, which 'leaves young, school age rape victims exposed to daily retraumatisation (sic) by being put in the same classrooms as their rapists'.

7. The Department received frequent correspondence (totalling over 100) in a similar vein throughout 2017, and again in 2018–19. In amongst the Department's responses, our client clarified the role of KCSIE and its role in keeping children safe, namely that it provides the framework for schools but is not intended to be a prescriptive document and cannot cover every eventuality. For example, on 28 March 2018, our clients noted 'statutory guidance is just that, guidance. It is guidance which schools must have regard to'. What this means in practice is that school leaders must by statute 'have regard to' KCSIE when drawing up and implementing their safeguarding policies but responsibility for safeguarding within a school rests with school leaders and, where appropriate, the relevant local authority. It should also be noted that the degree to which school leaders have 'had regard to' KCSIE is assessed through regular school inspection by Ofsted (or the Independent Schools Inspectorate in the case of some independent schools).
8. The responsibility for safeguarding within schools relies primarily on school leaders who must make decisions appropriate to the situation in which they find themselves having regard to the statutory guidance when doing so. KCSIE provides guidance to schools which amongst other things, includes how to handle reports of sexual violence and sexual harassment. Previous responses to [my name] also set out the process by which statutory guidance is reviewed and amended, i.e., following a public consultation (to which [my name] was and still is welcome to respond) which also requires cross government ministerial clearance on any changes.
9. Eventually, as a result of the vast engagement the Department had had with XXXX on the same issue, a decision was taken that further engagement with XXXX would cease and the Department informed XXXX of this decision in a letter of March 2019 – see attachment A.

Attachment A was the email sent by the civil servant on 3 March directly after publication in *The Times* of my open letter to the Secretary of State for Education.

In summary the Government's response to the PPAP was to promise a consultation which did not happen in the timescale they set out, and did not resolve the problem. It refused the opportunity to work collaboratively and there is still no new guidance for teachers. The Government response didn't even comment on the claim that young victims of sexual violence are suffering because their legal rights are trashed in school by teachers who understandably do not know one end of the HRA from the other.

The local authority and the DfE's Children's Commissioner

Alongside lobbying the DfE, I had also been trying hard to get my local authority to recognise its own legal duties under section 175 of the Education Act 2002 (the duty to safeguard and promote the welfare of school pupils) and the HRA (the duty to protect children from harm). The responses from the local authority were even more dismal and unintelligent than the responses I was used to from the DfE. There were many low points, but one which sticks in my memory was when the authority justified its actions/ inactions by quoting, in writing, section 26 of the HRA at me. There is no section 26 of the HRA. Local government officers should perhaps not be held responsible for not knowing about a victim's Article 3 and Article 8 rights initially, but they should be held responsible for not being open to finding out about how the HRA works; for the consequential failure to protect multiple victims of child sexual abuse from avoidable harm; for failing to engage positively with the public and Councillors concerned about this issue; for ignoring the evidence from a string of safeguarding failures; for circulating defamatory statements; for attempting to suppress public questions referring to safeguarding failure; for threatening the unreasonable behaviour policy simply because I asked for my reasonable questions to be answered; for sending a legal letter threatening me with arrest; for broken promises; for wasting public money; for obfuscations and endless delays. The institutional gaslighting I endured was also meted out to one Councillor who had the audacity to stand up repeatedly to officers on behalf of the public. As with the DfE, the Herculean efforts put into avoiding addressing the issue far outweighed the time and resources which would have been needed to fix the problem.

When our local authority's Children's Services were put into special measures after a string of high-profile failures and an Ofsted report which found it 'Inadequate' in every area, the DfE appointed a Children's Commissioner to come in and work out how the service could be improved. Her job was to understand what had been happening and suggest a way forward.

After four months in the post, she published a report for the Minister for Children. In the Executive Summary, in paragraph 1 of the section entitled 'Key Factors', she describes some of the contributing factors in the failure of Children's Services, and there I am. Identified as 'one mother'.

Later in the report, she writes this: 'The other issue that has taken up considerable time and resource is that of child-on-child abuse (previously known as peer-on-peer abuse) which has been a focus for some time, very strongly influenced by one mother's campaign to improve the way that this is dealt with.' Shall I publicly apologise here for taking up 'considerable time and resource' by drawing attention to ongoing human rights abuses in our schools which harm children? Or shall I point out that had the authority dealt with the issue when I first raised it years ago, no further time or resource would have been wasted? Shall I point out that the 'considerable time and resource' to which she refers includes time and resource put into attacking the messenger rather than dealing with the message? Shall I point out that far from this being a one-woman battle, there are a considerable number of other individuals, and organisations and Councillors, who have been battling this issue with the authority for years? Shall I point out that legal officers have refused to even meet with us for a discussion or to accept our offer to draft additional guidance for them?

One Councillor who had supported the public's attempts to prevent further breaches of children's human rights left a meeting at which the Children's Commissioner was present with the clear impression that the Council had been told by the DfE that it had 'done enough' and that the existing guidance was 'perfectly adequate'. The Councillor raised the point from Ofsted's 2021 findings that schools DID need additional guidance and asked the meeting why it thought this failing authority was doing better than anywhere else. During the subsequent discussion, reference was made to the fact that the DfE have had over 100 emails from 'THAT WOMAN!' That woman is me. The one who won't shut up about human rights abuses in our schools.

It has been an extraordinary thing to watch – the flailing of a Children's Services department which refuses an offer of help to fix a problem which harms children. Over many years, I have wondered what motivates such an incomprehensible and ultimately self-destructive response. My conclusion is that by improving its guidance to schools, the authority would have had to admit that it has made mistakes in the past which may have led to breaches of the HRA. In a defensive culture, hiding past errors appears to be more important than preventing future harm.

What is so extraordinary about the Children's Commissioner's identification of me as one of the key factors in the failure of this authority is that she had never even met me. I had written to her shortly after she was appointed, as follows:

> I would like to share some concerns with you about systemic risks to children in the county posed by a culture of cover up within Children's Services and Legal Services. I think the information is material to the decision you must make about the future leadership of Children's Services.
>
> I have observed the Council's response to a specific safeguarding failure involving my daughter, but what I think it is important to share with you, is not the specifics of that safeguarding failure, but what I have learnt about the systemic risks to children from the Council

response to (a) its own failures and (b) the public raising the alarm about generic safeguarding risks (c) the broken relationship between Members and officers.

She replied as follows: 'I will think about how I want to respond to this and come back to you this week.'

I never heard from her again.

Three months later, she identified me in her report as a 'key factor' in the failure of this authority. Where did her evidence come from? From the authority called out by High Court judges and Ofsted for failing children? From the authority which had paid £700 for me to have trauma therapy in late 2021 because, one assumes, they recognised they had treated me so badly?

Conclusion

The UK state is currently no more responsive to parents raising the alarm about individual or systemic risks to children than it was to the stark evidence presented for years that postmasters were being treated scandalously.

If you are unfortunate to become aware of state failings which are harming children and you feel moved to speak up for those children, know what you are dealing with.

As I mentioned in my introduction, it may help to think of the state as a lazy behemoth which will react badly to criticism or calls to action. It is likely to rise up against anyone foolish enough to attempt to prod it into action.

Before engaging, come to terms with the fact that the state is hugely more powerful than any individual or group of individuals and that this power imbalance allows the state to mistreat individuals and get away with it. Most individuals do not have the resources needed to assert their rights. It is the ultimate David and Goliath scenario, and David rarely wins.

It will help to be clear about what the state response is likely to be, and to prepare for the mind-bending gaslighting which you might encounter: delays, denials, silence, abdication of responsibility, buck passing, lies, promises which are broken, threats, accusations, vilification. If you are new to gaslighting, these tactics will come as a shock and have a particularly powerful effect when delivered on the headed notepaper of powerful state institutions. But knowing these are *standard* tactics will help manage their impact on you.

Cerebra's guide, *Accessing Public Services Toolkit* (Clements, 2016), was extremely helpful to me in understanding and coping with the state responses I was enduring; to read that these were typical state responses helped me understand that what was happening was 'normal' practice and not a targeted attack on me as an individual. Being able to label what was going on as gaslighting helped to keep it in a box. Remember that gaslighting is designed to destabilise you and render you compliant. A sustained period of gaslighting can induce trauma.

Confronting the state with compelling evidence of harm being done to children is generally not enough to win the argument and bring about change. When you can see the harm for yourself because either your own children are affected or you know other families who have been affected, it is acutely painful to be unheard. There is no clearer way of being told that you/those children do not matter. Once you realise that you/those children do not matter to the state, you feel isolated and vulnerable.

So, it is important to have in place a strategy/support network to help you cope with the emotional impact of state inertia. Understand that, over time, state inertia will become toxic to your wellbeing. After you've been banging your head against the same brick wall for years, your best friends and closest family will worry about the wisdom of what you are doing, and its impact on you and them. There have been a number of people on my journey at different times who have been my rock. I would like to thank them all, particularly my ever patient husband.

The state is not always responsive to threats to children, but it does respond rapidly to threats to its own people or institutions. The state is bothered by the press and the courts. Use these levers *from the outset* as reasoned arguments and evidence rarely make any impact.

Above all, do not attempt to go it alone. The state will see you as easy pickings. If you are fighting an issue which has affected your own family, you will be written off, as though the harm your own family has suffered has rendered you incapable of reason. If you are the female parent, you will get the label 'the mother', with all the misogynist connotations that word can muster. So, find others who will campaign with you, and organisations to work with, and journalists who are sympathetic and have time to invest. The state doesn't like adverse publicity, but at the same time, it knows the news agenda changes quickly, and it will simply sit out an embarrassing 48 hours of press coverage knowing that today's news is tomorrow's chip paper.

If you can, fight the issues with the help of a solicitor and the courts. In my experience, the state can ignore a question asked by an individual/organisation for years, but when the same question is posed on solicitor-headed paper, the question gets a timely response. Use the law to enforce change if you can.

If possible, find a way to bring about the change you need without action from the state. Do this instead of or in addition to challenging the state. I have made more progress in getting people to understand a victim's legal rights by running training workshops for teachers than by corresponding with civil servants.

My final piece of advice is to remember that society evolves slowly. When change comes, it seems to come quickly at the point of change, but there will have been a long trail to the change, the work of unseen hands over many years. Do not be disheartened if your effort seems futile; it will be part of the jigsaw. On the shoulders of giants.

This chapter was written in December 2023. The political backdrop to the story told here was a series of Conservative administrations.

We are now in a new political era in which the Labour MP Jess Phillips, who I mention as a fellow campaigner on this issue in 2018, is now Minister for Safeguarding in the Home Office. I have been reassured in writing that she will raise the inadequacy of the DfE guidance directly with the Minister for Children.

It will be interesting to see how quickly the behemoth responds to the evidence that schools need specific guidance on how the Human Rights Act should apply when a child reports a sexual assault by a school peer. Any further delays in filling this void will inevitably result in significant risk to children.

References

Anonymous (2019) 'I was sexually assaulted in school when I was 12. Here is my story', TES. Available from: https://www.tes.com/magazine/archive/i-was-sexually-assaulted-school-when-i-was-12-here-my-story [accessed 29 February 2024].

Clements, L. (2016, updated 2021) *Accessing Public Services Toolkit: A Problem-Solving Approach*, Cerebra, University of Leeds.

Department for Education (2018) *Keeping Children Safe in Education: Statutory Guidance for Schools and Colleges Education Act 2022*. Available from: https://www.legislation.gov.uk/ukpga/2002/32/contents [accessed 8 March 2025].

Hackett, S. (2014) *Children and Young People with Harmful Sexual Behaviours: Research Review*, London: Research in Practice.

House of Commons, Women and Equalities Committee (2016) *Sexual Harassment and Sexual Violence in Schools*, Third Report of Session 2016–17 (HC 91), London.

Human Rights Act 1998. Available from: https://www.legislation.gov.uk/ukpga/1998/42/contents [accessed 8 March 2025].

McNeish, D. and Scott, S. (2023) *Key Messages from Research on Children and Young People Who Display Harmful Sexual Behaviour*, Essex: Centre of Expertise on Child Sexual Abuse.

Ofsted 2021 Review of sexual abuse in schools and colleges - GOV.UK

Price, H. (2021) 'School rape culture: "her death could have been prevented"', BBC, 24 November. Available from: https://www.bbc.co.uk/bbcthree/article/b41fb362-6615-4e9b-950e-36859358e023 [accessed 29 February 2024].

Tahir, T. (2019) 'School "rapist" boy "raped girl, 13, in toilets after he was moved schools for sex attacks on two other pupils"', *The Sun*, 29 June. Available from: https://www.thesun.co.uk/news/9401424/boy-raped-girl-toilets-sex-attacks-other-pupils/ [accessed 29 February 2024].

West, R. and Issimdar, M. (2019) 'Boy convicted of sex assault on pupil allowed back to school', BBC News, 20 February. Available from: https://www.bbc.com/news/uk-england-essex-47201828 [accessed 29 February 2024].

Whitfield, L., Green, S. and Krys, R. (2016) *'All Day, Every Day' Legal Obligations on Schools to Prevent and Respond to Sexual Harassment and Violence against Girls*, London: End Violence Against Women.

Woolcock, N. (2019) 'Minister doesn't care, says mother of girl kept in class with alleged rapist', *The Times*, 2 March. Available from: https://www.thetimes.co.uk/article/minister-doesn-t-care-says-mother-of-girl-kept-in-class-with-alleged-rapist-dqw5lkdtg [accessed 18 July 2024].

6

Fabricated or induced illness: the controversial history, missing evidence base and iatrogenic harm

Andy Bilson, Alessandro Talia, Taliah Drayak, Mary Margaret (pseudonym), Sarah Smith (pseudonym) and Michelle Spence (the names of some co-authors have been changed to protect their and their children's identity)

Introduction

Since its inception in 2002, the definition of fabricated or induced illness (FII) has been widened and the indicators put forward to identify it have proliferated. This chapter focuses on the history of FII leading to its current incarnation, and the harm done by taking the approach developed by the Royal College of Paediatrics and Child Health (RCPCH) since 2002. It is co-produced with parents who have experienced harm caused by investigations and misidentification of FII.

FII and its predecessor, Munchausen's Syndrome by Proxy (MSbP), have a controversial history and an unsettled present. Although the term FII was coined in 2002, in 2009 the RCPCH (2009, p 11) reported an 'absence of universal agreement on the definition of FII'. In 2021, the RCPCH again acknowledged 'ongoing debate regarding terminology' (RCPCH, 2021, p 10) and offered a new definition (RCPCH, 2021, p 11), where FII is defined as 'a clinical situation in which a child is, or very likely to be, harmed due to parent(s)' behaviour and action, carried out in order to convince doctors that the child's state of physical and/or mental health and neurodevelopment is impaired (or more impaired than it actually is)'. Shortly following the publication of this revised RCPCH guidance, the British Association of Social Workers (BASW) published a practice guide which warned social workers about the danger of a range of illnesses being misidentified as FII; the lack of evidence for the indicators used to identify FII put forward in the RCPCH Guidance; and the likelihood of a high incidence of them 'identifying children where illness is neither fabricated or induced' (Long et al, 2022, p 2).

A history of FII

To understand what FII is and the way it has developed, it is necessary to start with its emergence after controversies about MSbP. Paediatrician Roy Meadow coined the term MSbP in 1977 for what he later described as 'journalistic reasons' (Meadow, 1995, p 534); that is, to publicise the issue. The paper described two cases where mothers fabricated their child's illness. In one case, Meadow reported that the mother poisoned the child with doses of salt, which eventually killed the child. In the other, he said the mother lied about her child's urinary tract symptoms, contaminating urine samples to make it appear as if the child was ill and causing innumerable and sometimes harmful investigations. According to Meadow, the parents had in common an 'insatiable appetite' (Meadow, 1995, p 535) for the attention of medical staff because of their child's illness.

By 1995, Meadow had become concerned that the term MSbP was being used too widely (1995, p 534), saying that it was being used for children meeting all these four criteria:

(1) Illness in a child which is fabricated by a parent, or someone who is in loco parentis.
(2) The child is presented for medical assessment and care, usually persistently, often resulting in multiple medical procedure.
(3) The perpetrator denies the aetiology of the child's illness.
(4) Acute symptoms and signs of illness cease when the child is separated from the perpetrator.

He went on to describe how these criteria 'lack specificity' and identified many different situations which were not MSbP, but met them, because a key element of MSbP missing from the criteria was that the carer fabricated the illness in order to gain attention from medical staff.
The controversy surrounding what became known as 'Meadow's Law' raises further concerns about the accuracy of the attribution of MSbP at this time, particularly in cases of child deaths. Meadow had started to link MSbP to cases of sudden infant death syndrome (SIDS). In his book, the *ABC of Child Abuse*, he states what came to be known as Meadow's Law: 'There is now substantial experience of mothers who repetitively smother consecutive children ... "One sudden infant death is a tragedy, two is suspicious and three is murder until proved otherwise" is a crude aphorism but a sensible working rule for anyone encountering these tragedies' (Meadow, 1997, p 29). This 'law' or 'working rule' became influential in paediatrics and social work and placed parents who had multiple children dying under suspicion of MSbP (Eminson, 2000, p 31). In 1999, Meadow published an article providing details of 81 cases in the UK where, over a period of 18 years, he

had advised, and where a child was judged by criminal or family courts to have been killed by their parents. These children's deaths had originally been thought to be the result of natural causes. He states (Meadow, 1999, p 11):

> The reason that more than half the reported families included more than one dead child is likely to be because the courts were impressed by evidence that it was highly improbable for two or more children to die in infancy of undiagnosable natural causes: 'if there is a 1/1000 chance of a child dying suddenly and unexpectedly of natural causes in the first year of life, the chance of two children within a family so dying is 1/1,000,000'.

Only months after the publication of this article, Meadow gave evidence in the case of Sally Clark, telling the jury there was a 'one in 73 million' chance of two children dying from SIDS in an affluent family. Clark's conviction was quashed in an appeal hearing in 2003 and the judges criticised Meadow's use of statistics. Alongside Clark, several other cases of women convicted of murder in which Meadow gave evidence were reviewed and convictions quashed, with widespread negative publicity about MSbP (for example, Sweeney and Law, 2001). In particular, Meadow's misuse of statistics such as the 1/1,000,000 cited above was challenged by the Royal Statistical Society (2001) and later by experts in genetics. The accuracy of paediatricians' diagnoses at this time is further questioned by an RCPCH questionnaire survey of its members (2002, p 62). This found that many paediatricians who worked in child protection had the view that 'a refusal [by parents] to accept reassurance is MSbP' and that 'a significant proportion of cot deaths are murder cases'. Other paediatricians considered that the subject of MSbP was dominated by a small number of over-zealous professionals. The scientific basis was seen to be 'anecdotal and uncontrolled', and they made statements including the following:

> ... medical opinions secure convictions, which are then cited as proof in scientific papers to secure further convictions.
> I just feel that MSbP is a bandwagon at the moment.
> The credibility of the profession is brought into disrepute by doctors who over-diagnose the condition.
> ... experts only appear for the prosecution, so that innocent parents cannot obtain medical support or defence. (RCPCH, 2002, p 62)

In 2002, against the background of the negative publicity, the Department of Health published new guidance which dropped the term MSbP and referred to the 'fabrication or induction of illness in a child' rather than using a 'particular term' because of disagreements about terminology. The 2002 DH guidance (HM Government, 2002, pp 5–6) defined FII as follows:

> There are three main ways of the carer fabricating or inducing illness in a child. These are not mutually exclusive and include:
>
> - fabrication of signs and symptoms. This may include fabrication of past medical history;
> - fabrication of signs and symptoms and falsification of hospital charts and records, and specimens of bodily fluids. This may also include falsification of letters and documents;
> - induction of illness by a variety of means.

However, it continued to promote the idea that there was a high risk of death or serious illness, saying that up to 10 per cent of children die and about 50 per cent suffer long-term morbidity because of FII (HM Government, 2008, p 10; the same figures are also cited in the Welsh Assembly Government's 2008 guidance).

Alongside the DH guidance, the Royal College of Paediatrics and Child Health published its own advice calling for the term Munchausen by Proxy to be abandoned. It took a momentous step in the history of the concept by aiming to promote early identification through recognition of 'warning signs' and called for a wide spectrum of behaviour to be considered FII, including: 'delusion, excessive anxiety, masquerade, hysteria, doctor shopping, doctor addicts, mothering to death, seekers of personal help or attention or financial gain, and those who fail to give needed treatment as well as those who treat unnecessarily' (RCPCH, 2002, p 9). The approach of confusing warning signs with diagnostic signs was criticised by Pankratz (2006, pp 90–1), who outlines how once 'warning signs' are identified, this starts 'an irreversible process of gathering more signs, which ends in a presumptive MSBP/FII diagnosis'. Many of these warning or alerting signs can be found in families where a child has a disability or illness, giving a large pool of potential candidates for misidentification of FII (Pankratz, 2006; Bilson, 2020; Gullon-Scott and Long, 2022).

The 2002 RCPCH guidance recognised that doctors can be off the mark in their diagnosis and stated that uncertainty about the origins of a child's symptoms is not rare, giving the example of a review that showed 9 per cent of inpatients and 24 per cent of outpatients were discharged without a confirmed diagnosis and saying that some disorders do not have objective physical signs or definitive investigations, and are often multifactorial (RCPCH, 2002, p 18). It recognised a danger that there would be families investigated over concerns about FII who are later 'found to have organic disease' (p 32) and called for treatment and support for these families and continuing medical review to aid recovery from the significant impact of the investigation. The guidance also recognised a 'difficult borderline' between fabrication and exaggeration of symptoms, but said that (p 17): 'the effects on the child of exaggerating symptoms, of obsessional protection from infections and allergies, of excessive medication, etc., are not necessarily severe in a child who is emotionally robust'.

In 2008, the government guidance was updated, although key elements remained unchanged, and it retained the definition above. The next year, the RCPCH updated its own guidance. This guidance further promoted early recognition of FII, and again broadened the definition, saying that the earlier approach had focused on severe cases where the carer was deliberately fabricating or inducing the child's illness, extending the definition to include cases with no deliberate fabrication or deception (RCPCH, 2009, p 7): 'In addition to these severe cases, there are others where a child may present for medical attention with unusual or puzzling symptoms which are not attributable to any organic disease and yet which do not involve deliberate fabrication or deception.' This widens the definition beyond the DSM-5 term Factitious Disorder Imposed on Another, as this requires 'identified deception' and from MSbP as defined by Meadow.

The RCPCH's 2009 guidance introduced a set of nine key indicators that should alert professionals and raise suspicion of FII. It also stepped away from the 2002 guidance, which expressed concern about the inclusion of 'exaggeration' as a criterion. 'Exaggeration of symptoms' had become a central element of the definition in the new guidance (RCPCH, 2009, p 7), although no evidence to support this change was offered. In this new broader category, FII was seen to be a spectrum of situations, including parents who are deliberately fabricating a child's illness, who are unduly anxious, or who misperceive or genuinely believe the child to be ill through to children later found to have a genuine medical condition. This widening of the definition was justified on an assertion without evidence that the harm faced by children was felt to be the same, regardless of the cause. No evidence was offered for this change, which reversed the view of the 2002 guidance that the harms caused by exaggeration are likely not to be severe. This assertion that the harm caused by someone deliberately poisoning their child to get attention from medics is the same as harm caused by an anxious parent challenging a diagnosis is clearly baseless. Such different issues require markedly different responses, but the assertion that they are all the same leads only to an investigative response where this guidance is followed.

The focus on awareness of the harm to families caused by misdirected investigations was substantially reduced, although the 2009 guidance did note that, in the spectrum of cases where concerns about FII may arise, there would be some cases where an unrecognised genuine medical problem becomes apparent. In these cases, the guidance said there was a risk of harm due to an 'inappropriate child protection process and delay in correct diagnosis' (p 9). Sarah Smith, a co-author with experience of misidentification of FII, gives an important indication of the harm that false allegations can bring:

> Twice we were caught up in this fear of FII stuff, and as a foster carer it not only destroyed my family life, it cost me my career. In the end, they labelled me anxious. Who wouldn't be anxious with a child suffering from brittle asthma and multiple allergies. I would never have believed what it was like to be on the receiving end of an investigation had it not happened to me. It was brutal.

Similar experiences of significant harm caused by misidentification of FII still abound as shown in Clements and Aiello's survey (2023).

In 2013, the RCPCH introduced the idea of 'perplexing presentations' (PP) in its handbook for paediatricians. According to this text, a PP occurs where one or more of the alerting signs of FII are present and there is no agreed medical explanation for the child's symptoms. The idea of PP was consolidated in the 2021 guidance, which defines them as occurring where there are alerting signs of possible FII, but where the state of the child's health is not yet clear and there is no perceived risk of immediate significant harm. PP have been introduced to promote early intervention even though the RCPCH admits there is no evidence on progression (RCPCH, 2021, p 17) and no evidence that if there is progression that the early intervention proposed in the guidance will prevent it (Glaser and Davis, 2019).

The 2021 guidance also provides its own idiosyncratic definition of medically unexplained symptoms (MUS), which requires both that the child's symptoms are unexplained and the 'parents acknowledge this to be the case' (RCPCH, 2021, p 11). This puts into the guidance the paediatricians' comments in the 2002 guidance that a refusal to accept reassurance is MSbP and ignores the acknowledgment of the limitations of medical diagnosis laid out in the earlier guidance and the criticisms of the term MUS that led to its exclusion from DSM-5 (Dimsdale et al, 2013, p 224).

The 2021 guidance asserts that understanding the parent's motivation 'is not essential to the paediatric diagnosis of PP/FII' (RCPCH, 2021, p 14), again substantially widening the scope of FII beyond the definition of MSbP. In addition, the guidance removed the warnings on the problems of misdiagnosis of illnesses; the harm caused by misdirected child protection involvement; and the need to support families put through child protection processes found in the earlier RCPCH guides. This combination of changes has been criticised for its likelihood of drawing many more children into the categories of FII and, even more so, PP (Bilson, 2020; Gullon-Scott and Long, 2022).

Evidence base for FII

Despite the term FII having been used for over 20 years, the RCPCH's 2021 guidance found an 'absence of published evidence' on it and developed its approach based on 'consultation and expert consensus' (2021, p 6), although the consultation had 'an absence of organisations representing key safeguarding bodies including social work education, and the police' (Long et al, 2022, p 4). The above discussion shows that MSbP is a substantially different concept from FII and thus research into MSbP is not directly transferrable to FII.

For this chapter, the authors carried out a search in the Psychinfo, Medline and PubMed databases in February 2023 and found 50 papers that included the term 'fabricated and/or induced illness'. Forty-four of these papers included no empirical research. Three papers presented case studies with none from the UK: a Zambian study describing poisoning with insecticide (Mwaba et al, 2022); a Spanish study describing individual subjects of poisoning (Gomila et al, 2016); and a Tunisian case study of twins with trocar needles inserted into bodies (Houas, 2019). Three papers presented a series of case studies: one paper concerning gastrointestinal problems and non-oral feeding in 65 children evaluated for medical child abuse in the US (Feldman et al, 2022); an Australian case series of two children with polymicrobial bacteraemia managed at a specialist hospital in 2015, subsequently identified as subjects of FII; and the third a case series of the psychopathology of the perpetrators in a series of 28 individuals with a 'putative diagnosis' of fabricated or induced illness referred over the 14-year period from 1996 to 2009 (Bass and Jones, 2011). This latter case series was the only one including UK based cases and covered a period starting before the term FII was used. In addition, there were two systematic reviews: one of abusive injuries identified in the ENT setting (Rees et al, 2017), which included studies where FII was indicated, and included three case reports from the UK, one of which was in the timescale for this review having been reported as a case of MSbP in 2004; and an international review of case reports and series covering 796 children published internationally since 1965 (Yates and Bass, 2017), most of which occurred before the term FII was used. There was also a narrative review of the literature on FII (although this mainly included papers on MSbP) produced for the National Society for the Prevention of Cruelty to Children (Lazenbatt, 2013, p 61) which concluded that: 'The growing body of literature on FII reflects the lack of clarity amongst professionals as to what constitutes FII, the difficulties involved in diagnosis, and the lack of research into psychotherapeutic intervention with perpetrators.'

None of the 50 papers searched had research into prognostic markers, the reliability or safety of rehabilitative or preventive regimens, or the specificity or sensitivity of the alerting signs being used to diagnose FII. In fact, Glaser and Davies (2019), who proposed these indicators, write that: 'While the alerting signs have been widely disseminated, they have not been tested prospectively for specificity and sensitivity' (p 10). Similarly, there is no evidence base for the RCPCH's recommended therapeutic, rehabilitative and preventive regimens. Again, Glaser and Davies (2019, p 10) state that 'the extent to which this can prevent harm to children, or progression to more damaging FII, remains untested systematically'. Thus, the evidence base for the RCPCH's FII guidance has none of the clinically relevant research into 'the accuracy and precision of diagnostic tests (including the clinical examination), the power of prognostic markers, and the efficacy and safety of therapeutic, rehabilitative, and preventive regimens' (Sackett, 1997, p 3) required for it to be considered evidence based.

Epidemiology

There is also a gap in the evidence base concerning the incidence and prevalence of FII (RCPCH, 2021, p 8). There are no official figures for the number of investigations and findings of FII and the above review found no epidemiological studies.

The most often cited epidemiological research (for example, Davis et al, 2019, p 110) is a survey of paediatricians carried out in the early 1990s prior to the use of the term FII (McClure et al, 1996). This survey identified 128 cases of MSbP, non-accidental poisoning or suffocation across the UK and Republic of Ireland in a two-year period between 1992 and 1994. It reported that 97 of these cases involved concerns about MSbP. The criterion to identify MSbP in the survey was weak. It asked paediatricians to report how many children they had seen about whom a child protection conference had been convened because of concerns about MSbP, non-accidental poisoning or suffocation. The purpose of a child protection conference is to decide if a child has been significantly harmed, so this criterion includes cases where the conference may have decided that MSbP had not been confirmed. The study sample also included an unspecified number of cases where the study's authors, rather than the paediatrician, classified the abuse as MSbP, so in these cases it was unlikely that MSbP was considered by the child protection conference (McClure et al, 1996, p 58).

The 128 children were mainly very young, with a median age of 20 months. The paper often did not differentiate between the three types of harm (namely, MSbP, non-accidental poisoning and suffocation), nor did later papers citing it. Thus, an annual incidence rate of 0.5 per 100,000 is often cited as the incidence rate of children having MSbP, but this includes all 128 children in the study. If limited to those cases which the authors suggested the case involved MSbP, the rate would be 0.38 per 100,000. Also, as mentioned above, Meadow himself reported a lack of specificity in MSbP's definition at this time and it was 'applied to a wide variety of abusive behaviour by parents' (Meadow, 1995, p 535), so this figure is likely to include children who did not suffer from MSbP. It was also published against the background of 'Meadow's Law' suggesting multiple child deaths were murders.

However, several sources suggest a large rise in parents being investigated for fabricating or inducing illness in their children. Davis et al (2019) state that paediatricians in larger hospitals have reported upwards of 50 cases under investigation. High and growing levels of investigations are being reported by organisations representing sufferers of a range of diseases and disabilities (for example, Action for ME, 2017; Autism Eye, 2018; Siret, 2019; Clements and Aiello, 2023; Long et al, 2023; and Ferguson and Hollingsworth, 2024) or difficulties (for example, Not Fine in School, 2018). Moreover, this rise is also reflected in news reports (for example, Grant, 2019; BBC News, 2021). Many of these sources claim that investigations frequently do not find evidence of FII and that they seriously harm families and children (for example, Colby, 2014; Siret, 2019). In a recent survey carried out in the UK discussed in Chapter 7 (Clements and Aiello, 2023), nearly 400 cases of alleged FII were identified. A significant majority of these cases (84 per cent) were ultimately discontinued, and almost all the children involved continued to reside with their parents (95 per cent). This supports the assertion that the application of warning signs would result in substantial misidentification of FII. While those promoting the dangers of FII often suggest that it is under-identified, this survey suggests the reverse: that there are high levels of misidentification.

Thus, there is no epidemiological data on FII on which to plan services or gauge the need for a response.

Deaths and serious harm due to FII

Much of the basis for the high profile of FII and PP over the period the concept has developed stem from the idea that it is associated with a high rate of mortality and serious harm. Thus, the RCPCH (2009, p 15) state FII 'is associated with significant mortality, physical illness, and disability. ... 6% of cases resulted in death and 7.3% of cases experienced long-term or permanent injury'. However, two of this chapter's authors (Bilson and Talia, 2025) analysed the NSPCC's national database of serious case reviews (SCRs) covering the period from 2010 to 2021. Serious case reviews are required in England for all deaths where child abuse or neglect was known or suspected. They found no deaths due to FII in SCRs published in this 12-year period and a literature review for the same period similarly found no UK-based child deaths reported in the literature. Thus, there appear to be no child deaths due to FII in England over a recent 12-year period.

Bilson and Talia found four cases where FII had been associated with serious harm leading to a serious case review over the same 12 years. They conclude that:

> Overmedicalization and/or medical errors were identified at an early stage in all four cases where serious harm was attributed to FII. The SCRs highlighted missed opportunities to respond to concerns about overmedicalization, which played a central role in the harm faced by the children. One further SCR identified a cluster of concerning practices in a single paediatric department, emphasizing that the focus on individual cases distracted from addressing this systemic issue. The focus on placing responsibility on carers, principally mothers, is criticized for potentially diverting attention from these medical shortcomings.

Iatrogenic harm

The literature focuses mainly on the potential harm that parents can cause to children, in cases of FII. However, a key reason for the RCPCH to call for the abandonment of the use of the term MSbP was the high-profile cases of parents having been wrongly imprisoned for murdering their children (RCPCH, 2002; Wrennall, 2007). The reports from parents' groups and charities discussed above illustrate a range of harms suffered following the misidentification of FII. In Gloucestershire, Siret (2019) found that negative impacts include missing treatment for undiagnosed illnesses, breaking up families, undermining the confidence and sometimes the health of parents, with the problems caused in this way impacting directly on all children in the family. It also led to distrust of the medical and social work professions. It also sits in records leading to ongoing problems with engaging with health services for the child and sometimes for the parents themselves. Thus, Mary Margaret says: 'Once my child's symptoms were called into question, mine followed. I was demonised for suggesting that conditions can run in families. Even after being cleared of FII and my child's diagnosis being established, this historical accusation remains on my health records hindering my access to care'.

There are several other organisations and groups that have identified similar issues relating to large numbers of children and their families. In Clements and Aiello's survey (see Chapter 7), parents detailed the trauma and lasting repercussions of this experience, aligning with reports from parents' groups discussed above. The experience of one of the co-authors similarly demonstrates this harm:

> We are a family of five living on our organic sheep and cattle farm in rural Scotland. We are ethnic mixed race dual-citizens and

I am a Muslim. We were referred to social work for 'FII' in 2018. I was accused of coaching my daughter to lie about her symptoms. Our daughters were diagnosed with a bowel condition by the head consultant paediatrician of the children's hospital before this happened. I was treated like a criminal and my daughter a liar. The social worker flooded us with a litany of accusations and it was as if the 'FII' accusation was the key that unlocked the flood gates and our little family experienced so much hatred. Before our eyes our confidant child shattered into a thousand shards of anxiety, terror and betrayal. She lost all trust in everyone but ourselves. School was hostile territory and none of us felt safe even in our own home. Our children's creativity, once so highly praised by the school, vanished. The moment a strange car or person was spotted arriving at our house the children will race upstairs in absolute terror and hide. For us, 'Fabricated and Induced Illness' was not about our children's wellbeing and health but a gateway that allowed certain people to act on their prejudices. The paediatrician proved the 'FII' to be false but we still had to contend with the flood of hate against our children and our family that poured out during and since the social work investigation. Our daughters immediately purged all Islamic and ethnic clothing from their wardrobe and scraped their natural hair into the high ponytail style favoured by their White peers. (Michelle Spence)

Unsurprisingly, few academic papers highlight mistakes made by professionals: 'From their position of privilege and power they remain completely oblivious to harm caused by a false accusation' (Michelle Spence).

Rand and Feldman (1999) undertook a literature review of cases of misdiagnosis of MSbP from 1966 to 1999. They identified seven reports of misdiagnosis in the literature and four new cases. These 11 cases of misdiagnosis included two child deaths wrongly attributed to MSbP. The misdiagnosis of MSbP led 'authorities to remove children from the home and/or bring criminal charges against an innocent parent' (1999, p 94).

Wrennall (2008) presented a case study in which the focus on FII and child protection processes led to harm to a child through significant delay in the diagnosis and treatment of the child's brain tumour (2008, p 1). Wrennall (2007) also outlines cases of false allegations and miscarriage of justice concerning Meadow discussed above. Van Gemert et al (2018) identified a case of misdiagnosed paediatric condition falsification leading to a child being placed for a long period in care. Because the nature of FII is that parents are thought to be lying or misrepresenting their child's illness, parents have no way to argue their case as their arguments are interpreted as further alerting signs. Thus, Taliah Drayak found:

When FII was first suggested, everyone acted as though they expected I would be a barrier. But I wanted to understand as much as anyone. The trouble was the only possible source of harm that was allowed to be considered in this process was that of harm by Mum, by me. Nobody was willing to even consider that a medical mistake could have happened.

Gullon-Scott and Bass (2018) warn of the likelihood that the behaviour of parents with autism can be misunderstood as FII. They give three case examples of mothers with autism whose behaviour was misidentified as FII and whose children had been removed into care or proceedings were under way. Parent groups (for example, McNeil, 2014; Siret, 2019) provide a series of cases where mothers were wrongly accused of harming their child and were investigated and in some cases had their child taken into care, as well having the major impact on families discussed above. Similarly, Saugstad (2020) highlighted the harm done to children suffering from Myalgic Encephalomyelitis (ME) who were taken into care because of misidentified FII. Speight (2020) also outlines his experience with children with ME in the UK, having been involved in over 50 cases subject to care proceedings due to FII/MSbP in the previous 30 years, none of whom became subject of a care order. Similarly, Colby (2014, p 1) reports that the Tymes Trust advised 121 families with a child suffering from ME who were facing suspicion of FII/MSbP and none of whom has been found to be at fault. Some families were said to have been 'bullied into allowing their child to be admitted to hospital for damaging regimes of active physiotherapy' (Speight, 2020, p 1), and families experienced investigations as overbearing and traumatic and were left fearful of taking their children to medical practitioners (Colby, 2014, p 6).

A recent survey of 387 families in the UK (Clements and Aiello, 2023) found that FII investigations were widespread across the UK, and the major finding was the severe and lasting trauma experienced by accused families regardless of the outcome of the allegation. Most investigations (84 per cent) resulted in no follow-up action and 95 per cent of the children remained living with their parents. Worryingly, half of the allegations followed a complaint made by a parent/carer. It also found that disabled parents were four times more likely to face FII accusations, raising concerns about Equality Act 2010 compliance. The profound impact of misidentification of FII and the self-fulfilling nature of the FII label is illustrated by Mary Margaret's experience of having her very ill child wrongly removed for two years:

> Once they made a decision there was no going back, no willingness to consider any alternative. I was guilty simple as, and my child's health deteriorated significantly which was put down to my child 'faking' their symptoms to protect me. Everywhere I turned looking for help, I found

closed doors. Professionals can literally do anything in the name of being concerned about a child. After a long battle, I cleared my name and my child was eventually returned 2 years later on hospice care. I will spend the rest of my life carrying the weight of the knowledge that this accusation and the significant change to my child's medical care for that period of time has almost certainly significantly shortened their life. I didn't just lose those 2 years with them, I think they have lost more than a decade of life they should have had.

The impact on both the child who was subject of an FII misidentification and the child's brothers and sisters is rarely considered, as illustrated by the account of Kaydence Drayak in Chapter 9 of this book. Michelle Spence shares her view of the impact on her children: 'Our eldest daughter was still riddled with anxiety. Our son now had a nervous breakdown. Our youngest daughter became withdrawn and depressed. Our children just had a bowel problem before FII, now they have much bigger problems.' Clements and Aiello's (2023) survey of parents misidentified as abusers who had committed FII discussed in Chapter 7 illustrates the significant harm done by misidentification of FII through the testimonies of hundreds of parents, the vast majority of whom had child protection proceedings dropped.

Alerting signs in current guidance

FII and PP are not illnesses, but rather clinical situations in which a child is deemed likely to be harmed. As such, they do not constitute an illness and cannot be diagnosed. This history of widening and changing the definition of what constitutes FII by the RCPCH has led to a wide range of alerting signs being written into local authority and national procedures and guidance across the UK (Long et al, 2020). The 20 alerting signs proposed by the RCPCH in 2021 are shown in Box 6.1. In addition to there being no evidence base for these alerting signs, they have several issues that frequently lead to misidentification of PP and MSbP.

Box 6.1: Alerting signs in RCPCH 2021 guidance

In the child:

1. Reported physical, psychological or behavioural symptoms and signs not observed independently in their reported context
2. Unusual results of investigations (eg biochemical findings, unusual infective organisms)
3. Inexplicably poor response to prescribed treatment

4. Some characteristics of the child's illness may be physiologically impossible eg persistent negative fluid balance, large blood loss without drop in haemoglobin
5. Unexplained impairment of child's daily life, including school attendance, aids, social isolation.

In the parent:

6. Parents' insistence on continued investigations instead of focusing on symptom alleviation when reported symptoms and signs not explained by any known medical condition in the child
7. Parents' insistence on continued investigations instead of focusing on symptom alleviation when results of examination and investigations have already not explained the reported symptoms or signs
8. Repeated reporting of new symptoms
9. Repeated presentations to and attendance at medical settings including Emergency Departments
10. Inappropriately seeking multiple medical opinions
11. Providing reports by doctors from abroad which are in conflict with UK medical practice
12. Child repeatedly not brought to some appointments, often due to cancellations
13. Not able to accept reassurance or recommended management, and insistence on more, clinically unwarranted, investigations, referrals, continuation of, or new treatments (sometimes based on internet searches)
14. Objection to communication between professionals
15. Frequent vexatious complaints about professionals
16. Not letting the child be seen on their own
17. Talking for the child/child repeatedly referring or deferring to the parent
18. Repeated or unexplained changes of school (including to home schooling), of GP or of paediatrician/health team
19. Factual discrepancies in statements that the parent makes to professionals or others about their child's illness
20. Parents pressing for irreversible or drastic treatment options where the clinical need for this is in doubt or based solely on parental reporting.

Identifying FII and PP using alerting signs comes with significant limitations, which can result in high levels of false positives, often harming both children and families (Clements and Aiello, 2023). These limitations are primarily due to:

1. Challenges in diagnosing various medical conditions
   Alerting signs 2, 3, 5, 6, 7, 8, 10, 11, 13 and 20 depend on an accurate diagnosis. For example, where the diagnosis is incorrect, there will

often be 'poor response to prescribed treatment'. The reliability of these signs is undermined by factors like the thoroughness of the physician's evaluation, their knowledge base, time constraints and biases. Misdiagnoses are prevalent, with error rates, according to Newman-Toker et al (2021) ranging from 2 to 69 per cent, with higher rates particularly occurring in complex or rare conditions.

A European study of eight rare diseases found that a quarter of patients waited between 5 and 30 years to get a diagnosis and 40 per cent received an erroneous diagnosis leading to incorrect medical interventions prior to an accurate diagnosis (Faurisson, 2004). While individual rare diseases are uncommon, there are many of them, and it is estimated that, on any one day, at least 3.5 to 5.9 per cent of the population are suffering from one of these diseases, with 69.9 per cent of them being exclusively paediatric onset (Nguengang Wakap, 2020). A crude comparison of this to McClure et al's (1996) estimate that 3.8 in a million children suffered from FII would suggest that there are over 6,000 children with a rare disease for every one suffering from FII.[1]

2. Warrior parents

The Lamb Inquiry suggested that the system turns parents struggling to get the right diagnosis and treatment for their sick child(ren) into ' "warrior parents" at odds with the school and feeling they have to fight for what should be their children's by right; conflict in place of trust' (Lamb, 2009, p 2). This system effect was confirmed more recently by Ofsted (2021). In this fight for their children, parents will be likely to trigger reporting signs 6, 7, 10, 11, 13, 14, 15, 16, 17 and 18.

3. Ambiguity in the alerting signs

These ambiguities require subjective judgement by medical staff, including the vague nature of signs like 'not able to accept reassurance', 'vexatious complaints' and 'inappropriately seeking multiple medical opinions'.

4. Difficulties in directly observing symptoms

Alerting sign 1 poses problems because numerous legitimate medical conditions, like migraines, lack objective confirmation for their symptoms. Additionally, the sign requires observation in the child's home, where intermittent symptoms may be easily missed. In hospital settings, limited medical personnel presence makes even episodic events hard to observe, making the absence of independent observation an unreliable criterion.

5. Exaggeration and misrepresentation

Alerting sign 19 is seen as a strong indicator of FII. However, studies indicate that it is not uncommon for parents to exaggerate or misrepresent their child's medical condition for a number of reasons, including how questions are asked or because they are anxious and wanting to get the

doctor to listen (Morley, 1995) and this behaviour is rarely indicative of fabricating an illness.
6. Medical disputes/controversies/developing knowledge

For a number of conditions, medical disputes, controversies or developing knowledge can lead to misidentification of FII because parents struggle to get a correct diagnosis and in some cases there is a dispute about the existence of some illnesses. For example, some parents are being disbelieved about their children having long Covid and this is categorised as FII (Munblit et al, 2022, p 1): 'The issue of not being believed is a common one, and the fear of being considered over-anxious and/or Munchausen's by proxy is very difficult.'

Disbelief and misinterpretations are widely reported in a range of illnesses, including, but not limited to: Autism (Gullon-Scott and Bass, 2018), Myalgic Encephalomyelitis/Chronic Fatigue Syndrome (ME/CFS) (NICE, 2021); Pathological Demand Avoidance (PDA) (Gullon-Scott et al, 2020); Ehlers Danlos Syndrome (EDS) (Ehlers Danlos Support UK, nd); Paediatric Acute-onset Neuropsychiatric Syndrome; Paediatric Autoimmune Neuropsychiatric Disorder Associated with Streptococcal infections (Pans Pandas UK, 2023); and long Covid (Munblit et al, 2022).

In summary, relying on these alerting signs for identifying FII and PP is problematic due to the inherent difficulties in diagnosis and the potential for misinterpreting behaviours commonly associated with complex medical conditions. This can lead to the misidentification of cases, causing harm to children and their families, particularly where undiagnosed or misdiagnosed medical conditions are prevalent.

Some indications of challenge and change

Despite this bleak history, there are some indications of effective challenges and change that need to be welcomed and expanded.

Shortly after the publication of the RCPCH guidelines, the British Association of Social Workers published its own guide (Long et al, 2022), which highlights the problems of over-identification using the alerting signs; warns about the likelihood of misidentification; and provides guidance and support to social workers to recognise and challenge misidentification of FII.

The National Institute for Health and Care Excellence (NICE) guidelines recognise that people with ME/CFS are not believed (NICE, 2021, p 71) and the symptoms of ME/CFS can be mistaken for abuse or neglect (sec 1.7.1). It specifically identifies that some of the RCPCH's alerting signs will be seen in families with a child with ME/CFS, saying they should not be interpreted as signs of abuse (sec 1.74). It also recommends that where a child with ME/CFS is being assessed for child abuse, they should directly involve health and social care professionals who have training and experience in ME/CFS (sec 1.7.2).

There is a growing recognition of the need to improve parental engagement and the Independent Review of Children's Social Care (MacAlister, 2022, p 23) recommended that 'where there are serious concerns, parents should have representation and support to help navigate the child protection process'. Pilots of parental representation have been included in the pathfinder programme as part of the government's implementation strategy for the review.

Conclusion

The history of FII, from its beginnings in the controversies surrounding MSbP, has been one of expanding thresholds for including families without evidence and with reducing concern for issues of false positives or the harm that misidentification can have on children and parents. This has led to an expanding set of unevidenced alerting signs which do not acknowledge the known shortcomings of medical diagnosis and that overlap with behaviours that are common in families with children with rare or difficult-to-diagnose illnesses. This combination of weaknesses leads to the patterns of over-identification of FII discussed in other chapters of this book.

The literature review reveals several significant gaps and concerns regarding the concept of FII and its associated guidance. Despite the term being used for over 20 years, there continues to be a lack of clarity on the definition of FII, and an absence of published evidence and research into key aspects of FII. The existing literature consists of a small number of case studies, narrative reviews and systematic reviews, many of which pre-date the use of the term FII. There is a lack of empirical research, diagnostic tests, prognostic markers and evidence for therapeutic interventions. The incidence and prevalence of FII remain uncertain, with a rise in investigations reported, but no epidemiological studies available. The issue of iatrogenic harm has been progressively removed from consideration in the guidance despite FII emerging from the controversy about parents wrongfully imprisoned for murdering their children. Accounts by parents highlight cases of misdiagnosis leading to wrongful imprisonment; delayed diagnoses and treatment of often serious medical conditions; family breakdown; serious impacts on parents' and children's mental health; and ongoing problems with health services long after the misidentification had been identified.

Note
[1] Taking the lowest band or 3.5 per cent and that 69.9 per cent are children, there would be 2446.5 per 100,000 children with a rare disease.

References

Action for ME (2017) 'Families facing false accusations: results of Action for M.E.'s survey'. Available from: https://www.actionforme.org.uk/uploads/pdfs/families-facing-false-accusations-survey-results.pdf [accessed 7 February 2025].

Autism Eye (2018) 'Parents bullied by fabricated illness'. Available from: https://www.autismeye.com/fii/ [accessed 7 February 2025].

Bass, C. and Jones, D. (2011) 'Psychopathology of perpetrators of fabricated or induced illness in children: case series', *British Journal of Psychiatry*, 199(2): 113–18.

BBC News (2021) 'Children's doctors given fabricated illness guidance'. Available from: https://www.bbc.co.uk/news/health-56253759 [accessed 7 February 2025].

Bilson, A. (2020) 'Comments on perplexing presentations (PP)/fabricated or induced illness (FII) by carers: RCPCH guidance'. Available from: https://bilson.org.uk/home/response-on-fii/ [accessed 7 February 2025].

Bilson, A. and Talia, A. (2025) 'Fabricated or Induced Illness (FII) in England: Examining Mortality and Serious Harm.'

Clements, L. and Aiello, A.L. (2023) *The Prevalence and Impact of Allegations of Fabricated or Induced Illness*, Cerebra, University of Leeds.

Colby, J. (2014) 'False allegations of child abuse in cases of childhood Myalgic Encephalomyelitis (ME)', *Argument and Critique*, July.

Davis, P., Murtagh, U. and Glaser, D. (2019) '40 years of fabricated or induced illness (FII): where next for paediatricians? Paper 1: epidemiology and definition of FII', *Archives of Disease in Childhood*, 104(2): 110–14.

Dimsdale, J.E., Creed, F., Escobar, J., Sharpe, M., Wulsin, L., Barsky, A. et al (2013) 'Somatic symptom disorder: an important change in DSM', *Journal of Psychosomatic Research*, 75(3): 223–8.

Ehlers Danlos Support UK (nd) 'Child protection and EDS'. Available from: https://www.ehlers-danlos.org/support/child-protection-and-eds/ [accessed 7 February 2025].

Eminson, D.M. (2000) 'Background', in D.M. Eminson and R.J. Postlethwaite (eds) *Munchausen Syndrome by Proxy Abuse: A Practical Approach*, Oxford: Butterworth-Heinemann.

Faurisson, F. (2004) *EurordisCare2: Survey of Diagnostic Delays, 8 Diseases*. Eurodis, Europe.

Feldman, K.W., Ambartsumyan, L., Goldin, A., Jenny, C., Wiester, R.T., Metz, J.B. et al (2022) 'Gastrointestinal problems and non-oral feeding in children evaluated for medical child abuse (fabricated and induced illness)', *Child Abuse Review*, 31(3): e2746.

Ferguson, L. and Hollingsworth, D. (2024) *Blamed Instead of Helped: How parents of autistic children experience parental blame when they approach services for support*. Association of Adult Social Services. Available from: https://www.wm-adass.org.uk/media/xprf2qx3/adass-autism-rep-oct24-final-fp7-approved-online.pdf [accessed 25 February 2025].

Glaser, D. and Davis, P. (2019) 'For debate: forty years of fabricated or induced illness (FII): where next for paediatricians? Paper 2: management of perplexing presentations including FII', *Archives of Disease in Childhood*, 104(1): 7–11.

Gomila, I., López-Corominas, V., Pellegrini, M., Quesada, L., Miravet, E., Pichini, S. et al (2016) 'Alimemazine poisoning as evidence of Munchausen syndrome by proxy: a pediatric case report', *Forensic Science International*, 266: e18–e22.

Grant, P. (2019) 'False allegations of fabricated illness "ripped family apart"', BBC News. Available from: https://www.bbc.co.uk/news/health-48151355 [accessed 7 February 2025].

Gullon-Scott, F.J. and Bass, C. (2018) 'Munchausen by proxy: under-recognition of autism in women investigated for fabricated or induced illness', *Good Autism Practice*, 19(2): 6–11.

Gullon-Scott, F. and Long, C. (2022) 'FII and perplexing presentations: what is the evidence base for and against current guidelines, and what are the implications for social services?' *British Journal of Social Work*, 52(7): 4040–56.

Gullon-Scott, F., Long, C., Eaton, J. and Russell, S. (2020) 'The need for a new approach to the identification of fabricated and induced illness', PDA Society. Available from: https://www.pdasociety.org.uk/wp-content/uploads/2020/02/A-new-approach-to-identification-of-FII.pdf [accessed 7 February 2025].

Houas, Y., Fitouri, F. and Hamzaoui, M. (2019) 'Fabricated or induced illness in twins associated with insertion of trocar needles into their bodies', *Paediatrics and International Child Health*, 39(3): 227–9.

HM Government (2002) *Safeguarding Children in Whom Illness Is Fabricated or Induced*. Department of Health.

HM Government (2008) *Safeguarding Children in Whom Illness Is Fabricated or Induced: Supplementary Guidance to Working Together to Safeguard Children*. Department for Children, Schools and Families.

Lamb, B. (2009) *Report to the Secretary of State on the Lamb Inquiry Review of SEN and Disability Information*. London: Department for Children, Schools and Families.

Lazenbatt, A. (2013) 'Fabricated or induced illness in children: a narrative review of the literature', *Child Care in Practice*, 19(1): 61–77.

Long, C., Coope, T., Hughes, S., and Hidson, K. (2023) *PANS, PANDAS and Fabricated or Induced Illness: A Guide for Social Work, Healthcare and Education Professionals*. Warwick: PANS PANDAS UK. Available from: https://panspandasuk.org/wp-content/uploads/2024/06/FII-Report-2024-PANS-PANDAS-Fabricated-or-Induced-Illness.pdf [accessed 25 February 2025].

Long, C., Eaton, J., Russell, S., Gullon-Scott, F. and Bilson, A. (2020) 'Fabricated or induced illness and perplexing presentations: practice guidance for social work practitioners', Unpublished report for BASW.

Long, C., Eaton, J., Russell, S., Gullon-Scott, F. and Bilson, A. (2022) 'Fabricated or induced illness and perplexing presentations: abbreviated practice guide for social work practitioners', Birmingham: BASW. Available from: https://www.basw.co.uk/resources/fabricated-and-induced-illness-practice-guide [accessed 7 February 2025].

MacAlister, J. (2022) 'The independent review of children's social care: Final Report', London. Available from: https://webarchive.nationalarchives.gov.uk/ukgwa/20230308122535mp_/https://childrenssocialcare.independent-review.uk/wp-content/uploads/2022/05/The-independent-review-of-childrens-social-care-Final-report.pdf [accessed 25 February 2025].

McClure, R.J., Davis, P.M., Meadow, S.R. and Sibert, J.R. (1996) 'Epidemiology of Munchausen syndrome by proxy, non-accidental poisoning, and non-accidental suffocation', *Archives of Disease in Childhood*, 75(1): 57–61.

McNeil, F. (2014) 'Parent, carer … victim?' *Autism Eye*, 13: 8–15.

Meadow, R. (1995) 'What is, and what is not "Munchausen syndrome by proxy"?' *Archives of Disease in Childhood*, 72(6): 534–8.

Meadow, R. (ed) (1997) *ABC of Child Abuse*. London: BMJ Publishing Group.

Meadow, R. (1999) 'Unnatural sudden infant death', *Archives of Disease in Childhood*, 80(1): 7–14.

Morley, C.J. (1995) 'Practical concerns about the diagnosis of Munchausen syndrome by proxy', *Archives of Disease in Childhood*, 72(6): 528–30.

Munblit, D., Simpson, F., Mabbitt, J., Dunn-Galvin, A., Semple, C. and Warner, J.O. (2022) 'Legacy of COVID-19 infection in children: long-COVID will have a lifelong health/economic impact', *Archives of Disease in Childhood*, 107(3): e2. https://doi.org/10.1136/archdischild-2021-321882

Mwaba, C., Chungu, C., Chola, R., Nkole, K.L., Wa Somwe, S. and Mpabalwani, E. (2022) 'Organophosphate insecticide poisoning with monocrotophos-induced fabricated illness in a 7-year-old girl with refractory seizures over a 4-year period', *Paediatrics and International Child Health*, 42(2): 83–8.

Newman-Toker, D.E., Wang, Z., Zhu, Y., Nassery, N., Tehrani, A.S.S., Schaffer, A.C. et al (2021) 'Rate of diagnostic errors and serious misdiagnosis-related harms for major vascular events, infections, and cancers: toward a national incidence estimate using the "Big Three"', *Diagnosis*, 8(1): 67–84.

Nguengang Wakap, S., Lambert, D.M., Olry, A., Rodwell, C., Gueydan, C., Lanneau, V. et al (2020) 'Estimating cumulative point prevalence of rare diseases: analysis of the Orphanet database', *European Journal of Human Genetics*, 28(2): 165–73.

NICE (2021) 'Myalgic encephalomyelitis (or encephalopathy)/chronic fatigue syndrome: diagnosis and management', NICE guideline [NG206]. Available from: https://www.nice.org.uk/guidance/ng206 [accessed 7 February 2025].

Not Fine in School (2018) 'Fabricated or induced illness (FII)'. Available from: https://notfineinschool.co.uk/fii#:~:text=FII%20is%20a%20potential%20allegation,not%20fully%20understanding%20the%20difficulties [accessed 7 February 2025].

Ofsted (2021) 'SEND: old issues, new issues, next steps'. Available from: https://www.gov.uk/government/publications/send-old-issues-new-issues-next-steps/send-old-issues-new-issues-next-steps [accessed 7 February 2025].

Pankratz, L. (2006) 'Persistent problems with the Munchausen syndrome by proxy label', *Journal of the American Academy of Psychiatry and the Law Online*, 34(1): 90–5.

Pans Pandas UK (2023) 'Fabricated or induced illness position statement'. Available from: https://www.panspandasuk.org/workinggroupstatement [accessed 7 February 2025].

Rand, D.C. and Feldman, M.D. (1999) 'Misdiagnosis of Munchausen syndrome by proxy: a literature review and four new cases', *Harvard Review of Psychiatry*, 7(2): 94–101.

Royal College of Paediatrics and Child Health (RCPCH) (2002) *Fabricated or Induced Illness by Carers*, London.

RCPCH (2009) *Fabricated or Induced Illness by Carers: A Practical Guide for Paediatricians*, London.

RCPCH (2021) *Perplexing Presentations (PP)/Fabricated or Induced Illness (FII) in Children: RCPCH Guidance*, London.

Rees, P., Al-Hussaini, A. and Maguire, S. (2017) 'Child abuse and fabricated or induced illness in the ENT setting: a systematic review', *Clinical Otolaryngology*, 42(4): 783–804.

Royal Statistical Society (2001) 'Royal Statistical Society concerned by issues raised in Sally Clark case'. Available from: https://web.archive.org/web/20021202172422/http://www.rss.org.uk/archive/reports/sclark.html [accessed 7 February 2025].

Sackett, D.L. (1997) 'Evidence-based medicine', *Seminars in Perinatology*, 21(1): 3–5.

Saugstad, O.D. (2020) 'Myalgic encephalomyelitis (ME) in the young: time to Repent', *Acta Paediatrica*, 109(4): 645–6.

Siret, D. (2019) 'An examination of fabricated an induced illness cases in Gloucestershire: a report from the Parent and Carer Alliance C.I.C', Parent and Carer Alliance. Available from: https://onlinelibrary.wiley.com/doi/10.1111/apa.15084#:~:text=Parents%20are%20accused%20of%20life,or%20even%20permanent%20detrimental%20effects. [accessed 25 February 2025].

Speight, N. (2019) 'Myalgic encephalomyelitis: time to repent', *Acta Paediatrica*, 109(4): 862.

Sweeney, J. and Law, B. (2001) 'Gene find casts doubt on double "cot death" murders', *The Observer*, 15 July. Available from: https://www.theguardian.com/uk/2001/jul/15/johnsweeney.theobserver [accessed 7 February 2025].

Van Gemert, M.J.C., Vlaming, M., Osinga, E., Bruijninckx, C.M.A., Neumann, H.A.M. and Sauer, P.J.J. (2018) 'Pediatric condition falsification misdiagnosed by misjudged weight growth from the curve of measured weights', *American Journal of Care Reports*, 27(19): 752–6.

Welsh Assembly Government (2008) *Safeguarding Children in Whom Illness is Fabricated or Induced (2008)* Cardiff. Available from: https://cysur.wales/media/grofqaa3/safeguarding_children_in_whom_illness_is_fabricated_or_induced.pdf [accessed 25 February 2025].

Wrennall, L. (2007) 'Munchausen syndrome by proxy/fabricated and induced illness: does the diagnosis serve economic vested interests, rather than the interests of children?', *Medical Hypotheses*, 68(5): 960–6.

Wrennall, L. (2008) 'Misdiagnosis of child abuse related to delay in diagnosing a paediatric brain tumour', *Clinical Medicine: Pediatrics*, 1: CMPed-S739.

Yates, G. and Bass, C. (2017) 'The perpetrators of medical child abuse (Munchausen syndrome by proxy) – a systematic review of 796 cases', *Child Abuse and Neglect*, 72: 45–53.

7

Managing the data: allegations that parents are fabricating or inducing their child's illness

Luke Clements, Ana Laura Aiello and Derek Tilley

Introduction

Any meaningful study of the phenomenon of 'parent carer blame' is bound to conclude that its origins are diffuse and that it is deeply embedded across the spectrum of statutory social welfare services. A paradigm example of this complexity emerged during the research programme described in Chapter 2: a programme that sought to better understand the causes, prevalence and impacts of social work practices that started from a premise that the parents of disabled children were neglectful and/or abusive (Clements and Aiello, 2021).

During the research programme, increasing numbers of parents reported that they and their families were traumatised by finding themselves accused of fabricating or causing or exaggerating their child's illness ('fabricated or induced illness', FII). FII can be characterised as an extreme form of parent blame and the fact that allegations of this kind had been made against significant numbers of families was surprising, given that (as discussed below) it is generally considered to be a very rare condition (McClure et al, 1996).

In consequence, it was decided that this aspect of parent carer blame should be the subject of specific research. The research considered situations where a parent, during their 'interactions with a public body such as a local authority, the NHS or an educational institution, believed that they had been accused of FII, or that things were said to them (or written) by a professional that implied that this might be the case' (Clements and Aiello, 2023, para 4.06). The research endeavoured to better understand the prevalence and impacts of professional suggestions/allegations of this nature.

FII background context

Bilson et al in Chapter 6 provide a brief history of the development of the concept of FII and the genesis of the current guidance as to the identification of its 'perplexing presentations' (published by the Royal College of Paediatrics and Child Health (RCPCH) in 2021). The guidance defines FII as: 'a clinical situation in which a child is, or is very likely to be, harmed due to parent(s) behaviour and action, carried out in order to convince doctors that the child's state of physical and/or mental health and neurodevelopment is impaired (or more impaired than it actually is)' (RCPCH, 2021, p 11). FII is not a condition listed in the current Diagnostic and Statistical Manual of Mental Disorders (DSM-5-TR) produced by the American Psychiatric Association and is not, therefore, a medically 'diagnosable' condition – it is at best a child protection label that describes a range of behaviours (*A County Council v M* 2005, EWHC 31 (Fam), para 175).

Methodology and methodological challenges

The research considered in this chapter commenced in June 2022 and culminated in a November 2023 report 'The prevalence and impact of allegations of fabricated or induced illness (FII)' (Clements and Aiello, 2023).

Between July and August 2022, Cerebra posted an online survey aimed at parent carers (parents caring for a disabled child) with the primary aim of assessing the impact that FII allegations were having on families. The survey (referred to below as the 'Cerebra survey') comprised ten questions and received 415 responses, of which 28 were discounted for methodological reasons, leaving a research sample of 387 responses.

Although the Department for Education database holds quantitative data on a wide range of child protection issues, it does not contain information as to the precise reasons for safeguarding action being initiated – for example, due to suspected FII. This too is the case for healthcare systems (an issue we explore further below). Faced with these challenges (in assessing the prevalence of FII allegations), the use of Freedom of Information (FoI) requests (to individual Children's Services authorities) appeared to be a potential method by which data of this kind could be obtained. However, at an early stage in the programme, we encountered researchers who had endeavoured, unsuccessfully, to capture FII prevalence data using this method. These had failed, as authorities either denied holding the relevant data or declined to provide it on costs grounds or relied on one or more of the exemptions in Part II of the Freedom of Information Act 2000 (for example, that the request concerned personal information relating to third parties).

The use of FoIs of this kind – even if Children's Services authorities had provided the requested information – could only unearth data relating to formal FII allegations that had been shared with a local authority for safeguarding purposes. However, the majority of the reports we received from parents concerned FII suggestions/allegations made by health practitioners or schools (Clements and Aiello, 2023, para 5.29). In relation to these, many of the families were uncertain as to whether they had resulted in an investigation by the Children's Services department (or indeed whether they had even been reported to that department): a situation we consider further below.

Within the timescale of the research programme it was, therefore, objectively impracticable to measure with any degree of precision the prevalence of FII allegations in the UK. It was considered, however, that a combination of a literature search, a search of local authority websites for relevant FII safeguarding policies and practices, and insights gained from the Cerebra survey could provide (in addition to evidence of the impact of FII allegations on families) an insight as to the prevalence of such allegations.

Safeguarding law overview

The Children Act 1989 provides English Children's Services' authorities with extensive powers and duties to intervene in the lives of families, where they have reasonable cause to suspect that a child is suffering, or is likely to suffer, significant harm. The basic duty in this respect is found in section 47 of the Act: the 'duty to investigate'. Where an authority has 'reasonable cause' to suspect that harm of this kind may be occurring, it is under a duty to ensure that inquiries are made to enable it to decide whether any action to safeguard or promote the child's welfare needs to be taken. In so doing, the authority must ensure that its inquiries and its subsequent actions are proportionate (Human Rights Act (HRA), 1998, Schedule 1, Article 8).

If it is decided that action needs to be taken, local authorities have a range of options – from placing the child on a child protection plan or instigating care proceedings to more consensual arrangements such as developing a child in need plan or accommodating the child.

As the statutory guidance 'Working Together' (HM Government, 2023, p 7) explains, the police, Integrated Care Boards (ICBs) and the local authority 'are under a duty to make arrangements to work together, and with other partners locally including education providers and childcare settings, to safeguard and promote the welfare of all children in their area'.

The 2023 guidance (p 89) emphasises that social workers should lead section 47 assessments with support from the police, health practitioners, teachers, school staff and other relevant practitioners in undertaking relevant inquiries. It follows that where one of the statutory partners has evidence-based suspicions that a child is suffering, or is likely to suffer, significant harm – they 'should' share this information with the local authority.

Learning of FII allegations

It appears that many families learn that they are suspected of FII not as a result of direct contact with Children's Services, but from comments/

intimations made to them by health or education practitioners or, indeed, by accident.

Lucy Fullard in Chapter 11 recounts her experience in hospital after the admission of her disabled daughter. Lucy sensed that the nurses were cold and 'blunt', but put this down to work pressures. She describes how in the nurses' station there was a large file containing her daughter's medical records and how her daughter, who was playing in that area, said 'that's got my name on it mummy'! Lucy opened the top of the records and saw on the front cover a prominent alert sheet raising safeguarding concerns about her having fabricated illness – and how her 'whole body went into immediate shock'.

Louise Parker Engels in Chapter 4 describes how a parent was so troubled by the 'funny looks' she got from receptionists when she took her children to medical appointments, that she asked Children's Services to 'confirm once and for all that she was not harming her children'. She then discovered that she was being investigated for FII, in part because the safeguarding doctor said that she claimed to know too much about health, due to claims of being a theatre nurse. It was subsequently shown that the doctor had mixed up her notes with someone else's (Parker Engels, 2020).

Amy in Chapter 10 describes how as a result of a request for her medical records she discovered an entry (which post-dated a complaint she had made) that expressed the need for involvement of the safeguarding team: a record that alluded to several of the 'perplexing presentations' in the RCPCH 2021 guidance; a record that she believes would be understood by practitioners as flagging up FII concerns 'without having the need to state this explicitly. A classic example of the secret language of parent blame used by such practitioners'.

2023 research findings

As the 2023 report records: 'No one reading the entirety of the research data could be in any doubt as to the study's most disturbing finding, namely the harm suffered by families who have experienced FII allegations' (Clements and Aiello, 2023, p 3), and at para 5.03:

> Time and time again, respondents described the impact of FII allegations using words such as 'trauma', 'trust' (as in 'loss of'), 'fear', 'scared', 'devastating' 'destroyed', 'suicidal', 'isolation' (in the sense of avoiding contact with health, social care and education services) and in terms of having to move homes and of lost employment. A striking characteristic of these impacts is the fact that they are generally described as long term/ongoing harms: harms from which the respondents believed that they and/or their partners and children will never recover.

Other relevant findings in the research included that:

- disabled parents appeared to be four times more likely to be accused of FII than non-disabled parents;
- 50 per cent of allegations of FII were made after a parent carer had complained about the actions of the relevant public body;
- of the survey responses, it appeared that most FII allegations (84 per cent) resulted in no follow-up action or were abandoned and that in 95 per cent of the cases, the child(ren) remained living with the parent; and
- NHS practitioners were the source of most FII allegations, followed by schools and then local authority children's services.

Data processing and 're-traumatisation'

One repeated and unexpected response to the Cerebra survey concerned the harm that many families had experienced as a result of the way their medical and social care records had been processed. This included not only the contents of the notes that had been uploaded by practitioners (in coding terms, the 'free text'), but also the difficulties the families had in getting these records erased when the FII allegations were, for example, shown to be mistaken or unsupported by the evidence or withdrawn (these examples are collectively referred to in the following analysis as 'unsubstantiated' allegations).

The 2023 report drew attention to these concerns, but did not consider in any significant detail the legal and practice implications of these responses. The analysis that follows seeks to address this omission.

Data protection concerns: an overview

A number of responses to the Cerebra survey reported that even when these allegations were shown to be without foundation, their health and social care records continued to flag up the fact that they had been suspected of causing such harm. Comments included:

> There is a note on my doctor's screen that pops up sometimes when I or my children visit the doctor saying something about safeguarding.
>
> I have tried to get this removed by complaining to [the] NHS Trust but they said they wouldn't as it was a data protection issue (which makes no sense!).
>
> You cannot get things removed from medical reports even if you can prove they are wrong and that is not right and worries me hugely.

Several families also referred to the harm that resulted from the fact that their NHS records (which included details of the unsubstantiated FII allegation) remained 'available to all'. Respondents described this experience in terms of being 're-traumatised' each time they encountered a professional who had access to these records. They spoke of avoiding visiting their GPs or hospitals save only in dire emergencies and of withdrawing entirely from contact with Children's Services – the welfare agency that ostensibly exists to support families with disabled children. Comments included:

> I don't feel able to seek support for this via my GP due to the safeguarding allegations and hate knowing that I am flagged up on a system in the same way that actual abusers are.
>
> I'm now scared to even speak to professionals, take my children to seek medical attention over fear & panic attacks & if I do, I'm instantly judged as safeguarding now still appears on my children's records which instantly affects the treatment my children get.
>
> We live in fear constantly now, I'm too scared to go to a GP or anything else for me and my child. If he's ill I try and deal with it at home now unless he's not breathing then I wouldn't have a choice to phone 999.
>
> This record is on my [child's] file for life ... I have no control of this, I appealed and they refused to remove it from my child's file even though it was a false allegation of FII. Whenever I see a doctor etc they read about the allegation ... so I feel like they are judging me. I feel physically and mentally violated.

Data protection: the statutory context

The Data Protection Act (DPA) 2018 and the General Data Protection Regulations (GDPR) control how personal information is used by organisations, businesses and governments. The Information Commissioner's Office (ICO) is the principal regulator in the UK charged with ensuring that there is compliance with these provisions. As part of this role, it issues online guidance, which is subject to amendment as and when required. The guidance considered in the section that follows is the version that was in force as at 30 August 2024.

The right to erasure

Article 17(1) of the GDPR provides for a right to erasure (subject to certain exemptions) where 'the personal data are no longer necessary in relation to the purposes for which they were collected or otherwise processed'.

A straightforward interpretation of this provision would suggest that when an FII allegation is made, the purpose for which the data was collected was to demonstrate that an allegation had been made. On this basis, where it becomes clear that the allegation is unsubstantiated, the presumption must be that there is no 'purpose' in retaining the allegation, and it should be erased. If this logic is not accepted, then one has to ask: 'in what circumstances – if any – could the fact that an allegation has been made, ever be erased?'

Problematically, the ICO guidance provides no advice on the scope of the Article 17(1) right (ICO, 2024a) as it might apply in situations of this kind, namely erasure of allegations that have become unsubstantiated. It simply states that the right to erasure applies if 'the personal data is no longer necessary for the purpose which you originally collected or processed it for'. There is, however, no guidance on what 'necessary' means (contrary to the position as regards special category data, outlined below). If, as noted above, logic suggests that the presumption must be that there is no 'purpose' in retaining the data, then it must also follow that arguments concerning necessity must also fall away.

To add to the lack of clarity, in relation to Article 19 – the right to the rectification of inaccurate data (discussed below) – the ICO guidance (2024c) expressly refers to deletion as a remedy when the right of rectification is exercised. Given that erasure and deletion appear to be the same thing, it is troubling that the guidance fails to explain when, in practice, it is appropriate to rely on Article 17 for erasure and when Article 19 deletion is to be preferred.

Special category data

For the purposes of Article 9(1) of the UK GDPR, 'special category data' includes data concerning 'health' and this contains an exemption to the general prohibition on processing in situations where (Article 9(2)(h)):

> processing is necessary for the purposes of preventive or occupational medicine, for the assessment of the working capacity of the employee, medical diagnosis, the provision of health or social care or treatment or the management of health or social care systems and services on the basis of [domestic law] or pursuant to contract with a health professional and subject to the conditions and safeguards referred to in paragraph 3 ...

In this context, it is instructive to consider the requirements of Article 9 not simply from the perspective of families against whom unsubstantiated allegations of FII have been made, but also from the perspective of individuals who have been the subject of incorrect medical diagnoses (accepting, as noted above, that FII is not a 'diagnosis').

ICO guidance on the meaning of the word 'necessary' (ICO, 2024b) in Article 9(2)(h) states that, in relation to the processing of special category data, 'it must be more than just useful or habitual. It must be a targeted and proportionate way of achieving that purpose [for which it is retained]'.

In view of the above analysis concerning the meaning to be attached to 'necessary' in the context of the Article 17(1) right, there would appear to be a strong argument that, legally, incorrect medical records and health-related allegations that have become unsubstantiated should also be erased.

It is of concern that the above-cited ICO guidance provides no indication as to when an allegation relating to health that becomes unsubstantiated or an incorrect medical diagnosis should be retained in relation to the right of erasure.

The importance of the right to have erasure in such cases is graphically illustrated by the tragic case of Zoe Zaremba. In June 2020, she took her own life, in part, as a result of her discovery 'by chance' when looking at her medical records that she had been described (wrongly) as having an Emotionally Unstable Personality Disorder. Zoe had sought to have this incorrect attribution changed, but her clinicians were not prepared to 'adapt to her distress'. The Assistant Coroner, in issuing a Prevention of Future Deaths report (Broadbridge, 2022), recorded that she 'withdrew from engagement with [mental health] services because she did not trust those entrusted to keep her safe, in part because of clinicians' failure to understand her autistic condition and their reliance on an unsubstantiated attribution of a mental disorder instead'.

Obligation on data controllers to erase

The right to erasure should not be interpreted as meaning it is only available if there is an application for erasure by the individual. This is because the enjoyment of the right can only be a practical and effective reality if the state, acting through the ICO, instigates a proactive system that ensures erasure.

Accordingly, the ICO guidance should require proactive erasure and require data controllers to have in place procedures (such as regular reviews of data held) to ensure that they remove allegations that are found to be unsubstantiated, as well as incorrect medical diagnoses. The failure of the data controller to proactively and swiftly erase inaccurate medical records, as noted above, was a contributing factor in the sad case of Zoe Zaremba.

The right to rectification

In relation to Article 19 (the right to the rectification of inaccurate data), the ICO guidance (2024c) states:

> It can be complex to decide whether data is inaccurate if it refers to a mistake that has then been put right. An organisation could argue

that the fact the mistake was made is an accurate thing to record, so it should record the mistake alongside the correct data.

Example

A doctor finds that a patient has a particular illness and notes it in their medical records. Sometime later, this diagnosis is found to be wrong. It is likely that the medical records should include both the initial diagnosis and the final findings because this gives an accurate record of the patient's medical treatment. As long as the medical record contains the up-to-date findings, and this is made clear in the record, it would be difficult to argue that the record is inaccurate and should be corrected.

This interpretation has been adopted by the relevant NHS England guidance (NHS England, 2022), which states that if the data recorded 'was correct at the time the entry was made but has since changed', then it is 'important that this is not amended'.

There is, of course, a certain logic (albeit misplaced) to this approach: a logic illustrated by the example it then provides – namely, 'there may be an initial working diagnosis which was, at the time of entry, clinically possible, but is later ruled out with a different confirmed diagnosis. Retaining the original diagnosis does not make the record inaccurate'.

The assertion raises more questions than it answers: indeed, it is questionable whether it answers any relevant questions. Why, for instance, is it 'important that this is not amended' and if the making of a data error is a 'fact', does it follow that it is important that it is not amended? More profound, however, is the apparent incongruity of the guidance with the mandate in Article 17(1) of the GDPR. As we argue above, the duty to erase arises where retaining the record is no longer necessary in relation to the purpose for which it was collected.

Guidance of this kind should provide a detailed explanation as to how the retention of data in such cases can be compliant with Article 17(1), and examples of when erasure, rectification and amendment should, in the ICO's opinion, occur and the principles that should apply in making difficult judgement calls. Guidance of this kind should not be used as a vehicle for providing logical flourishes buttressed by a single unhelpful example.

In the context of FII allegations, the guidance concerning Articles 17 and 19 is materially defective in a number of respects. Firstly, it fails to explain what should happen when there is a straightforward mistake – for example, due to a mix up of medical records. Secondly, it fails to address situations where there is cogent evidence to suggest that the allegation may have been malevolent, retaliatory or entirely subjective and without evidential foundation. Thirdly, it fails to address, in appropriate detail, the fact that in some situations the prejudicial effect of retaining 'accurate' information may materially outweigh and invalidate the retention of that information. Finally, it fails to explain what should be done when retention of the prejudicial but 'accurate' material can be justified provided significant restrictions are placed on its accessibility. Fit-for-purpose guidance would include a range of illustrative examples and guide practitioners and local data controllers on these important questions.

Mistaken data

Mixing up, misdirecting and misinterpreting medical records must occur relatively frequently in the NHS IT system – handling, as it does, over 1.3 billion messages a month and at times processing more than 3,200 messages a second (NHS England, 2023a). Such errors must also apply within social care and education systems – and it is clear from the cases we have had referred to us that such errors can, and do, result in mistaken FII allegations. A 2019 Local Government and Social Care Ombudsman (LGO) report concerned a doctor who agreed that a parent's behaviour raised FII concerns – but it transpired that he had confused her with another of his patients (LGO, 2019). In the same year, a BBC investigation noted that a similar error had resulted in a child being removed to a psychiatric unit almost 100 miles away from her family for ten months (Cave, 2019). While the logic of the above ICO and NHS England guidance would apply in such cases (namely, it was a fact that an FII allegation was made), it would appear to be wholly unjust in these cases for the FII allegation to remain on the records – even with an explanatory note to explain the circumstances. Parents who have been the subject of a safeguarding inquiry encounter additional consequential barriers (bureaucratic and attitudinal) – in many contexts, including in gaining or retaining employment that involves working with children. Since such work is highly gendered, a policy of not sanctioning erasure in such cases would have a disparate and adverse impact on women.

Baseless allegations

There will be cases where the allegation of FII is devoid of evidential foundation and cases where the evidence suggests that the allegation was retaliatory or indeed malevolent. In such situations, it would appear (for the reasons outlined above) to be wholly unjust for the FII allegation to remain on their records.

While the vast majority of health, social care and education practitioners must be assumed to act honourably, it is inevitable that this is not always going to be the case in a workforce in excess of 4 million. We know from many public inquiries that behaviour of this kind happens: 'defensiveness, denial and blame-shifting' (Kirkup, 2015); letters 'including inaccurate information

... including explanations which laid blame on the family' (Ockenden, 2022); practitioners giving 'misleading' and 'dishonest' evidence (Travers, 2024); the fact that 'not all professionals do live up to the high standards expected of them' (Francis, 2013); and organisational cultures 'of fear', 'of secrecy', 'of bullying' (Lansley, 2010).

We know too of cases where it has been suggested that a Children's Services authority had a 'FII label' 'fixation' (Independent Commission, 2023, para 3.4.3) and where it was decided that a social worker was 'actively trying to make [a] case fit the FII criteria' (LGO, 2021, para 17). We know too of a case where a straightforwardly malicious allegation against a parent could not be erased because it was a 'fact' that the allegation had been made (Cragg, 2024).

For a practitioner, the making of an FII allegation is, to all intents and purposes, an entirely 'risk free' act. The list of 'perplexing presentations' in the RCPCH 2021 guidance is so subjective and so wide that, as Gullon-Scott and Long observe (2022, p 4052), they 'scoop up anything that leads to a parent presenting frequently to professionals with concerns about their child and where the professionals are unable to identify a cause'. Indeed, even where there is an identified medical cause, this no longer excludes an FII allegation from being made (Eichner, 2016, pp 294–5).

Given these factors it is – objectively – almost impossible to imagine how a parent could establish that the alleging practitioner did not have grounds for a 'reasonable' suspicion. Many families believe, however, that in practice FII allegations are baseless, and in many cases, 'retaliatory'. A Department of Health and Social Care report (2021) referred to the 'repeated concern' voiced by parents and carers that they 'had been brought into the child protection process because of disagreements with practitioners' and the British Association of Social Workers (BASW) guidance (Long et al, 2022, p 10) refers to families reporting that 'concerns about FII are raised in the context of them requesting more support for their child or when raising a complaint'. A 2018 survey by the NGO Fiightback (2019) found that 58 per cent of the respondents (to a survey sample of 191 families) stated that their FII allegation followed a complaint that they had made about a school, a medical professional or other professional. Recent research (Clements and Aiello, 2023, para 5.21) found that 50 per cent of survey respondents (a survey sample of 387) reported that the FII allegations they had experienced were made after they had complained about actions of the relevant public body.

Amy, in Chapter 10, states: 'I believe I was set up for FII which was triggered directly after making a complaint' (about her son's care). Amy speaks of the secret language used by practitioners: of innuendo to flag up FII concerns 'without having the need to state this explicitly'. The secret language of physicians is, of course, legendary: language that 'casts doubt, belittles, or blames patients' (Cox and Fritz, 2022); language that questions 'patient credibility', portrays patients as 'difficult' and contains 'explicit doubt markers', such as 'supposedly', 'claims' or 'insists' (Park et al, 2021). Such behaviour is not, of course, confined to healthcare professionals. Shannon (2022a) refers to social care practitioners passing comments that can cause a 'lifetime of distress' and comments that are 'testimony not only to the power of the spiteful choice of words used to describe a fellow human being, but, moreover, perhaps the intent behind the words' (James et al, 2019, cited in Shannon, 2022b). Phrasing of the 'Mum is anxious' kind (Fisher, 2022): phrasing cut and pasted from the RCPCH list of perplexing presentations, not only has the potential to traumatise families when they get access to their medical records, but it also poses particular problems for families seeking the erasure of records. How is the ICO going to be able to require erasure of phrasing that, to the uninitiated, appears innocuous? This is a point to which we return below.

Human Rights Act (HRA) 1998

The DPA 2018 and the GDPR are not the only statutory mechanisms that restrict the way personal information is stored and processed. The Human Rights Act (HRA) 1998, and in particular Article 8 of the European Convention on Human Rights, also provide strong safeguards against inappropriate storing and sharing of such information.

Article 8 requires states to 'respect' (among other things) the private and family lives of individuals – and this has been held to include their personal records. Article 8, therefore, complements (and, in a number of respects reinforces) the provisions of the 2018 Act and the GDPR. By way of an example, in *Khelili v Switzerland* (2011) (a case that arose prior to the adoption of the GDPR) the issue concerned whether the police should erase historic records that described the applicant as a prostitute: something that they had originally believed to be true, but subsequently accepted that it was not. The European Court of Human Rights held that Article 8 required that the record be erased.

For the purposes of this chapter, the requirements of Article 8 are of relevance to situations where the record in question is not 'unsubstantiated' (as defined above, i.e. not being a record that has been shown to be mistaken or unsupported by the evidence or withdrawn) but is however data, the sharing of which is likely to be highly prejudicial and/or stigmatising for the individual in question. Examples might include an historic allegation that a parent had exaggerated aspects of a child's condition in order to shorten the waiting time for a medical appointment or a parent who had, many years earlier, experienced a single and mild episode of post-natal depression. As we note below, the process by which such records are encoded can result in minor occurrences, triggering major safeguarding 'pop ups' on medical and social services systems: red flags that alert health and social care practitioners that there are significant safeguarding concerns about the parent and their children.

Where a question arises as to whether prejudicial records of this kind should be erased, Article 8 requires that a 'proportionality review' be undertaken – as to whether the retention of the record is objectively 'necessary'. Such a review seeks to determine whether the prejudicial effect for the individual of retaining the information outweighs the state's interest in it not being erased.

The above-cited extracts of the ICO's online guidance (ICO, 2024c) and of NHS England's guidance (2022) provide little practical assistance to data controllers as to how the multifaceted process of a proportionality review should apply in such cases.

The ICO's guidance states, in effect, that the fact that a mistake was made is itself a fact and an accurate thing to record (alongside the correct data). The NHS England guidance states, in effect, that if the data recorded 'was correct at the time the entry was made' (namely, it was suspected that the person was an abuser), it does not cease to be a 'fact' even when it is shown to be untrue. This analysis may be metaphysically sound, but only as an abstract theory. In reality, such an approach ignores the stigma and the trauma that may attach to the initial attribution: a stain that can only be expunged by complete erasure. The GDPR Article 17(1) question is 'why is it necessary to retain the record?' The HRA 1998, in essence, delves more deeply, asking: (1) 'even if there is a legitimate reason for retaining the record, does this outweigh the right of the individual to have the record erased?'; and, if so, (2) 'is there a less intrusive way of retaining this record – for example by significantly restricting the number of people who are able to view this data (*Z v Finland* 1997)?'

Partitioning data

A proportionality approach to the value of retaining or erasing records (in this case, concerning past FII allegations) might appear to be a binary process – of deciding whether the benefits of retention outweigh the benefits that would result from its erasure. In practice, however, as the above analysis suggests, this is seldom the case. Problematically, neither the current ICO nor the current NHS England guidance discusses in any depth the issue of proportionality, let alone the issue of the partitioning of data.

In this context, the European Court of Human Rights has held that in difficult cases (namely, where there are strong grounds for both sharing and not sharing personal information) the principle of proportionality requires that a decision be made as to where the balance of interests lies and, if needs be, that there be recourse to an independent authority to make a final decision on this issue.

In *Gaskin v UK* (1989), the issue concerned whether the applicant could see confidential information on his social services record that had been provided to the authorities in confidence. It was accepted that he had a vital interest in seeing this, but also that the authorities had a vital interest in ensuring that the third party's anonymity was maintained – in order to ensure that third parties were not dissuaded from volunteering safeguarding information of this kind.

The court undertook a proportionality review, balancing the interests of the individual Graham Gaskin against the legitimate interests of the state. The court considered that in principle it was legitimate for the state to partition data: to have part of a person's social records that they could inspect without restriction, but that it was also legitimate for part of the file to be restricted (because, for example, it named third parties who had not agreed to waive their anonymity). The court, however, held that where there was conflict in relation to the closed part, there must be an independent panel capable of determining where the balance of interests lay and what restrictions should be imposed on access in such cases. Transposing this decision to the question of records recording past 'not unsubstantiated' allegations of FII, the issue of data partitioning appears to be of fundamental relevance where there are compelling arguments against erasure. As we discuss below, at present although the process limits the access of GP administrative staff to parts of a patient's records, this does not appear to be the case for medical practitioners, who by default have access to all of a patient's records (including the safeguarding data). This state of affairs is problematical not only from a proportionality perspective, but also from the perspective of the Caldicott Principles (HM Government, 2020) – Principle 4 of which stipulates that access to confidential information should be on 'a strict need-to-know basis' and that '[o]nly those who need access to confidential information should have access to it, and then only to the items that they need to see'.

These are all questions that engage fundamental human rights, and fit-for-purpose ICO and NHS England guidance would address these issues in the necessary detail – something that is currently not the case.

NHS data management systems

The NHS and Social Care IT platform 'Spine' supports the IT infrastructure for health and social care in England. It connects over 44,000 healthcare IT systems (NHS England, 2023a) and enables local authority social care workers to share details of children and young people in their care or on child protection plans (NHS England, 2024a).

Summary Care Records (SCRs) are a key element within this system. They contain important personal information for anyone who was born in England, or who has registered for NHS care in England. Whenever a GP's Electronic Health Record (EHR) for a patient is updated, the changes are synchronised to their SCR.

Access to Spine is gained by means of a smartcard which is used in conjunction with a passcode known only to the smartcard holder, via a smartcard reader. The smartcard is programmed to authorise which systems and the level of information each user can access. For instance, a user may be authorised to access the SCR, but limited to viewing the opening screen and not more detailed information.

GP administrative staff create EHRs using one of three commercial general practice clinical record systems (EMIS, SystmOne and Vision), all of which adopt standardised clinical terminology to create and update EHRs. Information is added to a patient's EHR either in the form of free text or a code (of which the vast majority are clinical codes). The information may come from a range of sources – for example, other healthcare professionals, patient or third-party correspondence, the police, government departments and safeguarding teams.

There are very many clinical codes, each of which consists of a short phrase (the 'concept') and a numerical code (NHS England, 2023b). In practice, it is not uncommon for a given concept to have other concepts expressing the same thing (namely, 'synonyms'). In relation to most medical disorders, choosing a synonym will not be a problem as the system will deliver the same code – for example, the words myocardial infarction or heart attack will produce the same code (NHS England, 2023b). Unfortunately, this functionality (in identifying correct codes) does not extend to the coding of childcare-related concepts. The standard systems do not, for example, contain an 'FII' concept or code, nor (as discussed below) do they have codes for some routine childcare concepts. In such situations, the administrative staff have to make significant coding decisions (which will often require an understating of childcare law) and the nature of the 'concern' or the child's condition will be in the text/scanned material entry.

In the context of safeguarding, information is generally uploaded to the EHR by GP practice safeguarding administrators (Royal College of Nursing, 2019). Training on using the clinical terminology systems (and therefore the use of safeguarding clinical codes) is entirely practice-based. Such administrators must have core competences regarding the entering of safeguarding information, which requires, among other things, the ability to differentiate 'between fact and opinion', but there is no requirement (for example) that they demonstrate an understanding of the issues surrounding miscoding and not removing safeguarding alerts when appropriate, nor (unlike clinical staff) that they have an understanding of the issues surrounding misdiagnosis in safeguarding/child protection. This failure is a cause of concern as the scope for miscoding is not inconsiderable. For example, there are separate codes for: (1) Child is cause for safeguarding concern; (2) Child at risk of abuse; and (3) Child at risk of neglect – so it would be possible for three different administrators to allocate three different clinical codes with different numerical codes for the same child.

System alerts and 'pop ups'

This, in itself, might not appear to be a problem, but some have the potential to trigger child protection alerts when EHRs are being viewed (NHS England, 2023c). Such alerts appear as 'pop-ups' for any practitioner viewing the SCR and these must be closed before the user can proceed to read or edit the record. As the Royal College of General Practitioner's (RCGP) 'Processing and storing of safeguarding information in primary care guidance' (2017, p 2) emphasises, it 'is important that all safeguarding information is coded as Major Active Problems so that all health professionals can be immediately aware when they access notes that this child/family/adult has particular vulnerabilities'.

The NHS England guidance (2023c) acknowledges that there are 'no statutory guidelines for applying and managing these alerts' and that 'the threshold for applying a safeguarding alert is subjective'. It then suggests that (in the absence of national guidelines) the threshold should be low. The guidance further advises that, in addition to 'GP practice staff involved in the care of a patient', there is a need to ensure that the safeguarding alerts are shared beyond the practice boundary 'as required'.

The lack of national guidelines and the fact that each GP practice is essentially a separate entity means that there is no consistent approach to the recording of safeguarding data. This point is acknowledged by the RCGP guidance (2017, p 2) in its reference to the fact that 'each practice will have their own unique way of how they handle information coming into the practice' – and also by NHS England guidance (2023c), which notes that the lack of statutory guidelines means that 'managing these alerts … can pose challenges and risks in ensuring the delivery of safe clinical care'.

Where an alert has been coded onto a patient's records, it will often be applied to the whole family (even if, for example, the concern relates to only one child) (RCGP, 2017, p 3). However, when the local authority decides that the child is no longer a safeguarding concern, the pop-up warning will continue until an additional code (a 'kill' code) is entered by the GP administrator. Not infrequently, however, it appears that local authorities fail to notify GP administrators of their decisions – meaning that alerts remain active (for whole families), possibly years after they should have been removed (Artus and Gibson, 2022, p 353). In consequence, unless GP practices have rigorous systems in place for periodically checking with children's social services to see if alerts remain appropriate, many will continue to pop up even though there are no safeguarding issues.

In this context, it is important to note that although the use of a kill code will stop pop-ups from appearing, they will have no effect on the text or scanned material on the ECH/SCR. This data will be visible to all practitioners who have access to the full record. Erasure/deletion of these materials would be dependent on the application of Article 17(1) of the

GDPR (discussed above). Given the current difficulties in obtaining full erasure, there appears to be no mechanism within the ECH/SCR systems to make access to such materials restricted – for example, by making it subject to authorisation being obtained by a third party.

As noted above, although the operating systems that underpin the EHRs are efficient in choosing the correct code for most medical disorders, this is not the case for childcare-related concepts. Artus and Gibson (2022) identify this problem in their discussion concerning the competency of administrators to choose the correct code in cases where there is more than one possibility. They suggest that this is, in part, due to 'the inconsistency among practices with alerts being managed by staff members with differing positions and approaches' – noting that due to the lack of adequate practice guidelines, 'GP practices will be adopting varying approaches in this area'.

An illustration of such an inconsistency concerns a request for information from a GP by children's social services in the context of an investigation under Children Act 1989, section 47 (namely, where the authority has reasonable cause to suspect that a child is suffering, or is likely to suffer significant harm). The request will be scanned and added to the patient's file and coded as a safeguarding issue. But, as explained above, the administrator will have a choice of possible clinical codes, for instance:

1. Child is cause for concern
2. Vulnerable child
3. Child at risk
4. Child is cause for safeguarding concern
5. Child at risk of abuse
6. Child at risk of neglect

It appears that the first three clinical codes do not result in an alert, but the final three do (North-East London Integrated Care Board, 2024, pp 19–20). We understand (from a personal discussion with a GP administrator) that the lack of guidance on these issues means that administrators have to make decisions based on very limited understanding of these concepts. The administrator added that the prevailing culture was 'risk averse' (due to media coverage of high-profile child protection cases) and had led to a 'better to be safe than sorry' approach: that in consequence the practice was to code in a way that resulted in a child protection alert on all letters received from children's social services – including, for example, a request from an occupational therapist for medical information in the context of assessing a request for a home adaptation.

A further and highly problematical issue arises in relation to requests for information in the context of a 'child in need' assessment (Children Act 1989, section 17) for a disabled child where support has been requested, but there are no child protection concerns. A 'child in need' is a legal concept and not one dreamt up by Charles Dickens or developed by the NSPCC. As Clements and Aiello note (Chapter 2), it is a difficult concept as it covers two distinct categories of children: those considered to be at risk of neglect or abuse, as well as all disabled children (Children Act 1989, section 17(10)).

It appears that there is no clinical code that covers 'section 17 assessments for disabled children with no safeguarding concerns'. We understand that in consequence administrators apply a child protection clinical code, such as 'Child is cause for safeguarding concern' or a 'Child in need' clinical code, both of which, it appears, trigger automatic alerts.

This understanding is reinforced by the RCGP guidance (2017, p 3), which states that '[a]ny child who is classed as a "child in need" also needs appropriate coding as a Major Active Problem'. In a similar vein, although guidance issued by Nottinghamshire and Nottingham City Data Leadership Alliance (2019, p 8) recognises that children in need may not have 'any safeguarding concerns', it nevertheless recommends that in relation to section 17 assessment requests, a 'Child in need' clinical code be used (and in consequence that an automatic alert be activated).

The automatisation of coding

The above analysis is predicated on the assumption that the data-coding process is (or should be) regulated at a primary care level by a competent administrator. It appears, however, that many thousands of GP practices use automated scanning systems to upload onto their records the very substantial volumes of data they receive. Docmangp is an example of one such system (Docman, 2024). What appears to happen when software of this kind is used is that when a GP practice receives a document (for example, a report from a diagnostic centre or from another health professional or from Children's Services), the software not only scans and uploads the material into the relevant medical system (for example, EMIS), it is also able to add automatically (through the use of 'word/phrase' recognition technology) the relevant codes. Although such systems have significant 'time saving' benefits for GP practices, their operational manuals stress the importance of administrator overview – to check that the codes that are assigned are correct. In practice, the evidence suggests that this essential overview is not always evident, with alarming consequences. For example, if a practice receives a document from Children's Services that contains the words 'Child Protection', there is a danger that the system may add, automatically, the 'Child Protection Plan' code. This code would then sync with the medical system and create an alert/flag on the patient record. Problematically, if the document scanned into the system has the title of 'Minutes Children's Protection Meeting', then (absent administrator intervention) the code and the alert will be triggered – even though the minutes might in fact record that the meeting concluded that there were no child protection concerns.

Such problems are inevitable within any data storage system – although, with increasing data flows and automation (allied to the use of alerts/pop-ups), their potential to cause significant (unintended) harm to large numbers of individual data subjects is very real. In this context, Artus and Gibson (2022), in their brief commentary on the shortcomings of safeguarding alerts systems for EHRs, conclude:

> There are no national or regional guidelines to govern the practical management of safeguarding alerts to govern issues such as the requirement for applying an alert, individual's consent, individual's confidentiality, and the professionals responsible for applying and monitoring them. This is leading to inconsistency among GP practices with a potential for incomplete or inaccurate information sharing, posing a risk of potential missed opportunities in protecting children and adults at risk, clinicians, staff, and other users of primary care services. The authors of the current article call for national, collaborative, inter-agency guidelines on the practical management of safeguarding alerts on EMRs.

It should be noted that concerns of this kind have also been identified in other nations – in relation to the use of electronic medical records to identify child maltreatment concerns. In a wide-ranging literature review combined with 'key informant interviews', Stilwell et al (2022) concluded that such systems were generally time and resource intensive and characterised by concerns about unintended consequences and harm to patients (including the impact of false positives and false negatives) and the challenges posed by 'institutional differences' – namely, health practitioners' relative lack of child abuse expertise.

Conclusion

There can be no doubt as to the trauma experienced by a parent who is wrongly accused of FII. There can be no doubt either about the fact that this trauma is also experienced by other family members, the child who was allegedly being harmed and their siblings, as Kaydence Drayak describes so vividly in Chapter 9.

The evidence suggests that FII is a rare or very rare condition and that, in the vast majority of cases, FII accusations are unsubstantiated. The evidence also suggests that parents and their families are traumatised, not only by wrongful allegations, but also by the fact that they and practitioners are regularly being reminded of the allegations: a form of systemic re-traumatisation due to the way that the data protection process currently operates and the enormous difficulties families experience in trying to have the data erased.

The information systems that underpin health, social care and education services are vast and complex – and their management often require difficult decisions concerning the reconciliation of competing interests. This is particularly the case where the traumatising record is replete with innuendo: with hidden and double meanings, with wounding words and phrases that speak to the unequal power relations between practitioners and parents. It is very doubtful that data protection regulations alone can address hurtful practices of this kind. One must hope that professional bodies will grasp this particular nettle and make provision for seriously dissuasive remedies to be imposed where language of this kind is used.

A reoccurring theme throughout this chapter has been the clear and compelling case that exists for revision (by significant expansion) of the umbrella data protection guidance issued by the ICO, NHS England and the RCGP.

Having practitioner 'alerts' may be of great importance in promoting multi-agency safeguarding action, but pop-ups of this kind must be properly policed. Families are being traumatised by alerts being wrongly triggered and, in consequence, deterred from seeing their GPs, visiting hospitals and seeking support from social welfare agencies. Inter-agency joint working failures (in this case, where the local authority silo fails to communicate with the NHS silo) are a fact of life. The system therefore needs to be adjusted to accommodate this – for example, by requiring a routine 'spring cleaning' by GPs to check that their alerts remain appropriate or indeed for all alerts to be time limited.

One final and important issue concerns the question of whether the state's data protection obligations, considered in this section, are proactive or reactive duties.

It is clear from the research that many individuals are unaware of the prejudicial and incorrect data that is held on their health, social services and education records. It would appear to follow that where an FII allegation has been found to be wrong, misguided, unfounded or unsupported by the evidence, then the relevant public body should take the initiative to ensure that the record is expunged – or, at the very least, that the fact that an FII allegation has been made is placed in a secure part of the records to which access can only be granted in exceptional circumstances.

There can be no doubt that the alerting signs identified by the RCPCH 2021 guidance are so subjective and so wide that they 'scoop up anything that leads to a parent presenting frequently to professionals with concerns about their child and where the professionals are unable to identify a cause' (Gullon-Scott and Long, 2022, p 4052). There can be no doubt that, in consequence, they result in very high levels of 'false positives' (namely, where an individual is wrongly identified as having a particular condition) (Long, 2008, p 27; Gullon-Scott and Long, 2022, p 4043).

Clements and Aiello (2023, paras 2.51–2.53) considered whether RCPCH 2021 guidance would be considered acceptable if it was a diagnostic screening test – which, of course, it is not (not least because FII is not a recognised condition for DSM-5-TR purposes). Their comparative assessment considered the UK National Screening Committee's (UKNSC, 2022) guidance as to when a targeted or population-wide screening programme is, and is not, generally appropriate. In relation to the key criteria, the RCPCH 2021 objectively failed. This was particularly so in relation to the requirement that: 'The overall benefits from the screening programme should outweigh the harms, for example, from overdiagnosis, overtreatment, false positives, false reassurance and uncertain findings.'

In the context of identifying FII, it is clear that the benefits are to be assessed in terms of the wellbeing of the child and not the parent who is being 'screened'. However, the evidence strongly suggests that the traumatisation experienced as a result of false allegations extends to the whole family, including the child for whose benefit the test is ostensibly being undertaken. The same observation holds true for the re-traumatisation resulting from the failure of the data protection systems to do what they are designed to do – 'to protect'.

We have somehow created systems that believe they exist in order to 'protect data'. They do not. They exist to protect individuals: to protect them from the harms that data can cause.

References

A County Council v M [2005] EWHC 31 (Fam), para 175.

Artus, M. and Gibson, J. (2022) 'Safeguarding alerts on electronic medical records', *British Journal of General Practice*, 72(720): 352–3.

Broadbridge, J.N. (2022) 'Regulation 28: Report to Prevent Future Deaths (North Yorkshire and York) Concerning the death of Zoe Emma Zarembra'. Available from: https://www.judiciary.uk/wp-content/uploads/2022/04/Zoe-Zaremba-Prevention-of-future-deaths-report-2022-0117_Published.pdf [accessed 13 August 2024].

Cave, R. (2019) 'I was accused of pretending that my daughter was sick', BBC News, 11 March. Available from: https://www.bbc.com/news/health-47500686 [accessed 20 August 2024].

Children Act 1989. Available from: https://www.legislation.gov.uk/ukpga/1989/41/contents [accessed 5 March 2025].

Clements, L. and Aiello, A.L. (2021) *Institutionalising Parent Carer Blame: The Experiences of Families with Disabled Children in Their Interactions with English Local Authority Children's Services Departments*, Cerebra, University of Leeds.

Clements, L. and Aiello, A.L. (2023) *The Prevalence and Impact of Allegations of Fabricated or Induced Illness*, Cerebra, University of Leeds.

Cox, C. and Fritz, Z. (2022) 'Presenting complaint: use of language that disempowers patients', *British Medical Journal*, 377(8335): article e066720. doi: 10.1136/bmj-2021-066720.

Cragg, S. (2024) 'Stella Creasy MP, erasing malicious complaints and Article 17 of the UK GDPR', Doughty Street Chambers. Available from: https://insights.doughtystreet.co.uk/post/102jba0/stella-creasy-mp-erasing-malicious-complaints-and-article-17-of-the-uk-gdpr [accessed 29 July 2024].

Data Protection Act 2018. Available from: https://www.legislation.gov.uk/ukpga/2018/12/contents [accessed 5 March 2025].

Department of Health and Social Care (2021) *Chief Social Workers for Adults and the Chief Social Worker for Children and Families A Spectrum of Opportunity: An Exploratory Study of Social Work Practice with Autistic Young Adults and Their Families*. Available from: https://www.gov.uk/government/publications/social-work-and-autistic-young-people-an-exploratory-study/a-spectrum-of-opportunity-an-exploratory-study-of-social-work-practice-with-autistic-young-adults-and-their-families [accessed 28 August 2024].

Docman (2024) 'Docman GP Electronic Document Management'. Available from: https://www.docman.com/what-we-do/primary-care/docman-gp/ [accessed 10 October 2024].

Eichner, M. (2016) 'Bad medicine: parents, the state, and the charge of "medical child abuse"', *University of California Davis Law Review*, 50: 205–320.

EMIS (2024) 'Managing child protection warnings'. Available from: https://www.emisnow.com/csm?id=kb_article&sys_id=9f08d9f2c3ed469cbeb93a0c050131c8 [accessed 30 July 2024].

Fiightback (2019) *False accusations of FII: A Report by Fiightback – March 2019: A Survey Involving 191 Families*.

Fisher, N. (2022) 'Mum is anxious. How anxiety is used to dismiss parents when their child is struggling'. Available from: https://naomicfisher.substack.com/p/mum-is-anxious [accessed 4 May 2024].

Francis, R. (2013) *Report of the Mid Staffordshire NHS Foundation Trust Public Inquiry: Executive Summary* (HC 947), London: The Stationery Office.

Freedom of information Act 2000. Available from: https://www.legislation.gov.uk/ukpga/2000/36/contents

Gaskin v UK 12 EHRR 36 (1989).

General Data Protection Regulations (GDPR) (EU) 2016/679.

Gullon-Scott, F. and Long, C. (2022) 'FII and perplexing presentations: what is the evidence base for and against current guidelines, and what are the implications for social services?' *British Journal of Social Work*, 52(6): 4040–56.

HM Government (2020) 'The Caldicott Principles'. Available from: https://www.gov.uk/government/publications/the-caldicott-principles [accessed 27 August 2024].

HM Government (2023) 'Working together to safeguard children: a guide to inter-agency working to safeguard and promote the welfare of children'. Available from: https://www.gov.uk/government/publications/working-together-to-safeguard-children--2 [accessed 27 August 2024].

Human Rights Act 1998. Available from: https://www.legislation.gov.uk/ukpga/1998/42/contents

ICO (2024a) 'Right to erasure'. Available from: https://ico.org.uk/for-organisations/uk-gdpr-guidance-and-resources/individual-rights/individual-rights/right-to-erasure/ [accessed 30 July 2024].

ICO (2024b) 'What are the rules on special category data?' Available from: https://ico.org.uk/for-organisations/uk-gdpr-guidance-and-resources/lawful-basis/special-category-data/what-are-the-rules-on-special-category-data/#scd5 [accessed 27 August 2024].

ICO (2024c) 'Your right to get your data corrected'. Available from: https://ico.org.uk/for-the-public/your-right-to-get-your-data-corrected/ [accessed 30 July 2024].

Independent Commission (2023) 'Report of the Commission to consider families' experience of Children's Services in Herefordshire'. Available from: https://www.herefordshiresafeguardingboards.org.uk/wp-content/uploads/2023/06/6.6.23-Herefordshire-Commission-Final-Report.pdf [accessed 13 August 2024].

James, E., Mitchell, R. and Morgan, H. (2019) *Social Work, Cats and Rocket Science: Stories of Making a Difference in Social Work with Adults*, London: Jessica Kingsley Publishers.

Khelili v Switzerland 18 October 2011; Application No 16188/07.

Kirkup, B. (2015) *The Report of the Morecambe Bay Investigation*, London: The Stationery Office.

Lansley, A. (2010) Mid Staffordshire NHS Foundation Trust House of Commons Hansard Volume 511: debated on Wednesday 9 June.

LGO (2019) Report concerning Leicestershire Partnership NHS Trust no 18 013 505a, 4 September.

LGO (2021) Report concerning Gloucestershire County Council no 19 014 556, 25 February 2020.

Long, C., Eaton, J., Russell, S., Gullon-Scott, F. and Bilson, A. (2022) 'Fabricated or induced illness and perplexing presentations: abbreviated practice guide for social work practitioners', Birmingham: BASW. Available from: https://www.basw.co.uk/resources/fabricated-and-induced-illness-practice-guide [accessed 7 February 2025].

Long, W. (2008) 'Munchausen syndrome by proxy/factitious disorder by proxy: a critical assessment for judges and lawyers'. Available from: https://autism.org/wp-content/uploads/2021/12/MSBP.pdf [accessed 6 August 2024].

McClure, R.J., Davis, P.M., Meadow, S.R. and Sibert, J.R. (1996) 'Epidemiology of Munchausen syndrome by proxy, non-accidental poisoning, and non-accidental suffocation', *Archives of Disease in Childhood*, 75(1): 57–61.

NHS England (2022) 'Amending patient and service user records'. Available from: https://transform.england.nhs.uk/information-governance/guidance/amending-patient-and-service-user-records/ [accessed 17 July 2024].

NHS England (2023a) 'Spine'. Available from: https://digital.nhs.uk/services/spine [accessed 30 July 2024].

NHS England (2023b) 'Clinical coding – SNOMED CT 2023'. Available from: https://www.england.nhs.uk/long-read/clinical-coding-snomed-ct/ [accessed 30 July 2024].

NHS England (2023c) 'Safeguarding'. Available from: https://www.england.nhs.uk/long-read/safeguarding/ [accessed 30 July 2024].

NHS England (2024a) 'Child Protection – Information Sharing (CP-IS) service'. Available from: https://digital.nhs.uk/services/child-protection-information-sharing-service [accessed 30 July 2024].

North-East London Integrated Care Board (2024) *Primary Care Safeguarding Handbook Improving Standards and Promoting Welfare for Children, Young People and Adults*. Available from: https://primarycare.northeastlondon.icb.nhs.uk/wp-content/uploads/2024/07/NHS_NEL-GP-SG-handbook-June-2024-v106.pdf [accessed 28 August 2024].

Nottinghamshire and Nottingham City Data Leadership Alliance (2019) 'Guidance on information sharing and issuing alerts to safeguard children in primary & community care'. Available from: https://customerportal.notts-his.nhs.uk/uploads/1065473/guidance%20on%20safeguarding%20children%20in%20primary%20community%20care%20v2.pdf [accessed 27 August 2024].

Ockenden, D. (2022) Final Findings, Conclusions and Essential Actions from the Independent Review of Maternity Services at The Shrewsbury and Telford Hospital NHS Trust HC1219, House of Commons.

Park, J., Saha, S., Chee, B., Taylor, J. and Beach, M.C. (2021) 'Physician use of stigmatizing language in patient medical records', *JAMA Network Open*, 4(7): article e2117052.

Parker Engels, L. (2020) 'Is this FII, or are school missing something?' Define Fine. Available from: https://www.definefine.org.uk/blog-3-are-school-missing-something [accessed 29 July 2024].

Regulation (EU) 2016/679. Available from: https://eur-lex.europa.eu/eli/reg/2016/679/oj/eng [accessed 5 March 2025].

Royal College of General Practitioners (RCGP) (2017) 'Processing and storing of safeguarding information in primary care'. Available from: https://northyorkshireccg.nhs.uk/wp-content/uploads/2021/03/rcgp-coding-advice.pdf [accessed 27 August 2024].

Royal College of Nursing (2019) 'Safeguarding children and young people: roles and competencies for healthcare staff'. Available from: https://fflm.ac.uk/wp-content/uploads/2020/12/007-366.pdf [accessed 27 August 2024].

Royal College of Paediatrics and Child Health (RCPCH) (2021) *Perplexing Presentations (PP)/Fabricated or Induced Illness (FII) in Children: RCPCH Guidance*, London.

Shannon, B. (2022a) 'Beyond blame', Rewriting Social Care, 23 April. Available from: https://rewritingsocialcare.blog/2022/04/23/beyond-blame/ [accessed 29 July 2024].

Shannon, B. (2022b) 'Just words', Rewriting Social Care, 3 June. Available from: https://rewritingsocialcare.blog/2022/06/03/just-words/ [accessed 29 July 2024].

Stilwell, L., Golonka, M., Ankoma-Sey, K., Yancy, M., Kaplan, S., Terrell, L. et al (2022) 'Electronic health record tools to identify child maltreatment: scoping literature review and key informant interviews', *Academic Pediatrics*, 22(5): 718–28.

The Chief Social Workers for Adults and the Chief Social Worker for Children and Families (2021) *A Spectrum of Opportunity: An Exploratory Study of Social Work Practice with Autistic Young Adults and Families*, Department of Health and Social Care. Available from: https://www.gov.uk/government/publications/social-work-and-autistic-young-people-an-exploratory-study/a-spectrum-of-opportunity-an-exploratory-study-of-social-work-practice-with-autistic-young-adults-and-their-families [accessed 5 March 2025].

Travers, R. (2024) 'Inquest touching the death of Jennifer Sharren Chalkley: Mr Richard Travers H.M. Senior Coroner for Surrey'. Available from: https://www.surreycc.gov.uk/__data/assets/pdf_file/0018/380106/J-Chalkley-Findings-and-Conclusion-01-May-2024.pdf [accessed 28 August 2024].

UK National Screening Committee (UKNSC) (updated 29 September 2022) 'Criteria for a targeted screening programme'. Available from: https://www.gov.uk/government/publications/evidence-review-criteria-national-screening-programmes/criteria-for-a-targeted-screening-programme [accessed 27 July 2024].

Z v Finland 25 EHRR 371 (1997).

8

Child protection and the experiences of autistic parents accused of fabricated or induced illness

Cathleen Long, Rachel Gavin and Esther Whitney

Introduction

The UK's child protection system is about ensuring the welfare of *every* child, providing them with high-quality and effective support as soon as their need is identified. While this is admirable because every child matters, and no child should be subjected to any form of abuse, there are significant flaws in the system whereby the needs of disabled children and autistic parents are being misunderstood and discounted. Across the UK, a high proportion of autistic parents (diagnosed, undiagnosed or self-identified) are being accused of exaggerating or making up their disabled child's difficulties, a term devised by the Royal College of Paediatrics and Child Health as fabricated or induced illness (FII). FII is *not* a diagnosis. However, many professionals confuse FII with Munchausen syndrome by proxy (MSbP), now redefined as factitious disorder imposed on another (FDIoA), which is an exceptionally rare psychiatric diagnosis (American Psychiatrist Association, 2013). The increase in accusations of FII is evidenced by the high proportion of inquiries two of the authors have received from parents, many of whom are autistic, requesting an independent social work assessment to assess their child's needs and potentially to challenge the misassumptions professionals have made about them, often because their parenting style is observed as deviating from the expected norm.

In the 1950s and 1960s, Bruno Bettelheim, who was thought to have become a self-styled psychologist, introduced the popular concept of a 'refrigerator mother'. He significantly influenced the fields of child psychology and psychiatry despite questions about his academic background debated in published research. Bettelheim's theory was that the 'refrigerator mother', an emotionally detached woman who presented as cold and uncaring, caused their child to be autistic. His fundamental belief was that 'the precipitating factor in infantile autism is the parents' wish the child should not exist' (Bettelheim, 1967, p 125). Leo Kanner (1949) trained in psychology and paediatric care and expressed similar beliefs to Bettelheim, proposing that parents of autistic children often appeared cold, obsessive and mechanical in their response to children. He later revoked these comments. Although this theory has since been retracted, its legacy lives on (Bennett et al, 2018). Despite the contemporary acknowledgment within society and within more recent literature and research, which supports that parents are not responsible for their child 'developing autism', there continues to be a long tradition of parent (most commonly the mother) shaming and blaming in the autism industry (Waltz, 2015). This is clear in the *Perplexing Presentations (PP)/Fabricated or Induced Illness (FII) in Children* guidance, which lists mothers as primary perpetrators (RCPCH, 2021), an assertion that is methodologically unsound and based on no tangible evidence (Gullon-Scott and Long, 2022).

Many autistic parents are lifelong caregivers to their autistic children, providing them with a secure, stable and loving home environment where they are accepted as themselves without imposing biased expectations about who their child 'should' be. Lizzie is an autistic parent who is an accomplished professional and the primary caregiver for her son. Here, she writes about her experiences of being a parent/carer, and the intricate and simplistic beauty of their relationship. Please note that all the names and identifying factors within case examples have been changed, with explicit consent given by each contributor.

Imagine ... a summary of the day in the life of a parent carer

Caring for someone with complex disabilities and health issues is hard work. It's very demanding non-stop, and it takes a toll physically, mentally, and emotionally.

I love caring for my son. He is non-verbal and shows off a lot of love. He really speaks through his eyes and sounds, and we do have a special bond. We spend a lot of time cuddling, laughing, and playing games together. We spend a lot of time fighting services and getting through every day on top of my daily demands as a carer.

I'm either administering his Epilepsy medications, military planning his day, undertaking personal care tasks for him, seeing to his education provision, dealing with his personal assistants, shaving him, feeding, and cooking for him, entertaining him, helping him transition from one micro or large transition to another, making sure he's safe at home and in the community with me, he doesn't understand danger. But loves the outdoors. He is 6ft and stocky and little 5ft me ensures his safety from road danger and more, meanwhile I'm working and fighting for others in his position, and still fighting for my own. I might be lucky enough to fall into bed by 1am. All I ask, is for action, for us not to have to fight like we do anymore. To every parent carer out there, I hear you.

Even though I love taking care of him it doesn't change the fact that it is exhausting. I have been waiting 20 years to have a conversation with him. However, there's other ways of communicating such as that look, that touch, that gentle push to guide me where he wants to be, that look under his eyes when he's not well, that vocal sound and hum when he is happy and content, that gentle stroke on my cheek when he knows I am not feeling 100%. It's our way of being, although I would still love that conversation to find out how he really feels and what he is really thinking. But how he really feels is shown beautifully in his smile he's giving me and the sounds he makes. Speaking is so overrated, there are hundreds of ways to communicate, and the spoken word is only one of them. What he really thinks is evident, is the fact he's always happy with me, comfortable in my presence and communicating what he likes/doesn't like. Although he may not be able to tell me with the spoken word, his beaming face tells me more than a thousand words couldn't.

Let's delve deeper ... please this is not any negative emotion towards professionals, it is simply a matter to give you the opportunity to reflect. Every day, I wake with the pure fear of his life and safety after my days. Can anyone really care for him like me? Will he be restricted once I'm gone, hurt by others, ignored when he can't say, can't communicate? Can you imagine having to worry about this? Can you imagine being petrified of dying and your child left behind. I do, every single minute of the day.

Can you imagine working all hours when he's asleep and with his day staff 9–4, and then caring on his return until the early hours to save for his future in the hope you can one day have your own supported living provision, developed, and managed your way, so you know your son and others like him are safe, happy, and content?

I'm a SEND [Special Educational Needs and Disabilities] mum, and I need you all, professionals, local authorities, health, education, and anyone else to please, stop and think and support us. Please stop the defensiveness and battle on top of my already exhausting days; day in, day out ... life is too short and challenging enough. To all professionals out there, remember you're accountable for your decisions in your own right as registered professionals, and codes of practice.

Please ...

From a knackered mum and parent carer!

FII accusations against disabled and autistic parents

Disabled parents of disabled children are four times more likely to be accused of FII than non-disabled parents (Clements and Aiello, 2023), which is indicative of widespread discrimination across the UK where organisations are failing to comply with the Equality Act 2010. Parents facing FII allegations are being accused of harming their children, when often, they are merely asserting their belief that their child has physical and/or developmental differences which others have not necessarily observed. It appears the number of autistic mothers accused of FII is increasing, with them feeling desperately perplexed about how to manage the 'charges' made against them. There are multiple reasons for the increase in the number of FII allegations, including the updated publication by the Royal College of Paediatrics and Child Health, *Perplexing Presentations (PP)/Fabricated or Induced Illness (FII) in Children* (RCPCH, 2021), an increase in autism diagnoses (Russell et al, 2022), and possible incentives to reduce budget expenditure during the austerity crisis for education, health and social care across the UK. Parents who once felt isolated and too ashamed to talk about their experiences of FII have a growing awareness about these types of allegations because others are publicly sharing their experiences, in person and via social media. There are new research initiatives, and the innovative creation of National Fabricated or Induced Illness Awareness Week in 2021.

The concept of FII and the content of the RCPCH guidance relied on 'extensive consultation and expert consensus from those with extensive clinical experience of managing these conditions' because of 'the absence of published evidence' (RCPCH, 2021, p 6). What this means is the RCPCH guidance is based on clinical opinion and *not* evidence-based research. According to the RCPCH, when a parent presents a child with a perplexing presentation, particularly when a medical condition is not understood, this can be an indicator that they are placing their child in 'a clinical situation in which a child is, or very likely to be, harmed due to parent(s) behaviour and action, carried out in order to convince doctors that the child's state of physical and/or mental health and neurodevelopment is impaired (or more impaired than it actually is)' (RCPCH, 2021, p 11). Despite various professionals believing FII is a clinical diagnosis, one which is synonymous with what was known as MSbP, it is simply a set of criteria professionals use to establish whether a parent is misrepresenting their child's needs by exaggerating or making up their difficulties. MSbP is now known as FDIoA and is cited in the Diagnostic and Statistical Manual of Mental Disorders, Version 5 (DSM-5), as when a 'perpetrator' falsifies physical or psychological signs or symptoms or induces injury or disease to assert another individual is ill, impaired or injured, and their behaviour cannot be explained by another mental disorder (American Psychiatric Association, 2013, p 325). FDIoA *does* exist, albeit it is rarely diagnosed. It requires an intent to deceive, with no other explanation for a person's actions and notably excludes anxious parenting (RCPCH, 2021, p 10).

An online article published by Autism Eye (2014) found that accusations of FII have increased, with some professionals openly viewing parental autism as a 'risk factor'. Research by Benson into autistic parents' experiences of children's social care describes how they came to realise that their diagnosis was considered as a 'perplexing' condition, with all aspects of their being 'pathologised; examined, unpicked, and analysed by baffled "outsiders"' (Benson, 2023). Autistic parents who come to the attention of social services have reported that they experience their lives being scrutinised, with the concept of 'non-normalcy' quickly being associated with 'risk': risk to their children (p 1448). These adverse experiences are not restricted to autistic mothers: autistic fathers also encounter practitioners who have failed to understand their different neurotype – practitioners whose default position is to view their neurodivergent approach to parenting neurodivergent children as harmful and not 'good enough' simply because it deviates from the 'norm'. This concept of discriminating against autistic parents is further supported by research findings of Alice Running and Danielle Jata-Hall. They identified that from 111 families who took part in the survey and were subjected to safeguarding procedures in relation to their child's presentation, alarmingly 76.75 per cent were neurodivergent parents (Running and Jata-Hall, 2023, p 26). The data within the survey identifies a common theme among professionals where neurodivergent presentations were misperceived as mental health issues and parental obstruction. Despite the centrality of social work intervention in the lives of many neurodivergent mothers, their plight remains largely absent in social work training and social work literature.

Here, Martha, an autistic mother, recounts her experiences of being accused of FII, which were, and remain, devastatingly traumatic for her and her family:

> After a series of unsatisfactory experiences of children's social care, Robert and I made a formal complaint. Thankfully, Rupert's head teacher was supportive, believing we were responsible, loving parents, which I found encouraging. The local authority decided to undertake a full assessment of Rupert's needs. We hoped this would be an impartial assessment where our family's position would finally be understood. I trusted this social worker and, when she asked about my childhood experiences, I shared my historical diagnosis of borderline personality disorder. If I could take this back, I would because this became my biggest downfall. Everything I did from then on was attributed to this judgmental, stigmatising diagnosis. Rupert was assessed by a paediatrician who could not ascertain any developmental or physical reasons for his behaviour. The paediatrician was incredibly dismissive when I talked about our experiences and how we were struggling to meet Rupert's needs. She looked at me and said, 'Mrs B, I believe you want me to find something wrong with your child.' She subsequently made a safeguarding referral to social services on the basis that I have

Fabricated or Induced Illness. From then on, I noticed a distinct shift in how professionals related to me. Our allocated social worker was always accompanied by a colleague, whereas beforehand this did not happen. She wouldn't reply to my emails or respond to telephone calls. I felt incredibly isolated and believed life was not worth living. I imagined killing myself to get away from the ever-growing nightmare. If I thought things were bad then, I soon realised they could get worse!

We ended up in Family Court where there was the imminent risk of losing custody of Rupert forever. It felt like everything was directed at me because I am 'personality disordered'. During the Family Court proceedings, a decision was made that Rupert needed to attend an autism diagnostic assessment. A clinical psychologist was instructed to undertake this assessment. I accompanied Rupert for the appointments so that Robert could look after Georgia and Dina. The clinical team assessed and diagnosed Rupert as autistic with a demand avoidant profile. To my utter shock, the psychologist suggested I undergo a diagnostic assessment. Apparently, the team had noticed behaviours in me which caused them to question whether I was also autistic. Robert and I funded a private assessment which confirmed that I am autistic, with attention deficit hyperactivity disorder; I am *not* personality disordered.

Thankfully, the FII allegations were dropped but what a hell of a journey it has been for all of us. I still feel intensely traumatised by the utter injustice we experienced as a family, and what I experienced as an autistic mother. I felt powerless and whatever I did or said made things worse. I know my story is one of many. It's a sorry and woeful system that allows this to happen.

What being autistic looks like

There are many descriptions about what being autistic looks like, with the DSM-5 stipulating this as a disorder characterised by a series of deficits in all aspects of social communication, and repetitive, restricted patterns of behaviour, interests and activities (American Psychiatric Association, 2013, pp 31–2). The National Autistic Society describes autism as a lifelong developmental condition that shapes how people communicate and interact with the world (National Autistic Society, 2024). A different explanation is that autistic people have 'differences in the development of their anterior cingulate cortex, a part of the brain that helps regulate attention, decision making, impulse control, and emotional processing … Autistic brains have unique connection patterns that deviate from what is normally observed in neurotypical people' (Price, 2022, pp 20–1). The term 'neurodivergent' is used to describe people who interpret information differently from the typical population. Beardon explains how the medical model identifies autism as a deficit which needs to be cured, whereas the social model recognises that an individual's problems emanate from society and/or their environment (Beardon, 2020, 2021b). He states that being autistic does *not* mean there is something 'wrong' with the person; they do not need to be 'fixed'. Beardon suggests that rather than referring to an autistic person as disabled, disordered or impaired, there needs to be a global recognition that most autistic people are disadvantaged by living in a society that does not readily understand them (Beardon, 2021a, p 17).

Over the past 20 years, there has been a growing awareness about autism which has led to an increase in the prevalence of people being assessed and diagnosed as such, as well as others self-identifying as autistic (Russell et al, 2022; O'Nions et al, 2023). At present, approximately 3 per cent of children and young people are diagnosed as autistic (O'Nions et al, 2023 and Stott, 2023). As the true rate of autism does not change across age groups, there are potentially 3 per cent of adults who would meet the diagnostic criterion. Gender differences play a big part in an autism diagnosis, with a much higher proportion of males assessed as being neurodivergent compared to females (Eaton, 2018, pp 22–3). Autistic mothers who are thriving might be unaware they are autistic and their unique perspectives are overlooked within literature (Fletcher-Watson and Happé, 2019). Furthermore, there is a notable absence of research pertaining to autistic mothers from Black, Asian and minority ethnic communities (Bobb in Carpenter et al, 2019). When autistic mothers are undiagnosed and unrecognised, this can negatively affect their need for understanding and support, leading to a potential negative perception of self and long-term implications on their mental health (Hull et al, 2017 cited in McCrossin, 2022, p 272). Pohl and co-authors found that autistic mothers were more likely to experience mental ill-health and greater parenting difficulties (such as feeling misunderstood by professionals, struggling with domestic responsibility) compared to non-autistic mothers (Pohl et al, 2020). Fletcher-Watson and Happé refer to the heritability of autism, which means there is a high probability that a parent of an autistic child could also meet the diagnostic criterion (Fletcher-Watson and Happé, 2019). Therefore, it is more likely that autistic mothers who find themselves in crisis will present themselves for diagnosis following their child's autism diagnosis.

Concerningly, many autistic women are initially diagnosed with a borderline/emotionally unstable personality disorder and more than 75 per cent with this diagnosis are women (Ussher, 2013). All too often, autistic women are being missed, misunderstood and misdiagnosed because all too often clinicians do not have sufficient training and expertise to recognise that a person they wrongly perceive as having a 'disordered' personality is autistic. An article published in *The Lancet* medical journal proposed that a whole generation of autistic people were misdiagnosed as having personality disorders, most of whom were marginalised women (Lai and Baron-Cohen, 2015). So why is this important? Price refers to research by Sheehan and co-authors, which demonstrates the stigma attached when an autistic person is misdiagnosed: 'Getting stuck with a personality disorder diagnosis also makes it very difficult for a patient to find affirming, compassionate mental health care, particularly if that stigma interweaves with sexism or misogynoir' (Sheehan et al, 2016 in Price, 2022, p 75). Remarkably, a diagnosis of borderline/emotionally unstable personality disorder is usually based on the assessment by an individual psychiatrist. One autistic parent described how a psychiatrist visited her soon after the birth of her second child and within minutes diagnosed her with a borderline personality disorder; 30 years later, this remains on her medical records and she continues to experience the stigma attached to what she refers to as a 'lazy' diagnosis. In comparison, an autism diagnosis requires a comprehensive assessment undertaken by a team of professionals who are trained and competent (NICE, 2012). Autistic women, who have previously been misdiagnosed as having a 'disordered' personality, continue to experience unwarranted discrimination when professionals choose to focus on their original diagnosis rather than accepting they *are* autistic. An autistic mother who was originally misdiagnosed with a borderline personality disorder details her experiences when she approached children's social care for support after leaving an abusive relationship with the father of her unborn baby:

> Holding it in; I've been holding it in for years. I really believed that children's and families social services were there to help and support, to keep families together, showing compassion and kindness. As an autistic person transition can be difficult to adjust to, when I became pregnant, I asked social services for help because I thought that they could help me adjust to becoming a mother. Help was far from what I received, instead they came into my life and instantly decided I could never be a 'good' enough parent. I was set up to fail, coerced, shamed, lied to, mocked, and openly discriminated because I am a disabled parent, by the very service that is supposed to provide help and support. Social services and the family courts obliterated my family and our trust in the system. Years later we are still coming to terms with our child's unlawful removal and the years we missed out on. Despite our child being returned to our care and years have passed, the impact on our family is visible every day. The fight to hold social services responsible is exhausting, we are damaged by their actions.

A high percentage of autistic people also have attention deficit hyperactivity disorder (ADHD). Dr Simon Bignell, a leading UK ADHD researcher, reports that potentially 80 per cent of autistic children have co-occurring

ADHD, who then grow up to become autistic adults with ADHD (Bignell, 2018). For people with ADHD, high stimulation is exciting and confusing because they can easily feel overwhelmed and overstimulated without realising this is happening until it happens. ADHD can cause difficulties with inhibition, regulating their attention and emotional responses. An ADHD diagnosis inaccurately implies a person has difficulties sustaining attention, when the reality is ADHD is not a deficit of attention but rather a challenge of regulating it at will or on demand (Nerenberg, 2020, pp 74–6). Another feature of ADHD can be a heightened sensitivity to criticism and being judged.

> Women with ADHD who have struggled for years with logistical challenges often develop a nagging sense of not being good enough, never being able to 'hit the mark' at home or at work, and they struggle with anxiety and depression. But many women with ADHD also use their gift for hyperfocusing to excel beyond their peers – in writing, research, art, and other areas. (Nerenberg, 2020, p 75)

Practice considerations for social workers when assessing and working with autistic people

A major research report has stressed that 'disabled children and their families within the UK are one of the most severely disadvantaged'. It is common for national and local policies to create a default position for those assessing disabled children with such policies to often assume parental failings (Clements and Aiello, 2021). The Case for Change, Independent Review of Children's Social Care, published in June 2021, highlights the acute problems families of disabled children experience, with 24 per cent of parent/carers providing upwards of 100 hours of care, with support only being offered once they reach crisis point. All too often, 'families with disabled children feel that they are navigating a system that is set up for child protection, not support' (Independent Review of Children's Social Care, 2021, p 29).

It is not uncommon for 'parenting advice' through a parenting course or 'Early Help' to be considered as the most appropriate or indeed the only response for working with families with disabled children. The purpose of 'Early Help' is to support children and to prevent children becoming at risk of harm, neglect or becoming a child in need. As disabled children usually need extra support to help them address the barriers they can encounter, it is difficult to apply the 'Early Help' model, particularly as short-term/time-limited intervention can be problematic for children with lifelong disabilities. There is no requirement for any social work professional to have expertise in assessing children with disabilities, something which is not adequately addressed in the *Working Together to Safeguard Children 2023* guidance (HM Government, 2023). Professional competency is vital if the needs of the child and caregiver(s) are to be accurately identified. It requires the assessor to be more than 'neurodiversity aware or affirming', as they must have the foundational knowledge and experienced perspective which is provided by engagement with the community in question. One autistic mother reported how their son's difficulties were automatically attributed to her parenting style and her 'lack of boundaries'. The requirement was that she (not her partner) attended a series of parenting courses which were not specific to neurodivergent children. She completed the course feeling that her parenting style was criticised and her competence as a mother devalued.

Social workers need to gain an in-depth understanding of an autistic person's experience and different styles of communication. They need to cast aside their own biases when evaluating different parenting approaches because autistic parents' parent differently, which does not automatically mean they are harming their children. When assessing and supporting neurodivergent families, there cannot be a 'one size fits all approach'. The delivery of dynamic social work support using professional competence and experience is critical. It is essential that social workers and other childcare agencies appreciate that any assessment of a disabled child requires professionals to adopt a different way of thinking and analysing the disabled child's needs, and the interfamilial dynamics because autistic people have a different way of thinking, rather than a deficient one. All too often, autistic people are held accountable when interpersonal relationships fail, particularly when the practitioner focuses on their perceived 'social deficits', unwittingly expecting them to mask (camouflage) their differences instead of adopting humility in the face of difference whereby they seek to build a rapport and understanding. The researcher Damian Milton describes how autistic people can have difficulties working out what non-autistic people are thinking, just as much as non-autistic people struggle to work out what an autistic person is thinking. This is referred to as the 'double empathy problem' (Milton et al, 2020), which is a cross-neurotype communication mismatch whereby autistic people and neurotypical people have different experiences of being, which shapes the way in which they communicate and empathise with one another. Communication cannot happen unless there are at least two people. To bridge the double cross-neurotype empathy problem, effort from both parties is required (Adkin and Gray-Hammond, 2023). Autistic-to-autistic communication is effective and better understood than neurotypical-to-autistic communication (Crompton et al, 2020), which probably arises from their shared neurology and cultural experiences.

Due to a notable increase in the number of concerns specific to FII across the UK, the British Association of Social Workers published the *Fabricated or Induced Illness and Perplexing Presentations: Abbreviated Practice Guide for Social*

Work Practitioners (Long et al, 2022). However, there is a paucity of research available which specifically examines autistic parents' experiences, and the prevalence of parental allegations related to FII when they approach statutory services for support. There is a valid argument against locating the issues of parental blame or FII at the feet of social workers or social work practice in general, given that epistemic injustice is a universal reality for marginalised groups within the statutory systems. One specification is that if professionals could gain a better knowledge of autistic presentations, autistic parents could avoid many of these highly stressful experiences. The following is an account of Ann's highly stressful experiences as a neurodivergent mother who was accused of FII.

> Ann was a barrister, who had recently left her career to look after her children full-time. Ann's children had been diagnosed as autistic with a Pathological Demand Avoidant Profile. Both children were also diagnosed with attention deficit hyperactivity disorder (ADHD), anxiety, sensory processing disorder, gross and fine motor skill delay, hypotonia, hyper mobility, Avoidant Restrictive Food Intake Disorder (ARFID) and sleep difficulties. They struggled with attending school and separating from their mother, presenting with 'challenging behaviour' at home and in the community, and family 'dysregulation'.
>
> Ann is an autistic single mother to two neurodivergent children. She advised her local authority that she was recently identified as autistic with ADHD. Ann has been subject to Parent/Carer blame and subsequently, accusations of exaggerating her children's difficulties and insinuations of child abuse, specifically when advocating for appropriate support for her children in education. Ann and her children were about to become subject to Child Protection following a referral from school to Child Protection services. Ann requested an independent assessment of her children's needs. Ann's children were presented as 'fine at school'. Ann came to realise that most professionals she encountered just did not understand her. Her direct manner and uncompromising honesty, her passion for niche topics, her propensity for correcting factual errors within professional reports, difficulty attending to some basic life skills (despite significant competency in other areas), were considered 'challenging' and she was deemed by professionals as 'anxious' and a 'mental health risk'.
>
> The hostile situations Ann encountered with health, education, and social care from the moment she initiated a Special Educational Needs and Disability Tribunal challenge with education, contributed to the significant difficulty and recurrent crises Ann experienced which led to a child protection plan being implemented. These traits became particularly problematic when Ann realised the difficulties that she

faced ensuring her children's needs were met and understood, as well as her own, would soon lead her to child protection matters. Both of Ann's autistic children, also with a Pathological Demand Avoidance profile, were presented to education by Ann with unmet education, health, and social care needs.

Ann's 'anxiety' was recorded in the social services records as the reason for her children's 'Perplexing Presentation'. Ann's 'persistence' in requesting support to help her and her children, was repeatedly being met with parental blame and no access to support or any form of practical assistance. In what Ann describes as desperation, following a significant level of repeated requested help from education and social care, she was made subject to a local authority policy which precluded her from sending emails or making complaints. She therefore commissioned independent assessments prior to referring for an independent social worker for help from independent professionals with experience working with children with a Pathological Demand Avoidant Profile. Whilst Ann found such assessments incredibly helpful, she needed support to deliver such recommendations directly with the children. They were simply a neurodivergent family that needed support.

Let's unravel what happened and why Ann's needs as an autistic mother were misunderstood. Many children who present with Pathological Demand Avoidance (PDA), or a PDA profile, mask their behaviours. Masking is a coping mechanism and is used in situations when a person is unsure about how to behave and adapt to fit in with others around them. For example, some autistic children hide their differences so they can adequately function in school (Kendall, 2020, p 28). PDA is characterised by extremely high levels of anxiety which underlies an individual's need to be in control to lessen their anxiousness. Their resistance to everyday demands and use of social strategies to avoid situations can be misinterpreted as 'a lack of parental boundaries', when the reality is the person's reactions are not intentional, their need to avoid demands are because they cause them distress, and their reactions are anxiety-driven. Often, there is a significant discrepancy between the descriptions of a child's behaviour at home and in school, or equally between different parental homes where parents are separated. These inconsistencies can make triangulation (using multiple sources of information to develop comprehensive understanding) harder, so it is vital to obtain detailed accounts from a variety of settings, teasing out information by asking further exploratory questions and looking for evidence of masking in all interactions, including with you during the assessment (PDA Society, 2022, p 16).

Ann's professional observations records noted; 'She gets fixated on things and if she cannot do them will become upset', 'She gets so strongly absorbed in something and will lose sight of other things', 'She often finds it hard to understand what is going on during a conversation', 'She has often been told that she goes on and on about the same thing', 'She says one thing and does another', 'She is constantly seeking more information, she is presenting as anxious', 'Her children are fine at school', 'She is impulsive', 'She is making her children anxious'.

Ann's difficulties staying on task meant that conversation and responses were not always on track, as she would veer off onto subjects that she was still processing. This meant that Ann had difficulty following conversations because, as an autistic woman, she considered each minute detail relevant to what was being discussed, even if it seemed unconnected to other people. Ann needed to fully understand and process a concept before she could 'file away' the topic and shift her attention to the next issue, meaning immediate answers were not possible for Ann and if she is put in a position where immediate answers were expected, her anxiety caused her to give an answer that she felt was expected, or she would shut down. Ann may later, after processing 'change her mind' or require more detail to process which is perceived as challenging or dishonest. She may then repeat the same information or request until she could fully understand the context enabling her to move on.

Ann needed support from a competent professional, not criticism of her parenting, to spend time learning and reprocessing what this new information meant to her, how her differing neurology impacts her and reprocessing a lifetime of experiences through an autistic and ADHD lens. Furthermore, like many carers, Ann did not have the practical support nor the understanding from those within the system designed to support families and the misinterpretation of Ann's communication continued. One could argue that Ann and her family were a family with unmet needs.

If Ann was in an unfamiliar environment or dealing with a situation where she did not feel understood, with lots of different people talking and different opinions to process, she was often unable to provide immediate answers when questioned. She struggled to understand the unwritten social rules or expectations, she was sensitive to the power imbalance where she felt she was being scrutinised whilst not necessarily understanding the motivations or perspectives of those doing the scrutinising. Ann reported feeling anxious and unsafe in that environment causing her immense distress.

Luke Beardon's Golden Equation states 'Autism + Environment = Outcome' (Beardon, 2021a, p 5). The experience of unmet needs within families with autistic parents and/or autistic children is common, with the importance of environmental factors overlooked. The time, lack of resources, training and levels of expertise within the system can impact the ability of schools, health provisions and social care to meet the needs of children and families that they are designed to support.

> Ann, a determined mother who, despite the criticism she faced from the system, fought her way through to ensure her children's needs were met. Professionals needed to understand and meet the needs of Ann's children, whilst she needed to be supported as a parent/carer to ensure her needs were also met. Whilst the 'welfare of the child is paramount', the main carer is central to the family unit with professionals needing to undertake a holistic assessment of the family, rather than solely focusing on the needs of the children.
>
> For Ann and her family, advice from occupational therapy sensory assessments on interoception was crucial. By understanding and providing independent social work support to meet the individual needs of each family member meant that Ann and her children received a service tailored through the lens of their autistic experience. This included communication and support planning. Consequently, Ann's children were 'removed' from the child protection register; however, the trauma of such experiences does not disappear.

The experiences of autistic parents accused of FII in the Family Courts

Autistic parents who have been accused of FII, which has sometimes led to their child/children being removed from their care, have described the injustices they experienced within Family Courts. One autistic mother said:

> Injustice lurks in places where transparency and accountability are forbidden. Within the family courts parents are 'gagged' under the guise of the 'protection of the rights of children'. However, many parents have experienced horrendous treatment within the family courts, and one would question whether 'children's rights' are really being protected by the family court system?

An autistic mother with no financial resources, who was not eligible for legal aid assistance to cover her legal costs, decided to represent herself in family court. She has written what happened:

> My experience within family courts as an openly autistic parent representing myself was horrific. The Judge was fully aware of my

autism but did not make any of the reasonable adjustments I needed. Within the family courts it is up to the individual Judge to decide whether reasonable adjustments are made. During proceedings I was treated less favourably by the Judge compared to the other non-autistic participants. Research [Sasson et al, 2017] has indicated that non-autistic individuals perceive autistic individuals negatively on first impression. Despite this it was almost impossible to complain, ultimately being an autistic parent within the UK family court system is a dangerous place.

Within the family courts autistic parents are, all too frequently, disabled, stereotyped and stigmatised by legal professionals who presume that having an autism diagnosis equates to inadequate parenting (McConnell and Llewellyn, 2002). Concerningly, recent research has highlighted that autistic parents are disproportionately becoming subjected to child protection proceedings, as well as growing numbers of neurodivergent mothers of neurodivergent children encountering treacherous experiences of social services (Clements and Aiello, 2021). Research into the lived experiences of autistic parents within the family court system has highlighted that family law professionals struggle to understand the barriers faced by their autistic clients – and that autistic parents reported having little to no support within the system, which led to them being misunderstood by the legal professionals, including Judges (George et al, 2018). In 2020, His Honour Judge Middleton-Roy provided guidance within a Judgement around the adjustments autistic parents may require to be able to fully participate within proceedings. He highlighted the importance of autistic parents being afforded *suitable, targeted, and attuned assessments* (*D and E (Parent with Autism)* 2020). Although this is a positive step forward, such guidance needs to be underpinned by training for family law professionals.

As independent social workers and expert witnesses for Special Educational Needs and Disability Tribunals, two of the authors have witnessed autistic parents who have opted to self-represent. Sometimes this has been painful to observe because the judicial system has its own set of rules which are not always explicit and can be confusing. Parents (autistic or non-autistic) can attend a tribunal, often with the expectation that they can finally tell their story in full. However, this is not how tribunals work and sadly autistic parents have discovered how traumatising the court arena can be. For example, one autistic mother referred to her 'neurodivergent family', which the judge quickly discounted by saying 'Aren't we all a bit neurodivergent?'

How can we change things?

What transpires is that there is an ongoing need for all professionals within social care, health, education and the Family Courts to access high-calibre training which focuses on the lived experiences of autistic families, including how the UK's child protection system can inadvertently become an incredibly traumatic and harmful experience for autistic parents of autistic children. Critically, social workers must be supported by their management, training and support systems to apply 'theory into practice' within frontline services, to ensure they deliver and uphold a competent system with is non-discriminatory and celebratory of difference. True cross-agency co-production must be at the heart of professional practice where autistic people are invited to have a central role in developing and evaluating cultural competence, not tokenistic 'awareness raising', which severs the matter at hand from its socio-political context.

History creates knowledge and understanding which is then built upon to enhance professional practice and to achieve successful outcomes. If we continue to position problems within disabled people and their families by subscribing to a medical model view, our ability to practise ethically is significantly thwarted. The 'blame' will always reside with the disabled person rather than acknowledging the need to change culture and environment to promote the wellbeing of everyone. In many years to come, one may wonder whether we might look back at the experiences of neurodivergent families of today and see where we went wrong in our support systems once this becomes our history. That day will likely come. One of the most dangerous phrases in language is: 'We've always done it this way.' The paradigm shift needs to start now in law, policy and guidance.

References

Adkin, T. and Gray-Hammond, D. (2023) 'Creating autistic suffering: the AuDHD burnout to psychosis cycle: a deeper look', *David's Divergent Discussions*. Available from: https://www.davidsdivergentdiscussions.co.uk/p/creating-autistic-suffering-the-audhd-burnout-to-psychosis-cycle-a-deeper-look [accessed 19 July 2024].

American Psychiatric Association, DSM-5 Task Force (2013) *Diagnostic and Statistical Manual of Mental Disorders: DSM-5™*, 5th edn, Washington, DC.

Autism Eye (2014) 'Parents accused of fabricated illness'. Available from: https://www.autismeye.com/parents-accused-of-fabricated-illness/#:~:text=The%20term%20used%20is%20'Fabricated,for%20attention%20or%20financial%20gain [accessed 19 July 2024].

Beardon, L. (2020) *Avoiding Anxiety in Autistic Children: A Guide for Autistic Wellbeing*, London: Sheldon Press.

Beardon, L. (2021a) *Autism in Adults*, London: Sheldon Press.

Beardon, L. (2021b) *Avoiding Anxiety in Autistic Adults: A Guide for Autistic Wellbeing*, London: Sheldon Press.

Bennett, M., Webster, A.A., Goodall, E. and Rowland, S. (2018) 'Understanding the "true" potential of autistic people: debunking the Savant syndrome myth', in *Life on the Autism Spectrum: Translating Myths and Misconceptions into Positive Futures*, Singapore: Springer.

Benson, K.J. (2023) 'Perplexing presentations: compulsory neuronormativity and cognitive marginalisation in social work practice with autistic mothers of autistic children', *British Journal of Social Work*, 53(2): 1445–64.

Bettelheim, B. (1967) *The Empty Fortress: Infantile Autism and the Birth of the Self*, New York, NY: Free Press.

Bignell, S. (2018) 'Autism across the lifespan', University of Derby. Available from: https://www.derby.ac.uk/blog/autism-across-lifespan/ [accessed 19 July 2024].

Bobb, V. (2019) 'Black girls and autism', in B. Carpenter, F. Happé and J. Egerton (eds) *Girls and Autism: Educational, Family and Personal Perspectives*, Abingdon: Routledge.

Clements, L. and Aiello, A.L. (2021) *Institutionalising Parent Carer Blame: The Experiences of Families with Disabled Children in Their Interactions with English Local Authority Children's Services Departments*, Cerebra, University of Leeds.

Clements, L. and Aiello, A.L. (2023) *The Prevalence and Impact of Allegations of Fabricated or Induced Illness (FII)*, Cerebra, University of Leeds.

Crompton, C.J., Ropar, D., Evans-Williams, C.V., Flynn, E.G. and Fletcher-Watson, S. (2020) 'Autistic peer-to-peer information transfer is highly effective', *Autism*, 24(7): 1709–10.

D and E (Parent with Autism) [2020] EWFC B18 (11 May 2020).

Eaton, J. (2018) *A Guide to Mental Health Issues in Girls and Young Women on the Autism Spectrum: Diagnosis, Intervention and Family Support*, London: Jessica Kingsley Publishers, pp 22–3.

Equality Act 2010 (2010)The Stationery Office. Available from: https://www.legislation.gov.uk

Fletcher-Watson, S. and Happé, F. (2019) *Autism: A New Introduction to Psychological Theory and Current Debate*, 2nd edn, Abingdon: Routledge.

George, R., Crane, L., Bingham, A., Pophale, C. and Remington, A. (2018) 'Legal professionals' knowledge and experience of autistic adults in the family justice system', *Journal of Social Welfare and Family Law*, 40(1): 78–97.

Gullon-Scott, F. and Long., C. (2022) 'FII and perplexing presentations: what is the evidence base for and against current guidelines, and what are the implications for social services?', *British Journal of Social Work*, 52(7): 4040–56.

HM Government (2023) *Working Together to Safeguard Children 2023: A Guide to Multi-Agency Working to Help, Protect and Promote the Welfare of Children*.

Hull et al 2017 cited in McCrossin, R. (2022) 'Finding the true number of females with autistic spectrum disorder by estimating the biases in initial recognition and clinical diagnosis', *Children (Basel)*, 9(2): 272.

Kanner, L. (1949) *Child psychiatry*. Charles C. Thomas.

Kendall, E. (2020) *Helping You to Identify and Understand Autism Masking: The Truth Behind the Mask*, Andover: M & R Publishing.

Lai, M.-C. and Baron-Cohen, S. (2015) 'Identifying the lost generation of adults with autism spectrum conditions', *The Lancet Psychiatry*, 2(11): 1013–27.

Long, C., Eaton, J., Russell, S., Gullon-Scott, F. and Bilson, A. (2022) *Fabricated or Induced Illness and Perplexing Presentations: Abbreviated Practice Guide for Social Work Practitioners*, May, Birmingham: BASW.

McConnell, D. and Llewellyn, G. (2002) 'Stereotypes, parents with intellectual disability and child protection', *Journal of Social Welfare and Family Law*, 24(3): 297–317.

Milton, D.E.M., Heasman, B. and Sheppard, E. (2020) 'Double empathy', in F. Volkmar (ed) *Encyclopedia of Autism Spectrum Disorders*, New York: Springer.

National Autistic Society (2024) 'What is autism?'. Available from: https://www.autism.org.uk/advice-and-guidance/what-is-autism [accessed 19 July 2024].

Nerenberg, J. (2020) *Divergent Mind: Thriving in a World That Wasn't Designed for You*, San Francisco, CA: HarperOne.

NICE (2012, updated 2021) Autism spectrum disorder in adults: diagnosis and management. Clinical guideline (CG142).

O'Nions, E., Petersen, I., Buckman, J.E.J., Charlton, R.A., Cooper, C., Corbett, A. et al (2023) 'Autism in England: assessing underdiagnosis in a population-based cohort study of prospectively collected primary care data', *Lancet Regional Health Europe*, 29: article 100626.

PDA Society (2022) 'Identifying & assessing a PDA profile – practice guidance'. Available from: https://www.pdasociety.org.uk/wp-content/uploads/2023/02/Identifying-Assessing-a-PDA-profile-Practice-Guidance-v1.1.pdf [accessed 26 July 2024].

Pohl, A.L., Crockford, S.K., Blakemore, M., Allison, C. and Baron-Cohen, S. (2020) 'A comparative study of autistic and non-autistic women's experience of motherhood', *Molecular Autism*, 11(1): 1–12.

Price, D. (2022) *Unmasking Autism: The Power of Embracing Our Hidden Neurodiversity*, London: Octopus Publishing Books, pp 20–1.

Royal College of Paediatrics and Child Health (RCPCH) (2021) *Perplexing Presentations (PP)/Fabricated or Induced Illness (FII) in Children: RCPCH Guidance*, London.

Running, A. and Jata-Hall, D. (2023) 'Parental blame and the PDA profile of autism', PDA Society. Available from: https://www.pdasociety.org.uk/wp-content/uploads/2023/02/Parental_Blame_PDA_Research_Report_Running_JataHall.pdf [accessed 16 July 2024].

Russell, G., Stapley, S., Newlove-Delgado, T., Salmon, A., White, R., Warren, F. et al (2022) 'Time trends in autism diagnosis over 20 years: a UK population-based cohort study', *Journal of Child Psychology and Psychiatry*, 63(6): 674–82.

Sasson, N.J., Faso, D.J., Nugent, J., Lovell, S., Kennedy, D.P. and Grossman, R.B. (2017) 'Neurotypical peers are less willing to interact with those with autism based on thin slice judgments', *Scientific Reports*, 7(1): 1–8.

Sheehan, L., Nieweglowski, K. and Corrigan, P. (2016) 'The stigma of personality disorders', *Current Psychiatry Reports*, 18(1): 1–7, cited in Price, D. (2022) *Unmasking Autism: The Power of Embracing Our Hidden Neurodiversity*, London: Octopus Publishing Books.

Stott, J. (2023) 'Autism in England: assessing underdiagnosis in a population-based cohort study of prospectively collected primary care data', *The Lancet Regional Health*, 29(1): article 100626.

Independent Review of Children's Social Care (2021) *The Case for Change*, London: Department for Education.

Ussher, J.M. (2013) 'Diagnosing difficult women and pathologising femininity: gender bias in psychiatric nosology', *Feminism & Psychology*, 23(1): 63–9.

Waltz, M. (2015) 'Mothers and autism: the evolution of a discourse of blame', *AMA Journal of Ethics*, 17(4): 353–8.

9

A sibling perspective on fabricated or induced illness

Kaydence Drayak

In the beginning – something has changed

Perhaps, it is best to start at the beginning, the 'before' times: everything in my life is itemised – the 'before times'; the 'during times'; and the 'since times'. Here is my story, as a big sister, who had lost to an FII investigation and then recovered from foster care, a baby sister.

My life in the before times was wonderful. I was just a kid who liked to play netball, and had a lot of younger siblings that would drive me crazy, but who I loved dearly. We would play outside, running around like hooligans, we played imaginary games, we would swim in the sea. Life was pretty good, I loved my life, I don't think I really knew how good I had it. Then life got harder, my sister became really unwell.

When FII begins it's hardly ever as simple as an accusation being made, a wee investigation being carried out, and a swift collusion and action. From speaking to others who have experienced FII and reflecting on my experiences, it feels like it is often handled poorly, at times unprofessionally and always inhumanely.

As a sibling and child when the life-altering event of an FII allegation occurs, you don't know exactly what's going on. In fact, when most adult events happen, children seldom get the full story. This time, my parents were also in the dark – although we didn't really understand this and often felt worried they were keeping important information secret from us. It is only in hindsight that we can appreciate that none of us were able to predict what would happen.

The lead-up to the trigger being pulled.

The chaos being unleashed by an FII allegation is, I imagine, unique to every case – but in mine the trigger was my sister's illness. She was sick and she was getting sicker and sicker. There were countless visits to the hospital and many, many medications that she had to take. We tried our best not to fall asleep at night because we were always worried that an ambulance might pull up outside and we might not see our mother and sister again for days or even weeks. We knew something was wrong and didn't really understand it, but we became good at cleaning up vomit and doing whatever it took to make our little sister happy.

Then came the day when my sister became very unwell and she disappeared almost for forever. For real – we almost lost her life and then we lost her into foster care. This was the day a doctor decided that was my mother's fault.

We didn't know this at first. At first everything was just 'off'. As a child, you know when you are not told that something is wrong. All the adults were being weird, the doctors were acting standoffish and even rude, teachers kept a closer eye than you could really explain away, social workers arrived and entered our house unannounced all the time, and most importantly to me – my parents were scared. It's not a nice thing to say, I think, because it feels like I'm somehow undermining their bravery, strength and even how fiercely they love us: but my parents were not weak and they are still strong. The air was thick with worry and all the safe certainty that had always been before went away. We could see it in the way they walked, the change in their voices and the change in priorities. Children are connected to their parents and we could feel that they were terrified as any human being would be. But we didn't fully understand why and we didn't know what we were going to do about it.

My siblings and I began walking around like balls of stress and silliness. We began doing weird things to prepare for this unknown. Something unknown was building up and all we knew was we were not ready. We cleaned every inch of the house even when we didn't have the time. We hid cereal boxes, because maybe social workers think you should only have two boxes of only the healthy kinds in the cupboard. Quickly hide the Cocoa snaps, lest they decide that is the straw that breaks the camel's back in their report. Generally, I couldn't relax, not for a second and it felt as if my skin didn't fit me anymore.

During – the FII investigation is officially announced

When it happened, after all the waiting, all the weirdness and stress, it happened too quickly and all at once. A social worker came and sat on our sofa and smiled as she said my sister would not come home. We already hadn't seen her in months, it already had begun to feel like she was a dream I had had a long time ago.

And so we came to understand our sister was gone.

And our mother was a stamped, certified and officially designated monster.

The rage I felt was overwhelming. I took care of my sister too, but nobody asked me. I had known my mother my whole life and nobody asked me. I cannot tell you how my mother survived it, she is truly the strongest person in the world and I will never believe otherwise. Instead, let me tell you how I and my siblings did. Once the accusation was made, my sister was gone completely to us. We did not get to say goodbye and neither did anyone else. It felt like we as siblings had no role, no value at all to my sister's life.

We began collecting information trying to understand and hopefully fix whatever it was that had gone wrong. What we knew:

We knew our sister had been taken by the social workers.

We knew somehow and in some way the doctors had made a big mistake.

We knew that this whole experience was a secret and we were not to speak about it to anyone.

And we knew that everyone was saying horrible, terrible things about my mother much louder than they thought they were.

As siblings, we stuck together, shared our pieces of the puzzle and spied on the adults who were only getting weirder. The social workers who we now knew were actually evil monsters – my siblings and I cleverly puzzled this out all by ourselves thank you – were seemingly constantly in our home. They want to talk to us alone. My siblings and I also knew we could NEVER leave one of us alone with them, we'd be dragged off wouldn't we?[1] Worse still, my mother kept trying to side with the social workers. She invited them into our home. She asked them to come play games and activities with us to get to know us. She told us things like the social workers were trying to help figure things out so all of us children, including our lost sister, would be safe. She said it was their job to care about children. It became hard to trust even my mother. Why was she taking the side of the people who were trying to hang her? We felt in a way like we needed to protect our naïve mother. She always tries to see the best in people even when there is nothing good there to see.

Looking back, I can see clearly that my siblings and I stopped trusting professionals. We learned never to trust professionals ever again. How could we when they held such a radically different and painful view of reality? They told us that things had happened that we were confident had never happened. The professionals told us things we knew to be true were false in their reality. The truth was we had a choice to make – we either had to trust ourselves and what we actually experienced or we had to trust strangers. These strangers were inconsistent, they changed their minds, they made promises and didn't keep them, and they seemed to hate the person we loved so dearly. It wasn't a hard choice actually. Our mother had raised us to believe our thoughts and feelings were important. She raised us to believe that we mattered. To these professionals, we certainly didn't feel like we mattered. Needless to say, we decided to trust ourselves. We knew we weren't allowed to say any of this. We learned that to stay together we would have to keep what we actually thought and felt a secret, and we learned to isolate ourselves from everyone except each other.

This will undoubtedly feel like repetition, but we could not understand or forgive the fact that none of the professionals ever asked us what we thought.

Actually, after telling us our sister wasn't coming home, the social workers and professionals never acknowledged our lost sister to us again. Every single one of them behaved like they were pretending she had never existed.

Meanwhile, we were far too afraid to ask.

It became clear to us that our parents were instructed never to talk to us about anything to do with real life. We worked out that these professionals thought our parents were clearly just going to manipulate our fragile undeveloped brains, as if we were incapable of having our own views and thoughts independent of our parents. We were under the impression that the monsters that stole and ate – was the working theory[2] our sister, were untrustworthy and we came to this conclusion all on our own.

They seemed to have no trouble telling us our parents were monsters. Takes one to know one, right?

Contact – seeing our sister again

Our parents eventually 'earned' Contact. I feel it was earned because it was not automatic for our parents, they had to constantly engage and deliberate with professionals to see their own child, they showed up to every hearing, every children's panel, they came for everything so they could see my sister again. I also believe I must capitalise the word Contact. Because the word grew. It grew and it grew until it meant nothing like what the word once meant to me as a young child. I might have wanted to make contact between my foot and a football in a match, but it bore no resemblance to the experience of a forced, supervised visit with my now estranged sister.

Let's be clear, at first we weren't allowed to go to Contact with our parents, just like the rest of the big important meetings that decided our fate – the last place silly children should be – but our parents, the only people left who cared about us, fought to let us come too. It was in this fight for Contact that I first realised the FII accusation had grown and it had spread from my mother to us children. We couldn't be alone with our sister either it seemed, because maybe we might hurt her too. Nobody believed us, nobody listened, but rather than assume the best in us, we were also presumed guilty until proven innocent.

When my parents managed to achieve Contact with our sister and us, siblings, it was a mixed blessing. It was a blessing because it meant for the first time in a very long time we would see our sister again. We missed her very much. I do believe it would have been easier to go on if they had cut off a piece of me, I think we all felt this way. Our sister belongs to and with us and we belong to and with her. She is us and we are her. How hard is that to understand? And how painful it is to be denied what should be a human right to be with your own (Citizen's Advice, 2024).[3]

So, we got to see her at Contact.

The way Contact works is quite strange. We were limited to how many could attend. I guess they forgot that we had spent our whole lives together, but initially, our parents could only bring a few of us at a time. Those chosen to attend – could you think of a better way to cause division between siblings – would show up at the agreed-upon time, the nightmares – the latest pet name we had chosen for the social workers and social work support – would be there watching us and writing things down. It was weird. It was intrusive. It made us feel bad about ourselves.

Our sister would show up an hour late and we would play for whatever time we had left. Every time we saw her again, she felt odd. Like she wasn't really sure who she was anymore. And little by little over the course of an hour, she would come out of her little shell and we would meet her again. By the end of the Contact, our sister would cry and beg us to take her home and the nightmare she lived with would physically drag her away to their car. It made me feel bad that I didn't run after her and stop them. But I knew it would in a way make everything worse.

Contact was stressful. It had moments of love and almost like a memory of the happiness we once had coming to the surface. But it was fleeting. And it was heart-breaking to have to keep grieving the loss of our sister after each Contact.

I love my sister. I hated Contact, but I would never have given it up.

Meanwhile – our parents were fighting for our sister back

We knew and could see our parents were fighting to get our sister back. My mother seemed to be forever putting care packages in the post to my sister, spending hours on the phone to who I don't know, but it was all very serious. My father devoted his energy to trying to get our family the right legal support and every other day felt like they both had to go away to a meeting.

Consequentially, we lost our parents during this time too. It wasn't just our sister the FII investigation stole. It stole our Mum too. Our parents spent entire days in court every other week. This process was unimaginably horrific, because they spent all their time listening to people call them monsters, unable to fight back, only to come home and be expected to work full-time, look after the kids and play host to our invaders – our latest theory was that the social workers were actually in fact demons looking to collect all the children and put them in evil zoos – and in order to get children they wore the parents down one meeting and hearing at a time.

While our parents were home, it felt as much as like they were gone even while there. There was no fun, there were no silly conversations and drop everything and head to the beach adventures. Everything was overshadowed by the FII investigation. With all this going on, we were not doing so hot ourselves. We were discovering very young that having our home and life invaded any time, any place with no warning shattered the childish illusion of both safety and privacy. Our bedrooms were not our own when social workers could insist on coming in whether we liked it or not. Our mother was too afraid of standing up for us to social workers and it felt like they could do whatever they wanted. Our life was their business, not ours, and we felt like the least important thing – for we felt fairly sure we must be merely things to them – in the equation. We didn't have any privacy or autonomy in our lives and we knew very well without anyone saying so that any reason that these people could find to take the rest of us away or indeed ruin my sister's chances of returning would be taken. This felt it had to be true, after all our sister had disappeared for a reason that we knew to be untrue. What else could be said or accused next? Nobody seemed to ask them to prove anything, but we had to answer so many questions and it felt like our parents were trying to justify everything we did. We knew we had to be perfect. Our family depended on it and that meant pretending, all of the time. Pretending not to be anxious. Pretending not to be angry. Pretending to be okay with feeling small, powerless and invaded. Pretending that we understood their reality, which was so vastly different from our own lived experience.

In meetings – voice

A child like me
By Bunny, aged 9

You see a child like me and I think you don't even see me at all.
You hear a child like me and you don't hear me at all.
You visit a child like me and you don't even see me, like I am
    not even real.
You think you know me but you don't know me at all.
You make big decisions in my life when I don't even want them.
You act like my family aren't real people.
You have meetings about me and I am not invited.
You say you care about me but you don't.
You say you care about me and my family and you don't.
You think things that aren't true and accuse us of it.
You don't know a child like me.

For almost all of the meetings, we were not invited. The important adults were off making the most important decisions about us and we weren't even allowed to come and listen. Our parents would go away for what felt like all day and on lots and lots of days. Some of the stuff I could sort of understand, but most of it I didn't really understand. I was worried about the police being there and whether that was a sign they were there to take us away. I felt and had presumed everyone at the meeting was there to be against our family.

A dear friend, who wished to remain anonymous, whose family was attacked by an FII accusation explained her perspective:

> My social worker claimed my mum had 'Munchausen's by proxy syndrome' and was fabricating and inducing mental illness in me …. During my time in 'care' I was forbidden to attend any of my hearings. Despite writing over thirty letters and begging my social workers to let me go, the answer was always no. This was so I wouldn't be able to tell the truth. I still don't feel safe: I think I'll never feel truly safe (even now I am home).

The interviews my siblings and I were forced to attend were just bizarre. The room, the clothing, the conversation is just normal enough that it makes you question why you feel so deeply uncomfortable, but it was like stepping into another reality. After the interviews, we compared experiences between us. When they picked each of us up in the police car, none of the adults spoke to us. It was just a child alone in the back of a police car, while the police and social worker spoke to each other. Once in the room, they had all these cameras and microphones. We felt like they were desperate to have us say or do something incriminating. The interviewers kept saying how they were hot and cold, and hot and cold, and hungry. It was weird and I can't help but wonder if they were trying to convince me they were human. There were two interviewers to each of us, individually as children. We were not allowed a support person. We were not allowed an advocate. It felt like because of the 'seriousness' of the FII investigation, we stopped being children in need of support. There was no room for kindness and empathy in an FII investigation. Right down to a 6-year-old boy being interviewed alone, two against one. Again, because FII investigations are taken so extremely seriously, we were taken alone to a location we didn't know. I didn't recognise the building. I didn't know if I left the building how I could get back home. I didn't even know if they were going to bring me home.

Onwards – I can't go on, I'll go on

Being a big sister or big brother comes with an element of built-in responsibility. Some society enforces, but a lot of it is personal. In our family, we all want to be the sort of brother or sister that stands up for each other. We want to be someone each other can rely upon. We take pride in being loyal friends. We all feel enormous guilt at how our sister was forced to leave with no explanation. We weren't allowed to explain that we wanted to take her home but couldn't. We all fear that she must've thought we didn't love her anymore. It hurts to imagine how it must've felt that she was the only one who couldn't go home.

I remember hating that my parents wouldn't kidnap her. I was convinced that the only right thing to do was drive to where they had her, steal her back. We fantasised that as a family we could go live in another country with fake names. For all of us, we didn't care what we had to do, we only cared that we had our sister back.

The social workers were still around way too much. At some point, we stopped even trying to explain our views to them because we were too tired and nobody wanted to listen. My siblings and I were so good at pretending not to be mad, not to be anxious, not to be upset – pretending to be absolutely fine and normal – that we began to forget who we were. The one thing that never dulled was that we failed to protect our sister and that we hated ourselves for it. After many months, we sort of stopped talking. We were dedicating what little energy we had left to just getting through. It is exhausting living in defensive mode for a prolonged period of time.

There are memory gaps of this time. Sometimes your heart hurts too much to let yourself remember. While I can't tell you exactly what happened, I know our trust was broken, we had lost both parents and a sister, and we were all alone in the world because we had learnt that everyone else is too dangerous and untrustworthy.

At long last – victory

One day, we got up and it was a day like all the others where we drag ourselves through our routine feeling pretty desolate. Our parents had a hearing, and it didn't appear like it was any different from any other hearing. Our parents didn't have some kind of special optimistic look, they both looked like they felt pretty defeated. The crazy thing about this was just like there wasn't any advanced warning at the beginning, it didn't feel like there was advanced warning at the end. Like a switch being flicked on and off without too much thought for what happens either way. Our parents went to court and that day we won and my sister came home. Suddenly, our mother was de-monstered. Being monstered left scars; I don't actually think it was that simple for her or for any of us. It felt really surreal. When you have a new baby in the house there is a feeling as though this brand new person we have just met has both been the piece that has always been missing, but also like I can't imagine life without them. Surely, there never was life before we had them? Our sister coming home felt like that. Only this was a person I had already been missing for what felt like years. This was a person who had been a part of our lives before. We were really, really happy to have her back. When she was away, it was all stress, all suffering – and when she came back it was like it was just surreal happiness. Yet, that happiness was thinner than the happiness used to be, because we didn't believe even after she returned that she wouldn't vanish again. After all those days of grieving for her, could she really be home?

Eventually it did sink in, and as quickly as they came, the social workers left. Patting themselves on the back at a job well done. Unfortunately, they didn't return us back to the way things had once been. I did not have friends anymore. When my sister was sick I could at least talk to my friends. They could understand my sister having to visit the hospital. But you can't exactly say social workers are accusing my mother of abusing my sister. Truth be told, you aren't even sure what you are allowed to say. I tried once to talk to a friend, and then they just ghosted me. I never heard back from them until years later when they simply asked me, how's your sister? Which was hard to even begin to pick up where we left off, much less with that last message having gone unanswered for years sitting between us. Trying to pick things back up is hard. I no longer knew who I was, my siblings had changed too and our sister did not return as the same person who left. We were all different, slightly broken people.

Of course, I understood why my sister had changed, she had been utterly traumatised and abandoned, I remember thinking how much worse she must've had it. I didn't believe that I would have survived what she went through. She did survive and I'll never stop being thankful.

We had our parents back, although they needed to heal as well. Slowly and clumsily, my mother helped us put ourselves together, learn how to be ourselves again, and get to know our sister who we could finally tell we never wanted to let her go.

Future – the aftermath

The lasting effects of FII are countless and my family and I will never not be affected.

My siblings and I will never trust professionals fully. I will never allow any of my siblings to be without a family member by their side ever. At least now, I can say we are happy together.

One side effect of this FII experience is that we have difficulty connecting to others who have not experienced FII. If I was to try to explain these things to my peers, I fear they would think I'm insane, 'professionals would never do that!', 'that can't be allowed!', 'social workers aren't like that', 'your mother must have deserved it!' We are isolated, and I fear that to almost anyone in the world apart from my siblings and parents, I must seem to be a closed-off, distrustful and strange young girl.

My sister explained this well:

Before this happened, I couldn't imagine this happening to anyone. In fact, I still struggle to wrap my head around that this happens to other people. If I had to divide my life into chunks I would have to cut my life in two: before and after. Before, my life felt like one long holiday, and since it has been never ending stress and anxiety. While I have gotten my life back, I never get to go back. I feel like I didn't know about problems or bad things in the world, until this happened. And since, bad things feel real and terrifying. I am terrified all the time.

In a way, FII kind of made me grow up immediately. More anxious, it took issues I had and multiplied them. I hate being out of control, and this was an experience of absolute powerlessness. And overall it was hard because we were just trying to grow up and stuff and then it catapulted us into systems that didn't have time for growing up, they just steamrolled in and then back out.

In trying to heal, I have found advocacy, I felt I never had a voice, that those who had never met me or my siblings were making decisions about our lives without us. I firmly believe in the mantra 'nothing about us, without us', so I am and intend to continue working with people and organisations to support those with lived experience (particularly young people), to have a voice and make sure those making decisions hear what they have to say. That's what I feel would have made a difference for me and my family, our situation would never have happened if someone had actually listened to us tell them what we wanted and what was actually happening, instead of them blindly operating in our 'best interests' – a term I have come to despise.

If we were to try to find the positives in the FII investigation, it would be that we did work out what made our sister so poorly and that she is well now. However, that could have been done without a mountain of trauma and pain. The other positive thing is the people we have met. We have made some wonderful friends, and met some amazing people. People who have helped to restore a little of our faith in humanity. One of those people is a friend I made, a sister herself, who was the victim of an FII accusation and separated from her Mum and sister. I will leave you with her poem.

Dear Child Away From Your Family,

I can't even possibly imagine how you must be feeling right now because although our situations are similar every situation is unique to that individual and their family, but I can take a pretty good guess at what it might be like for you. I do know you must feel absolutely terrible, as though part of you has been stolen and as if your heart has been ripped out your chest. I can at least say I know what it's like to feel like that because I felt that way every day and night for the 18 miserable months I was in the 'care' of my local authority. I won't go into detail but yes as you probably guessed I was stolen from my mum. The social workers lied to the sheriff about my family and my mum and as a result an order for the social workers to take me was granted. I consider this method to be nothing more than legal kidnapping. It's the most horrible thing in the world, being in care and being without your family – I know, I've been there. But please believe me, THIS WILL END. You will survive this. Keep breathing and get through the days, remembering each day brings you closer to the day you will get back home. Two years ago I was in the same position as you: alone, miserable, scared and desperate, desperately longing for my family, and I never truly thought I would ever be happy again, but I am …. There is no quick fix for this and I'm sure you already know that but slowly but surely and over time your scars will begin to heal, your broken heart will mend and your soul will grow braver, wiser and more full of love than it ever had been before this experience. Your trauma will always be part of you but trust me, the memories WILL fade and even though it doesn't seem like they will ever leave you now, they will. Nothing will ever be worse than what you have already survived. Remember one day this will all be over and it will just be a bad, bad, bad memory but it won't be your life. Hold on. This will end. And one day, somehow, no matter what, I promise you, this will only be a memory.

Best wishes, A Child Who Was Kidnapped Too.

Notes

[1] This is a story about a true experience and no offence is intended as I try to convey how we felt as children. This is not targeted at any individual and is intended to be read in the context of a child's experience of the world.
[2] Again, child's perspective – chill out, we are pretty sure social workers do not in fact eat children.
[3] This is actually a human right under Article 8 of the Human Rights Act (1998).

References

Citizens Advice (2024) 'Your right to respect for private and family life'. Available from: https://www.citizensadvice.org.uk/law-and-courts/civil-rights/human-rights/what-rights-are-protected-under-the-human-rights-act/your-right-to-respect-for-private-and-family-life/ [accessed 18 July 2024].

Human Rights Act 1998.

10

Parent blame and the NHS

Amy (pseudonym)

Introduction

My son, Joe, is 16 years old and autistic. He received his autism diagnosis when he was 15. From early childhood, he experienced multiple difficulties, which led us into the medical system and into interactions with paediatricians and other healthcare professionals within the NHS.

Background

Joe is my first-born child. I had a difficult pregnancy, followed by a complicated birth, which resulted in an emergency cesarean. Joe therefore entered the world in a traumatic fashion, he had experienced some pressure on his head and was subsequently delivered very swiftly in theatre. He was well after birth.

From a tiny baby, Joe demonstrated a high level of irritability, he had a high level of energy and movement, he didn't like to lie flat, he disliked being swaddled, and as he progressed through the early years, he would become distressed if he was restricted in any way, such as in his car seat, buggy and highchair.

Joe hit his developmental milestones early or as expected. However, a notable difference was his high level of activity day and night. He constantly sought interaction with his environment and found it very difficult to 'switch off'. It was like his brain needed to be engaged with sensory information all of the time. This allowed him to learn concrete facts quickly, such as numbers, the alphabet and names of objects, but then the basic everyday tasks such as drinking from a cup and getting dressed were much more problematic and challenging for him. Consequently, Joe's skills often seemed to be 'out of sync'. This led to difficulties in being able to self-soothe and self-regulate, he had significant sleep difficulties, he had a restricted diet due to intolerance to certain textures, smells and taste of foods. Joe also had problems with certain types of motion: he was sensory-sensitive to clothes tags and shoes, he was averse to certain noises of pitch of sounds and he also showed signs of obsessional tendencies.

Our health visitor described Joe as a 'high needs' child. As parents, we made huge efforts to establish routines for Joe which provided stability and predictability for him. However, many of the conventional strategies used with children to help to facilitate resolutions to some of the childhood difficulties mentioned simply didn't work for Joe. It was evident to us that his needs were different. Strategies that were also recommended to us also tended to be tailored for children whose needs were quite different.

As Joe's mum, I was able to acknowledge to myself and to people close to me that Joe had differences and this was also recognised by those people. Outside of my close circle, I was very reluctant to speak to anyone at all about his difficulties, including other parents and health professionals. I had fears about lack of understanding, therefore was highly driven to manage Joe's differences myself without professional input.

When Joe was 5 years old (by which time I also had a second child), his difficulties had escalated on multiple levels, predominantly around eating, sleeping and experiencing strong sensory intolerances that were impacting significantly on him and on family life overall. It is at this point that I spoke to a GP, who signposted me to the school nurse. The conversation I had with the school nurse was positive and I felt that my concerns were heard and understood. The school nurse referred my son to a paediatrician. This began a six-year arduous journey of navigating the paediatric and medical system.

Paediatrics

Joe had multiple difficulties, and different departments dealt with different medical aspects of those difficulties. He was sent around the paediatric system like he was a ping-pong ball, being bounced from one service to another. This, I now realise, is not uncommon, particularly for children with disabilities and children with various medical needs. In consequence, I attended all the services that Joe was 'sent to', as recommended by the paediatricians.

Joe attended a sleep clinic, a sensory service (where he was identified as having sensory processing difficulties), he had hydrotherapy to help with water aversion, he was diagnosed with Tourettes as he experienced tics, he had longstanding leg pains and so was under the rheumatology service, where he was diagnosed with hypermobility, pain sensitivity and severe muscle tightness warranting physiotherapy. The clinics attended were therefore very specific to Joe's needs at a given time. There was also a question mark raised about autism.

Joe also had longstanding and persistent avoidance of many foods due to sensory intolerances, leading to a restricted diet. This caused some vitamin deficiencies at various times, and likely impacted on his other difficulties at various times and to varying degrees. His eating difficulties escalated when he was 10 and I was concerned that his health was becoming more compromised. It is at this point that I flagged up my concerns regarding his level of food restriction and turned to the rheumatology consultant for direction as to what to do next. I did this very specifically due to the rheumatologist having previously recognised that my son's needs did not always present 'typically' and that he might require an alternative understanding outside of the medical 'norm'. Rheumatology was also a service that was involved with my son at the time – and they were already aware of his eating difficulties.

Child and Adolescent Mental Health Services (CAMHS)

Joe was referred by his paediatrician to the CAMHS Eating Disorders Team for an assessment for Avoidant Restrictive Food Intake Disorder (ARFID). Unfortunately, this referral became problematic and led to misconceptions about what my son's needs were. This put me in a position of having to address concerns with a team that I subsequently discovered did not welcome feedback. This then created a conflict between parental views and the opinions of medical professionals, and also formed the roots of parental blame: blame that started specifically after I raised concerns about Joe's care within CAMHS services.

Accessing CAMHS in the first instance was troublesome. ARFID is a much less known eating disorder than anorexia and bulimia and is also fundamentally different from both of these conditions. It was necessary, therefore, that the assessment and treatment approach should be appropriate to ARFID. The Eating Disorders Team did not take this view and insisted that he be assessed and treated in line with anorexia.

Rather than reading the referral and listening to what I considered to be Joe's needs, CAMHS adopted a standardised 'scattergun' approach to his assessment – sending out a number of inappropriate questionnaires. I tried, without success, to confirm with the team what my son's needs were and the reasons for his referral, but it became clear that it lacked an understanding of ARFID and was intent on proceeding with an anorexia assessment regardless.

After researching ARFID myself, I had contacted multiple professionals across the UK who had experience of working with this condition. These communications confirmed that ARFID should not be assessed or treated in the same way as anorexia: that this was not merely unhelpful, but it was also harmful and risked making the situation worse. My concerns about CAMHS' approach had been validated by professionals who did have specialist knowledge of ARFID, and I believed therefore that I was right to protect my son from an inappropriate assessment approach.

Unfortunately, CAMHS did not share my view. Prior to the assessment at CAMHS, I had communications with a specialist doctor and team leader of the Eating Disorder Service. My intention was to discuss my concerns amicably, but the responses I received gave the impression that as a parent I should not be questioning their approach: that they knew better, and my opinion was completely irrelevant. All trust had broken down. This was the team my son had been sent to for support. He was struggling with his health and as his parent I believed that I had to safeguard his wellbeing, and equally safeguard him from having his care mismanaged. I also knew that if I did not proceed with the assessment Eating Disorder Service proposed, then I could be accused of obstructing my son's care. It was an impossible position to be in.

After much deliberation, I did go ahead with the assessment and made it clear at the outset that their questioning needed to be appropriate for my son. As Joe was unaware of the difficulties that had arisen with the team, I wanted to give him a chance to obtain help for his ARFID if it was possible. The outcomes of the assessment, based on the opinions of the Eating Disorder Team, was that Joe had a severe eating disorder and he was given a diagnosis of ARFID. The proposed actions were to arrange dietetic input, to arrange gastroenterology input, to have regular medical monitoring as he was considered to be 'medium risk', and he was to receive individual therapy. Due to Joe's needs and age, it was specified and agreed that therapeutic input would initially focus on relationship building only via play sessions and that direct questioning was to be avoided.

Although the assessment process had been turbulent, I was apprehensive but hopeful that the outcomes and proposed actions would be helpful to Joe. Unfortunately, this also went wrong. He attended his first play session, only to be taken into a huge meeting room without any toys and was asked questions for one hour: in other words, the opposite of what he had been informed would happen. Understandably, this resulted in the team losing Joe's trust and in him disengaging before he got started. There was confusion about who could provide dietetic input as there was no current dietician. The referral to the gastroenterologist was forgotten about (which I discovered months later). Joe's written diagnostic report specified a diagnosis of ARFID, but it appeared that the criteria used to come to this conclusion were based on the criteria for anorexia. His care had ultimately failed.

Joe did not return to this service. I was left in a precarious position as he did need to be monitored. I therefore had to raise concerns and try to secure some kind of alternative care for him.

Raising concerns

I raised my concerns with the Patient Advice and Liaison Service (PALS) to explain my family's experience of trying to access care appropriately, and of Joe's subsequent experience of attending the service. My ultimate aim was to find an amicable solution swiftly. Joe would not be returning to CAMHS, but he did need support and treatment due to medical risk factors associated with his ARFID that the clinicians had identified. I also hoped that by raising concerns it may prevent other families from having a similar experience. After discussion with PALS, I lodged a formal complaint via the NHS complaints department, which turned out to be another experience fraught with difficulties.

The complaints department was presented as being there to resolve complaints with 'transparency' and to support complainants. In reality, their actions presented the opposite vibe. The NHS have a timeframe in which to formally respond to complaints; however, the department I was dealing with repeatedly disregarded this and followed their own agenda. I received multiple evasive responses and apologies for delays, and these communications became the norm.

As the NHS perform their own internal 'investigations' and are essentially allowed to investigate themselves, this automatically puts complainants in a disempowering position and at a disadvantage considering that it holds the records that can prove or disprove a complaint. In order for a formal response to be drafted regarding the issues I raised about Joe's care, this would have required Joe's medical records held by CAMHS to be reviewed. The formal response outlined the following outcomes:

- my complaint was partially upheld on the basis of 'communication failures';
- it was agreed that alternative medical management would be set up by CAMHS;
- it was agreed that alternative treatment for ARFID outside of CAMHS services would also be set up, also to be done by CAMHS management;
- it was agreed that letters would be sent to professionals involved in Joe's care explaining that Joe had left the eating disorder service due to service failure and not due to non-engagement with services.

There was no acceptance that there had been a service failure and multiple errors were overlooked. However, at least alternative care had been promised and it was my main concern that Joe could access the appropriate care that he needed.

Months passed and none of the outcomes and proposed resolutions was put in place by CAMHS. No alternative medical management was put in place, no alternative treatment was sought, no letters were sent to any other professionals involved in Joe's care. In fact, nothing at all was done. This left my son without any care, therefore successfully failing him all over again. When I pointed this out to the complaints department, CAMHS then proceeded to attempt to set up monitoring with my son's neurologist who had no experience of ARFID with a request to organise a sensory assessment. This was not the agreed plan. Joe had already had his sensory needs assessed and spent three years within the sensory service from which he had been discharged as it had been accepted that they could not support him with ARFID (hence why he had been referred to CAMHS in the first place). CAMHS were fully aware of this and yet were going to send him around the same unsuitable system again. I had to intervene again and point out the inappropriateness of CAMHS' unagreed solution.

I then embarked on my own path of finding alternative care for Joe. I had communications with Great Ormond Street Hospital (GOSH), who agreed to accept a referral for Joe, but the referral had to be made by a paediatrician. Unfortunately, this meant that I had to rely on the same hospital to refer to GOSH. I asked that this be done, and the hospital agreed to support the referral. This, however, did not happen and I subsequently discovered that the delay was not the result of a simple omission.

This process spanned many months and during this time Joe was left without any care at all by the hospital who had informed me themselves that he needed to be monitored due to his condition. Joe was struggling. I asked the GP to monitor him on a basic level as I was not willing to fail him, unlike the local hospital who had failed him repeatedly.

I took my son's case to the Parliamentary and Health Service Ombudsman (PHSO) who agreed to investigate my complaint. This process took many months and was not straightforward. However, the outcome of their investigation upheld my complaint. The PHSO made the following findings:

- eating disorder treatment in CAMHS had been stopped due to NHS failings;
- alternative care agreed by CAMHS was not delivered;
- Joe's health was not monitored appropriately;
- Joe had been left without care while in a 'high concern' category;
- care was below expected standards and there was maladministration;
- a referral to gastroenterology had been forgotten, which was an additional failing;
- General Medical Council (GMC) guidelines in regards to documenting medical records had not been followed.

The PHSO made recommendations to the Trust to improve their services. I had no faith, and to this day, have no faith at all that services or any of the practices we encountered will be improved. I have shut down from this NHS Trust who failed my son: an NHS that then, in my opinion, proceeded to attempt to destroy my integrity as a parent and to lay the blame at my door instead of facing up to their failings and taking responsibility for them.

Information governance and medical records

I requested a copy of my son's medical records from the NHS Trust. As data is protected under the General Data Protection Regulation (GDPR), there are regulations concerning accessibility to records, including timeframes for disclosure of records and other rights, such as to rectification of records. The NHS is bound by the GDPR; however, its actions suggested that it views itself as immune to such regulations and appeared to follow no regulations at all. Its practices were evidenced by the difficulties I encountered obtaining my son's records. These included:

- multiple missing records, particularly linked to my complaint;
- 'misfiled' records across departments;
- missing medical facts, including physical examinations and treatment outcomes of consultations;
- records unsigned by health professionals involved;
- removal of my own signature from a document I sent to them;
- removal of patient-identifying details from some records;
- my 'right to rectification' requests were completely ignored.

I have considerable concerns about the many records that have factual inaccuracies, and quite specifically records that linked to my complaint. I have difficulty in believing that all of these result from simple mistakes. In addition to this, I subsequently discovered that months after raising concerns and after leaving CAMHS services due to its failures, a 'retrospective' entry was made in the relevant records: entries that, in my opinion, can objectively be characterised as parent blaming and raising the spectre of FII. This was due to the documentation referring to 'maternal anxiety' and a 'long presentation to different clinics' (these being the clinics that my son had been sent to by paediatricians, and therefore attended as a result of these referrals).

Professional Standards set out by the General Medical Council (2023) do not support the making of 'retrospective' entries months after an event. It is clear from my analysis of the relevant records and from my discussion with my GP that no concerns about my parenting or of any other safeguarding issues had been raised about me or my family prior to my complaint.

I contacted the Information Commissioner's Office (ICO) about the Trust's handling of my data request. It agreed that GDPR had been breached and issued an infringement letter to the Trust. Unfortunately, this made little difference, so gave a strong impression that, in practice, the GDPR simply does not protect medical records even if regulators become involved. In my opinion, this empowered the NHS Trust to continue violating GDPR regulations, and so it did. It became clear to me, through interactions with both the Trust and the ICO, that although it is stipulated that I had rights under the GDPR, in reality I effectively had none, and this indirectly let my son down again.

Making sense of the NHS records

As I write this chapter, I realise that I have spent several years seeking disclosure of the relevant healthcare records, analysing (and cross-correlating) the records that have been disclosed and endeavouring to understand why other records have not been disclosed. During this process, I have been given an extraordinary range of excuses as to why records (that clearly must exist) have not been disclosed. I have been told that key documents 'may have been misfiled'; that emails cannot be located; that the delays in disclosure I have experienced 'were not intentional' and I have been given documents in unreadable formats. Documents that I had been told 'could not be located' were, however, readily available (and provided) when I asked my GP. On analysis, these documents directly contradicted other records that characterised my actions as blameworthy – and this appears to me to have been the clear pattern woven by this process. Documents that contradicted the narrative of blame were not disclosed (could not be found, etc). This view was, for me, reinforced by the fact that, in some cases, I already had copies of the relevant 'unfindable' documents and could well understand why the 'system' might be reluctant for me to see them; these records which attributed no parental blame, also written by the same NHS Trust and in some instances the same clinicians, were missing.

It can be incredibly distressing to read what a practitioner has recorded about (for example) a meeting: when the practitioner says one thing, but records something quite different and when my son or I are not given any opportunity to rebut what has been written. It is even more distressing to read entries that were clearly made retrospectively. One such entry (which post-dated my initial complaint) made deeply upsetting and unfounded suggestions about my motivation and my anxiety, and the need for involvement of the safeguarding team. It is a record that touches on several of the 'perplexing presentations' detailed in the much-criticised Royal College FII guidance (RCPCH, 2021; Gullon-Scott and Long, 2022). It is a record that I believe would be understood by the health and social care practitioners who read the note as flagging up FII concerns without having the need to state this explicitly. A classic example of the secret language of parent blame used by such practitioners. I contested this documentation and was informed on multiple occasions that NHS management would respond to my concerns. This was another empty promise, as there has never been a response: a failure that I interpret as clear confirmation that this innuendo was without foundation and should never have been written. I requested that this record be rectified under the GDPR; the NHS responded to my request with deafening SILENCE.

Over this period, I have come to realise that my experience is far from unique. I have encountered many other parents who tell a similar and no less disturbing story. Time and time again, I hear of families being traumatised by the inaccuracies and allegations that they discover in their records – allegations of which they were unaware and for which they were given no opportunity to refute. Families that have had complaints about NHS malpractice upheld (as I have), only for the findings to be ignored by the NHS – with impunity; families that have had complaints about NHS malpractice upheld by the PSHO (as I have), only for its recommendations to be ignored by the NHS, with impunity; families that have had complaints about NHS failures to disclose data upheld by the ICO (as I have), only for the findings to be ignored by the NHS, with impunity. Like so many such families, I have come to realise that the NHS is unaccountable and that regulators such as the PSHO and the ICO appear to be paper tigers who lack the will (and probably the resources) to enforce compliance with their findings – and that this is something that the NHS knows full well. The injustice to people on the receiving end of this is profound and damaging.

Implications of raising concerns

This experience has taught me a number of things. I learnt a lot about NHS complaints handling and the lengths that the NHS will go to in order to avoid accountability for failings of care. Fundamentally, I learnt of the vast power imbalance between parents such as myself and the 'system': a system that has been exposed on many occasions as exploiting that power imbalance without any boundaries or conscience and which has shown itself prepared to use gaslighting and scapegoating as tools to deflect valid criticisms. For me – my understanding of this state of affairs and my experiences have forged a deep mistrust of all medical services across the board and I now can never feel any basic safety at all with services: this is not reversible.

My son has a basic right to have his medical information recorded accurately and I believe that his rights have been violated. I have a parental right for my character not to be casually undermined, without being given any opportunity to correct the record. This is the price that I have paid for raising valid concerns about my son's care.

Alongside this is the general demoralisation I have felt at being made out to be somebody I am not. It only takes one person to sow a seed (and for this to be placed on internal records read by a range of practitioners) for this to escalate. I gave up my career and postgraduate studies when my son was young so that I could be there for him and look after his needs. His needs led me into the medical system, I did not put myself there by choice. My son has a disability, and I am being blamed.

Further considerations and reflections

The problems we encountered in services predominantly occurred when my son was referred to CAMHS for an assessment for ARFID. Unfortunately, ARFID is not well known generally or among medical professionals, and this leaves open the risk of misunderstanding or misdiagnosis. Lack of knowledge of ARFID is a barrier for many families who seek care for this condition. I think this is one factor that played a part in the failures of care for my son. More research and understanding are needed to help to break down this barrier.

Organisations such as the PHSO and The Patient's Association have publicly recognised that NHS complaints procedures are often problematic for complainants who raise concerns about their own care or care of a family member, and can often come up against a strong defensiveness when attempting to resolve concerns. There have been numerous NHS scandals that have been publicised in the media, some that have not come to light until years later, and some that have had serious consequences for patients involved. It is commonly known that the foundations of these scandals lie within a deep-rooted culture to cover up mistakes, deny events and use power to manipulate records to mask the truth. I believe this is a factor that played a role in our experience too.

There is also the issue of parental blame. When I raised concerns about my son's care and consequently got blamed, I truly believed that I was the only mother who this had happened to, which pushed me further into silence. I have since discovered that I am not only one of many who this has happened to, but that unfortunately parental blame is common practice among children's services. The great work that Luke, Ana and their colleagues have done by highlighting these complex issues in this book is invaluable.

One of the points that has been raised specifically in relation to FII is that there has been a notable increase of FII referrals to social services, a large percentage of referrals are made by paediatricians and 50 per cent of these allegations are made 'after' a parent has raised concerns in some way about their child's care within services (Clements and Aiello, 2023). It seems that this is also going unchecked. For me, this flags up serious questions about true motives for making such extreme and damaging allegations and whether FII allegations are being inappropriately used as a default position in attempts to deflect or remove accountability for poor care or to cover up failings in healthcare settings. Perhaps more research is needed to understand the true nature of FII referrals. If an organisation or particular healthcare setting makes repeated FII allegations against multiple parents/families, then one would hope that this is, or should be, grounds to investigate why this is happening.

Another thought is 'safeguarding'. An FII allegation is a safeguarding concern against a parent. If a false FII allegation is made and it causes damage to a family, this will inevitably cause emotional harm to the child involved. Shouldn't this avoidable harm be considered a safeguarding concern in itself created by the professional involved? My guess is that it is not viewed this way and families will have to carry the can regardless, so allowing professionals to walk away unscathed.

I believe I was set up for FII which was triggered directly after making a complaint about Joe's care. My belief stems from the specific theme that emerged across all NHS departments – to fail to disclose records that undermined such a supposition.

I take heart in two things. Firstly, the retrospective entry I note above that gave the impression of FII also documented in the same sentence that my 'non-engagement' with services was a safeguarding concern. These two concerns are completely contradictory, so it seems that CAMHS could not make their own mind up as to what they intended to accuse me of. I view this as cracks in their professionalism and an attempt to cover their backs. Secondly, when looking back at these traumatising times, I remind myself of the following quote written by the relevant NHS Chief Executive: 'The complaints process usually runs parallel to any clinical treatment or medical support being provided to the patient to ensure consistency and continuity of care. It appears that our communication was not sufficiently joined up between the different departments involved in your child's care.' Exactly. Absolutely correct. I would like to thank Luke and Ana for allowing me to use this space to share my story, and hope that by doing so, I can contribute something to the area of 'parental blame' so that further discussions can be opened up to help and support other families who find themselves 'parent blamed'.

Lasting impact

I was never outright accused of FII and neither any member of my family nor I have been approached by or had contact with social services or safeguarding. However, the innuendo of FII became clearly evident after raising valid (and proved) concerns about my son's care and service failures. Interestingly, the NHS were transparent in wanting me to witness this documentation (as they sent it to me), while withholding records that would directly refute this innuendo. The realisation that in my opinion, I was being gaslighted by abuse of power on an intentional and collective level by medical professionals, has been wholly damaging on both parental and personal levels, which has had multiple and lasting implications. The trust and integrity that is core to any medical care, and which is also reflected in the upholding of GMC Professional Standards, has simply been obliterated for me.

However, I would like to end by saying that my son is unaware of the situation regarding the NHS and the fight to get him the care he needed.

I continued to search for appropriate care for my son and did find an independent therapist who could meet his needs. He is doing OK, and ultimately, that is all I wanted.

References

Clements, L. and Aiello, A.L. (2023) *The Prevalence and Impact of Allegations of Fabricated or Induced Illness*, Cerebra, University of Leeds.

General Medical Council (2023) *Good Medical Practice*.

Gullon-Scott, F. and Long., C. (2022) 'FII and perplexing presentations: what is the evidence base for and against current guidelines, and what are the implications for social services?', *British Journal of Social Work*, 52(6): 4040–4056. https://doi.org/10.1093/bjsw/bcac037

Royal College of Paediatrics and Child Health (RCPCH) (2021) *Perplexing Presentations (PP)/Fabricated or Induced Illness (FII) in Children: RCPCH Guidance*, London.

11

Forging an Alliance

Lucy Fullard

Our Alliance is born, not of fear, but of hope. It is an Alliance that advances what we are for, as well as opposes what we are against.
Kennedy, Address before the Canadian Parliament in Ottawa, May 1961

The beginning

Our daughter was born in 2001. She was a twin, but I lost her twin a few days before going into labour. We already knew that one of the twins would have significant disabilities, but it was the healthier of the twins that died. When I went into labour, she was rushed into the neonatal intensive care unit. We were new, young parents, and looking back there was so little care and compassion because we were immediately thrown into a system focused on process.

At the time, I thought that the care we were receiving and the way it was being given was the same for everyone. I had never experienced the world of disability before. I always believed that people looked after one another and that there were systems in place to always protect people from right and wrong and to uphold people's rights in law.

My daughter was really sick when she was a young baby and needed frequent emergency admissions to hospital and many surgeries. It was a difficult time.

Due to the complexity of my daughter's conditions, she was under lots of different teams, but they never seemed to speak to one another, and I learned very early on that I had to advocate for her and coordinate everything and that it was a full-time job on top of all the care that was required.

What seemed clear was that although there are experts in certain conditions or different departments, such as in urology or surgery or neurology, many of these teams do not seem to consider or do not like to work with other consultants. Many children with complex healthcare needs may not only have one condition. Who takes the lead in situations like this? One consultant told me that it is like having a bus with too many different drivers.

Boundaries and ownership of decision-making were often a key concern. Coordination, or rather a lack of it, and communication were extremely poor. Hospital letters sent out after clinic or on discharge from hospital would arrive many months later, and this left me having to relay information to different health teams. This was never a role that I was trained for or one that you even want to do when you are terrified for the health of your child; when you are so sleep-deprived that you almost enter a sense of survival mode; and one when I was still grieving the loss of my daughter.

When we entered the hospital system, I used to feel that we were entering a bubble and that within that hospital bubble you would get lost from the outside world. My life was nothing like other families around me. No one helped me navigate all of these different systems. I felt responsible for my daughter's disabilities, even though I was not, and when I look back now, I realise that the way I was treated was a continual reinforcement of the view that my daughter cost the public purse too much money and that this was therefore my fault. I was so lucky and blessed to be a mum to a beautiful girl who has taught me so very much; however, I can honestly say that the system has been the hardest part of the journey.

I remember on one occasion just after my daughter was born, she required a cannula to be put into her head because there was no other access to her veins at the time. To do this, they had to shave a small part of her head, with her beautiful blonde curls. I was devastated and I found this so overwhelming that I went outside after the procedure to get some air. Once getting outside the hospital, it was a normal busy day and I sat down on a bench outside crying. The professor of the foetal medicine unit that had been looking after my pregnancy happened to walk past at this point, and stopped and asked me how my daughter was doing. I told him that she was currently having a cannula in her head and his reply is something that I'll never forget. Without any warmth, care or compassion, he told me bluntly that he had offered me an abortion and then carried on walking.

Being at a hospital miles away from home was really hard, away from my support network, away from my other children, away from all the little things that are important to your life, such as access to a comfortable bed, access to a healthy meal, access to clean clothes with a washing machine that you can use any time you want. You lose control of your own lives. As a parent carer, planning became impossible. My other children always asked me, when are you coming home? It broke my heart to frequently not know the answer.

Challenging the 'system'

On one admission, my daughter was at the nurses' station colouring at their desk, and I felt that the nurses at the time were really blunt and quite cold, but I assumed that it was because they were tired, and that this is just the way they were because they were so focused on what they needed to do for their patients.

On the nurses' station was a huge file of my daughter's medical records. I remember my daughter commenting, that's got my name on it mummy! While I sat next to her, I opened the top of the records and saw on the front cover a prominent alert sheet raising safeguarding concerns about myself regarding fabricated illness. My whole body went into immediate shock. I went to the toilet shaking uncontrollably, terrified of what I had just seen and so confused as to how anyone could think so terribly of me when we were in a situation that we had absolutely no control of, whatsoever. We were entirely dependent on a system that didn't understand my daughter's needs, and yet it was seeking to blame me for symptoms they didn't understand.

This incident resulted in an upheld complaint and apology from the hospital, with the surgeons confirming, in writing, that there were no remaining concerns due to the requirement for necessary surgery.

There is so much possibility for children with complex needs to be misunderstood at any point within the system. I remember the local health visitor telling me (when my daughter, who was very premature, had just come home from hospital) that she looked like an underfed baby. The fact that she had five abdominal stomas at the time did not seem to factor into her knowledge. There was no explanation or advice given to us as new parents as to how to manage all of these differing opinions and types of expectations. The end result, though, was always parental blame.

As my daughter got slightly older, she still struggled to put on weight, and had frequent infections and also further major surgeries. My daughter was often sick and often refused food. I asked for help as we didn't know what to do. The response was always 'just give her anything she wants, even chocolate buttons, it doesn't matter; she will eat if she's hungry ...'. The hospital clearly felt at the time that I was making a mountain out of a molehill. I tried everything to get her to eat. I used to try every food, we used to play crazy distraction games while trying to feed her, but nothing worked. I remember a psychologist coming onto the ward to see my daughter and she said it was over her feeding issues. I asked her to please try herself to feed my daughter, just to see how it was. I remember she started feeding her a yoghurt. My daughter ate some spoonfuls, and the psychologist looked at me and started telling me that I was the problem. Just at that moment, my daughter started vomiting and not just a small amount, but the whole of the yoghurt and all of her previous milk feed. The psychologist stood up, left the room and went to get a nurse to clear up the mess. She didn't come back into the room, she left the ward and I never saw her again. There was no apology.

Many years later, my daughter's large bowel was removed. It was found that the muscles within the bowel couldn't coordinate and contract properly, and so had become so swollen that the bowel was then useless. It had to be removed and she was given an ileostomy. From here on in, it was so much better. Finally, we had the reason why eating had been such a problem!

When my daughter was at home, she needed a huge amount of care. It was impossible to do that on my own and so I needed carers to help, and this involved social care assessments. Social work assessments were difficult, the social worker did not understand the complex medical conditions and the process was not explained. I thought that it was like all the other different systems that you have to apply for and then my daughter's level of need would equate to a level of provision. I asked a lot of questions as I didn't understand what was happening. They didn't like me asking questions and they certainly didn't give me any information about my rights over the process or the timescales that I should expect. I found the process a hugely traumatic experience because my life was frequently examined purely because I had a disabled child and that, within the process, I had to want the social worker not only to understand the disabilities, but also to consider that I was a good parent. And I had to do this within the very short time that the social worker was with me. How hard is that? I lost count of the number of social workers we had, so that knowledge and understanding was frequently lost. When you are going through a really traumatic time, any extra stress makes life unbearable – yet, at your lowest moment, when you are dealing with such significant health issues, you're meant to find the time to lay out your life to a stranger in order to enable your child to get the care that she needs.

In 2016, my daughter was significantly unwell and required major surgery in a London hospital with two surgeons travelling across London to operate. Just before this, I had developed pneumonia and pleurisy and couldn't perform my daughters' medical procedures. I contacted the social worker to be told that she had gone on maternity leave without letting us know. As a result, a new social worker was eventually allocated, but, in the meantime, no extra help was provided despite legal letters.

I remember that I was spinning far too many plates. My husband was working very long hours to try and keep us afloat, so he could not support me at home. The continuous appointments and fluctuating health of my child was a real worry, and the inability of her school to provide the care she required meant that she was often not at school. I was in a battle with school, as it was not being inclusive: it was failing to provide the necessary support and it was not doing what it was required to do under her Education, Health and Care Plan. At a parents evening, the teacher did not know about her diagnosed learning difficulties or of the previous major surgeries that she had had. The school was simply focused on her attendance, and the impact on their statistics, and not on the reality of my child's needs.

I was exhausted from continuous lack of sleep and had a serious chest infection and was in significant pain. I had two hospital appointments prior to the social worker arriving at my house, and I had to collect my son from school at 3pm. I was rushing around; as usual, there were not enough hours in the day. I didn't have time for another appointment to lay out my family story to yet another professional, but had to jump through this hoop to try and get some more respite. I felt under immense pressure to make the house look immaculate as this was also likely to be judged, even though I was asking for more help.

When the social worker arrived at the door, at that very moment, I realised my child's stoma bag had leaked. There was a strong smell, but I knew that I needed to answer the door. I answered the door … and burst into tears. After the social worker came in, I cleaned up my child and was running out of time due to having to collect my son as the social worker had also arrived late. There had been no apology.

I remember her first question was who else could help me from my family? If that had been a possibility, then I wouldn't have asked for extra support. I felt like I was in the worst kind of job interview; the level of stress was horrendous as this person was here to scrutinise my life and had the power to rip it apart. The questioning was cold and aggressive. I was significantly unwell, and my child had major surgery coming up. I was then told that parents of disabled children must do large amounts of care and they 'just have to get on with it'. She asked me to leave the room so that they could be on their own with my child to ask them some questions. A stranger, without any medical training. I felt like I was being treated like a criminal. I didn't know what to do or where I should go in my own house. When I was called to be allowed back in to see my own child, I was asked by the social worker to show them my child's bedroom. I did so and they then left. I felt like our home had been violated. I was left bewildered, confused and devastated. No extra respite was provided.

When, finally, a new social worker visited, well outside statutory timescales, she clearly did not understand the disabilities and I was once again accused of fabricated illness. This became the defence of judicial review proceedings. At the time, we were only being given one hour of care in the morning and one hour of care in the evening at £10 per hour. There was no one that was going to come to our house with the skills and experience that was needed in complex care for £10 for one hour. They would likely pay more in petrol than they would earn for the small shift. We had to fight for a better rate of pay and more hours to meet my daughter's needs and attract anyone interested in the role.

When this was settled, extra care was provided, and an apology and retraction issued regarding the FII accusation. It was found in the subsequent complaint investigation that the social worker had only recorded information to suit her view, appeared to have been 'actively trying to make this case fit the FII criteria', was 'overzealous' and 'inexperienced'. This also included an assessment that included what I consider to be character assassination and was found to misquote health professionals and falsify information. It came out that she had even contacted professionals and questioned diagnoses at a time when my daughter was waiting for major surgery. We believe this may have caused a delay in securing the surgery date when she was in significant pain.

Our complaint was upheld through the complaints processes and then through the local government ombudsman. Prior to this, Ofsted had inspected the local authority and raised concerns over the integrity of the senior leadership team. At this time, the social worker and the team manager left the local authority.

The impact on our family has been immense throughout this experience. The whole family has suffered trauma. The fear that was experienced from individuals abusing their power will never be forgotten. It even led to us doubting our own judgements regarding our other children's health in case we were flagged as possibly fabricating anything else. We thought that the social worker and her managers would not stop until they took our children away because we were challenging the system. My son had been complaining of stomach issues and we really questioned seeking medical advice over this, such was our fear by now of the system. In the end, when he was in a lot of pain, we took him to hospital, and it turned out his appendix was failing. As they took him to theatre, it ultimately burst. Imagine if we had not taken him in!

The knock-on effect of a fabricated illness accusation can last many years as it remains on the child's and often the mother's records. The problem is that with a disabled child they often need many medical appointments and treatments and therefore this dangerous narrative can continue. This means that when a new professional takes over a case, their judgement is immediately clouded. We certainly found this to be the case and it took a lot of fighting to ensure that the local authority records were remedied, and a retraction statement was issued and an apology with a letter to all professionals involved. This painful process took almost three years.

My husband says that we needed someone to give us light, someone to give us help in one of the worst moments of our lives. When we required protection from abuse, there wasn't any. In all other areas of life, the risk of experiencing abuse is recognised – for example, abuse in the workplace, abuse by health professionals, police officers, teachers – but for reasons that escape me, there appears to be no consideration that the abuse might come from someone who has chosen to work in social work.

Forging the Alliance: the vital importance of 'independence'

'Coming together is a beginning, staying together is progress, and working together is success'

In 2017, I started a Facebook page. At the time, I was quite a social media novice. I didn't know many other parent carers. I was isolated, and I wanted to reach out and see if there were any other people who were in a similar situation to me or who needed help.

The Facebook page took off immediately and within two weeks we had over 130 families saying that they were in the same position. Within a month, we were asked to be the Local Parent Carer Forum and were offered funding. This was like a snowball effect. More and more people joined and so many families shared that they were being accused of fabricated illness. So many families had very similar issues. So many families were being treated so badly by the very systems that are meant to be supporting them.

The Department for Education (DfE) provides annual funding for one Parent Carer Forum in each local authority area in England. The funding is not available for any campaigning work (Contact, 2024) and our local authority wanted us to sign a contract that in order to receive our funding, we were not allowed to challenge them. At the time, we were told by an adviser that our role was to 'stroke' the local authority and a previous manager of carer services explained that 'in the past parent-carer voice was funded by the authority, but there was pressure not to be negative and when we said things they didn't want to hear – the contracts went elsewhere. It's vital it is independent'.

Due to the extent of the issues we had uncovered and the deep mistrust of the families of the 'system' that we were supporting, we felt that our independence of that system was essential. With no funding for the group at the time, we rejected the Parent Carer Forum agreement and the funding that came with it, and we walked away.

A broken system needs challenge to improve, or more significantly, in our experience, it needs challenge in order to want to make the effort needed to change. We knew that in order to help the families that the system was failing so badly, we needed to be independent and to be able to challenge the authority when it was appropriate (without the very real fear of losing our funding).

Independence of the system became central to our work and ethos. One family said, 'the group online is wonderful because it's the only local space that is truly independent and truly not local authority or educational affiliated, so the honesty and directness, and ability to believe in people's good faith, is fairly unique'.

An influential comment I came across at the time (sadly I can't remember who said it) was that 'to be unafraid to challenge must drive the need to remain independent. You cannot be yourself when living in someone else's pocket. The power to change and the action needed to do it, simply won't happen in the shadows and fear of towing the line'.

Being independent is literally the difference between being suffocated and stagnant or forward-thinking and free to grow. Some of the many comments made by Alliance members on the value of independence include:

- Independence is critical in order for parents to be able to trust ... it is likely that they will have experienced non independent 'support' (or lack of) before they join and therefore trust is already eroded.
- Independence gives families the confidence to share, knowing there is no judgement, only support from those with 'lived experience'.
- VERY. utmost importance. I have been let down by so many services, and my daughter has been let down by even more. And I realise that in this financial climate it is hard; however, being tied to funders who have strings attached to change things or don't allow you to support families also need to be avoided too. Need to find some monied philanthropists who just want to see things better for us.
- Independence is crucial to ensure the rights of the most vulnerable in society are not only upheld but championed too.

By rebalancing power and increasing transparency of the system and accountability, this offers protection to the families that we support and has also driven improvements locally.

Something truly magical started happening. Even though families were sharing the most terrible experiences and situations, they were helping one another navigate the systems that had affected them so badly and, in that process, they were feeling this was in some way helping their recovery from what they had experienced. Families with disabled children helping other families with disabled children; families with younger children entering the system could be guided by others; families with lived experience, understanding other people's experiences and knowing how to navigate that system. Knowing the right people to talk to, the right people who will listen. There is no guidebook for any of these different routes for equipment or support. The group was growing so quickly.

The Parent and Carer Alliance turned from a Facebook page into a community interest company in 2018, having secured some funding from independent funders, the wonderful Barnwood Trust and the National Lottery. We were able to build our community. Without this essential independent funding, we would not have been able to help so many people. The work of the Alliance started to take shape. Our first report into fabricated illness was shared across social media, local news, 'BBC Radio 5 Live Investigates' and local TV.

The Parent and Carer Alliance aims are to ensure that families whose children have additional needs:

- feel less alone, more recognised and supported;
- are better prepared and informed; and
- are able to champion getting the needs of their vulnerable children met.

We work to ensure families are given a real opportunity to have a voice in the decision-making processes which affect their lives and to feel more confident in championing getting the needs of their families met, and run events and host webinars to enable increased understanding of legislation and rights to support. In addition, we provide a service that gives practical advice on how to ensure rights to support are met and contribute valuable lived experience when working on local and national projects to improve services. We also provide safe spaces for families to meet virtually, and face to face, to share their experiences with others experiencing the same challenges, who truly understand, to alleviate loneliness and have fun.

The Alliance has now grown to over 2,100 members with 1,300 active members receiving daily support and posts on the Facebook page have increased by 76 per cent. There have been 4,775 comments and 6,702 reactions within a few weeks, over a recent busy period. At the start of last year, we faced a 159 per cent increase in requests for support.

The needs of our community of parent's carers and children and young people provide the drive and the focus for all the work of the Alliance. Their response to what we provide, in terms of attendance at events, requests for advice and support, growth of the associate and Facebook memberships, and their feedback, give the direction and scope for our future focus. One family summarises their experience of the support provided by the Alliance:

> This can be such a lonely an isolating path, and service providers tend to sound so confident when telling you something isn't possible, or won't happen, and do not even try. I love the support and kindness shown to one another by everyone in the Alliance, and the understanding of how hard it is to negotiate the services paid to support us. It means a huge amount, just knowing you aren't alone. And that's before you get into the amazing levels of specific knowledge you can access the advice given from other people's experiences too.

References

Contact (2024) 'What is parent carer participation?'. Available from: https://contact.org.uk/help-for-families/parent-carer-participation/what-is-parent-carer-participation [accessed 2 April 2024].

Kennedy, J.F. (1961) 'Address before the Canadian Parliament in Ottawa', 17 May. Available from: https://www.presidency.ucsb.edu/documents/address-before-the-canadian-parliament-ottawa [accessed 28 August 2024].

12

Conclusions: The way forward

Luke Clements, Ana Laura Aiello, Louise Arnold and Lucy Fullard

Introduction

What these many, varied and fascinating chapters tell us is that parent blame is a deep-seated, complex and gendered phenomenon. It is experienced in all manner of situations, not least in the interactions that parents have with the institutions and professionals whose support they require.

Parents have many such interactions and parents of disabled children may have many more: sometimes hundreds more and with specialists in multiple disciplines. Every negative interaction has negative consequences: trust is undermined and parents become more hesitant about further interactions. Although many parents of disabled children seek to challenge the way they are treated/categorised, they remain 'surrounded with proximal blame', and inescapably dependent on institutional and professional resources (Blum, 2015, p 240).

Every public inquiry and every media story about child neglect has ramifications – every policy designed to protect children from harm has ramifications: consequences and unintended consequences that invariably increase the number of interactions and the suspicions of state officials of parents and parents of state officials. And yet, all too often, these policy initiatives treat complex systems as simple and linear, and advocate solutions that result in disproportionately adverse consequences.

Clements and Aiello (Chapter 2) cite the Munro Review's finding (2011, para 1.16) that the cumulative impact of child safeguarding reforms had 'led to the heavily bureaucratised system' that, in effect, undermined the effectiveness of the child safeguarding system (Munro, 2011, para 1.16). What the Munro Review failed to appreciate was that its radical proposals to animate the child protection system would have unintended and adverse impacts on the system charged with supporting disabled children and their families.

Simple linear policy responses to complex problems litter the pathways that parents must tread in order to get the support that a responsive state should provide. Policies that mandate bedroom searches simply because a family seeks essential support; policies that advocate child removal on 'any iota' of evidence of harm (Zahawi, 2021); policies that treat anxious parents as abusers if they seek a second medical opinion based on internet research; policies that assume parental failings because a neurodivergent child behaves differently in school.

For many parents, particularly parents of disabled children, there is an apprehension about interactions – and for some there is a dread: a dread that if their child has a bruise – that taking her to a doctor may mean that they lose her forever through heavy-handed care proceedings – and that not taking her may be fatal – if the bruise is (as they suspect) a sign of meningitis.

Front-line practitioners working with children and their managers know that if something tragic happens to one of the children with whom they have professional interactions, then the natural tendency of the organisation and the media will be to seek someone to blame. These fears have inevitable organisational consequences – which, all too often, involve exporting the risks to families. These are disempowering relations – with each interaction reinforcing the power disparity between practitioner and parent – between the observer and the observed.

So, what then can be done?

Listening to families and children

Many common themes run through the accounts in this book. Perhaps the most important is that those responsible for the policies and practices that impact on parents should put 'listening to families' at the heart of everything they do: listening, gaining trust and responding positively. And, in turn, that all practitioners should understand how the system that parents have to navigate generates trauma: how a significant number of parents who are desperately anxious about their child's difficulties feel constantly rebuffed, belittled and intimidated by the system and by the enormous power differential it embodies. To understand that parent carers live under a microscope: they are forever being observed – the subject of the professional gaze – in all manner of settings, under a veil of suspicion that can be experienced as particularly traumatising by parents caring for children with complex disabilities.

'Trust' is a word used time and time again – as a benchmark measure of success and failure. Baker et al (Chapter 3) refer to family members having difficulties in trusting practitioners – and in consequence being cautious or rejecting even the well-intentioned initiatives – and to the downward spiral that then ensues. The families' actions engender a defensive response from practitioners who fail to grasp that this is a symptom of the family's history of being let down by services; the practitioners then label this defensiveness as problematical, which the family then interprets as yet further evidence that the practitioners cannot be trusted: thus setting up a vicious circle of mistrust and family blame.

Drayak (Chapter 9) describes how none of the social care professionals listened: that none asked her or her siblings what they thought and that in consequence they 'stopped trusting professionals': that the 'truth was we had a choice to make – we either had to trust ourselves and what we actually experienced or we had to trust strangers' – which, unsurprisingly, 'wasn't a hard choice'. Reflecting on these traumatic failings, she describes this in terms of trust: that neither she nor her siblings will ever trust professionals fully.

Amy (Chapter 10) also describes the enduring impact of the parental blame she experienced in terms of forging 'a deep mistrust of all medical services across the board' and of never again feeling any basic safety at all with services, adding: 'this is not reversible'.

Fullard (Chapter 11), when describing the genesis of the Parent and Carer Alliance, speaks of the deep mistrust of their family members of the statutory 'system'; of the vital importance of the Alliance being seen to be truly independent of that system; of the families that have previously experienced non-independent 'support' and in consequence that their trust has been eroded.

The negative impact of not putting 'listening to families' at the heart of everything that children's practitioners do is difficult to over-estimate. The impact on parents is the tip of the iceberg, when one considers the impact that this has on those who bear witness to the systems' inhumanity: the generational impact on the whole family, the children, their children and the wider family networks. If we consider instances such as the families with disabled children humiliated and alienated by the highly intrusive social care assessment process, which all too often results in the provision of no meaningful support; the parents threatened with prosecution because their neurodivergent child is traumatised by a hostile school environment and 'school refusing'; the mothers wrongfully accused of FII – and many more – we are talking about very large numbers indeed. Trust, once lost, is hard to recover.

For senior practitioners charged with reviving a failing children's service – 'reorganisation' is all too often seen as the panacea. It is simple, fast, well-tested, and almost always a failure. Building trust by listening to families, by involving families in reformulating policies and addressing past injustices takes considerable time and requires many careful changes to policies and practices. It is complex, slow and seldom attempted, but can only lead to improvements.

Reframing risk

The Munro Review spoke of the need for a fundamental review of the approach to risk in the context of child protection (2011, para 4.30). It cited the findings of a House of Commons Health Committee (HCHC) report (2009, p 9) that 'most harm was not done deliberately, negligently or through serious incompetence but through normally competent clinicians working in inadequate systems'. The Munro Review proposed a 'systems approach' be taken to the issue of 'risk' – that instead of a 'blame culture, where people try to conceal difficulties, it is better for people to discuss problems so that they can be managed or minimised' (at para 4.29).

While medical and social care practitioners were the central focus of the Munro Review and the HCHC report, the need to reframe risk has been a core theme emerging from the contributions to this book. Reframing risk in terms of pointing to the system generated failures (for example, disabled children without essential support, without equipment, without a school place) instead of considering the parents as a risk.

A 'systems approach' requires policy makers and practitioners to 'zoom out' (Chapman, 2004) and to see the wider picture. To understand the unintended harms that have resulted from the 'cumulative impact of child safeguarding reforms' and in consequence to question whether an exclusive focus on risk is indeed an effective way of 'safeguarding' children.

When thinking about the term risk, 'health and safety' is often the scenario where most people would think it applies, and the Health and Safety Executive (HSE, 2024) advises that, at minimum, this requires an employer to:

- identify what could cause injury or illness (hazards);
- decide how likely it is that someone could be harmed and how seriously (the risk); and
- take action to eliminate the hazard, or if this isn't possible, control the risk.

In the HSE's opinion, the assessment of the level of the risk is dependent upon the likelihood and the extent of harm: it is not dependent on who may be causing it. This approach is highly instructive when applied to the Royal College of Paediatrics and Child Health (RCPCH) FII guidance (2021) and to the contexts of many parent blame practices. As Bilson et al note (Chapter 6), the guidance is silent about the serious harms that can result from the misidentification of FII – its only focus is the risks posed by parents, albeit that the extent of the harm resulting from misidentification may well be far greater than the risks resulting from FII. The same observation holds true concerning the 'one-size-fits-all' assessment process for all 'children in need', that Clements and Aiello (2021) argue has the effect of 'institutionalising parent carer blame' into social care practice. In the relevant central government guidance, there is no acknowledgment that highly intrusive assessment practices that may be appropriate where there is evidence that a child is at risk of abuse – may cause disproportionate harm when applied to disabled children and their families where there is no such evidence. For many such families, the experience of seeking social care support services is negative: of barriers to assessments (refusals, misdirection and delays); of being 'risk assessed' as to the risk that they pose to their child; and of then being denied support. The current assessment process is silent as to the trauma that can result from such an approach – its focus is the risks posed by parents, albeit that the extent of the harm resulting from the 'one-size-fits-all' assessment process may far outweigh the harms it seeks to avoid.

Reforming cultures

Much has been written about the top-down managerialism that dominates the NHS, most children's services authorities and many education settings. These organisations run on a command-and-control business model predicated on the twin goals of budget management and target hitting. Despite promoting themselves as 'people first' and person centred orientated – the unspoken reality for many of those who work within or seek support from without, is that these are systems that put people second.

These are inefficient and often unpleasant environments: harmful for their workers and those who for whom they ostensibly exist to support. These are environments where, as Baker et al (Chapter 3) describe 'professionals focus on difficulties' and 'perceive families in essentially negative terms' as 'a collection of problems and diagnostic labels'. In advocating for a major shift in the way services to families are structured, Baker et al give the following example:

> a typical response when families ask for support for their child who has a learning disability is to recommend that they attend a parenting course. The implication is that their parenting skills are deficient. We need to move away from this deficit model to a more supportive investment model: we know families provide significant, often lifelong, care, support and advocacy, so it would make sense to invest in them, acknowledging and enhancing their considerable skills, expertise and knowledge and valuing them as essential partners.

A significant element in reforming unhealthy organisational cultures of this kind involves liberating front line practitioners, by encouraging them to exercise professional judgement and then respecting their decisions to (for example) provide timely services. The Munro review (2011, para 7.19) warned that organisational policies that denied practitioners such powers could have a 'disproportionate effect on child and family social work services': that this was an example of management practices having unintended, negative consequences.

In this context, Engels (Chapter 4) highlights the importance of practitioners being 'professionally curious and to question beyond assumptions'. That instead of adopting a default assumption of 'parent carers neglecting their children, fabricating their SEND and health needs [and] refusing to send their children to school' to question whether in fact the 'families need support' and whether the 'children have needs that are not being met within school?'

As Seddon (2008, p 52) has observed, a healthy (and indeed a cost effective) organisational culture is one that focuses on value – and that, counterintuitively, a focus on costs 'drives cost up'. Seddon also demonstrates that where demand appears to outstrip resources, creating administrative barriers to frustrate that demand (ie managing costs) also 'drives cost up'. People complain, people make repeat applications, staff become demoralised, families can't cope and fall into crisis and in need of hospital beds, expensive care placements, and so on. In unhealthy organisational cultures the system overshadows families and requires them to jump through all manner of hoops before even starting the process of seeking support. It leaves exhausted parents without support and then blames them for their failing to cope.

There is, in consequence, a need for health and social care organisations to be aware of the traumas experienced by many children and their families. In one sense this is now happening, with several NHS bodies and children's services authorities publishing local 'Trauma Informed Policies': publications that stress the importance of practitioners being aware that many people who have need of their support, have had traumatic experiences – for example, traumas arising out of adverse childhood experiences, domestic violence, mental health difficulties and so on. However, what these (otherwise welcome) documents fail to acknowledge is that many users of public services identify their most traumatising experiences as the way they have been treated by the public bodies that they had approached for support. There is, therefore, a pressing need for public bodies, not only to take responsibility for the harm families experience when attempting to navigate their inaccessible, siloed, systems but also to dismantle and, in line with HSE's directive (2024), to take action to eliminate this hazard – the hazard of systems' generated trauma.

Challenging the beast: power inequalities

Many of the accounts in this book, make reference to the manifest (and inevitable) power imbalance between parent and state. Payne (Chapter 5), in her conclusions, warns parents that before locking horns with local authorities or state departments – that they must 'come to terms with the fact that the state is hugely more powerful than any individual or group of individuals and that this power imbalance allows the state to mistreat individuals and get away with it'. That in consequence they need to be prepared for 'mind-bending gaslighting ...: delays, denials, silence, abdication of responsibility, buck passing, lies, promises which are broken, threats, accusations, vilification'.

Amy (Chapter 10) describes how she has experienced first-hand the 'vast power imbalance between parents ... and the "system": a system that has been exposed on many occasions as exploiting that power imbalance without any boundaries or conscience and which has shown itself prepared to use gaslighting and scapegoating as tools to deflect valid criticisms.'

Even in the most benign social welfare support system, there is no obvious way that the power imbalance between the state and the individual can be erased. The state need not be the lazy, petulant, arrogant behemoth that Payne describes, but its huge power will inevitably have a significant and intimidating impact on all who attract its gaze. In relation to child safeguarding issues, the inequality is most obviously the power of the state to remove children from their parents and its financial, legal, and administrative resources that can make contesting such action, very one sided. It also includes: its privileged access to influential networks; its ability to exploit its information advantage – its understanding of the way the system works; the status disparity of a large public body compared to a single overwhelmed parent; the power of its practitioners to record on central, widely disseminated, databases details of their accounts/narratives of interactions with the individual and so on.

There is no general duty on local authorities to ensure that parents involved in the child protection system have advocacy support and legal aid is only available once formal proceedings in the Family Court have commenced. Long (2024) refers to the sense of powerlessness experienced by parents when subjected to investigations and their lack of trust in child social workers. This, she argues, feeds into the struggle to participate in the process – such that they may effectively disengage – with the consequence that their 'non-engagement, or poor engagement, can result in an intensification and escalation of child protection involvement': that this can include children being taken into care 'not because they are unsafe or in danger, but because parents are unable or unwilling to engage with the system'. To address their sense of being marginalised/disempowered, Long proposes that (as a minimum) there be a duty to provide advocacy support for parents at child protection conference.

On a wider scale the evidence suggests that support from truly independent parent carer groups is of enormous value to parents who find themselves in conflict with a health, social care or education authority (Clements, 2020, p 104). One such group, the Parent and Carer Alliance (see Fullard, Chapter 11 above) speaks of the real difference made by its independent advocacy service – where families feel that some of the enormous power imbalance is addressed by having external validation and by providing a level of outside scrutiny of the workings of the system. The Alliance's feedback from parent carers and observation reports that the value of independent support is not limited to individual cases, vital as this is. That when parents and carers come together, they can begin the process of 'rebalancing power': by the increasing transparency of the system, by highlighting its failings and by increasing accountability. A single parent complaining about her family's experience is easily ignored or characterised as a one-off failure by an authority. However, when an independent support group prepares a report that demonstrates that the complaint is not an isolated example, but evidence of a widespread policy failure and/or a problem of the culture within the authority, this can result in systemic change – sparing individual families the ordeal of having to spend hours in front of a computer, framing a complaint and away from their children. Despite the rhetoric of 'learning from individual complaints', many public bodies don't. However, collective complaints, especially those that attract significant media coverage, can change systems. In this respect, the Alliance would point to changes concerning local procedures for FII (Siret, 2018; Cave, 2019) and special educational needs provision.

Operationalising change

Guidance and guidelines

The need for effective guidance is a refrain that echoes through many chapters in this book. A call for discrete social care guidance concerning the assessment and support of disabled children; for fundamentally revised FII guidance; for guidance concerning the retention and coding of health and social care records; for effective guidance concerning the protection of young people after peer-on-peer sexual abuse.

Good guidance is of huge importance to practitioners – in that it explains, in non-legal language, what the law requires and what in practical terms public bodies need to do. In theory, developing and publishing the fit-for-purpose guidance that these chapters have identified as necessary should be straightforward. And yet, all too often, the process proves to be tortuous and the resulting document materially defective. The RCPCH guidance on FII (2021), considered in Chapters 6, 7, 8 and 10, is a paradigm example of such a flawed process. As the relevant chapters in this book attest, the impact of this guidance has been to traumatise the very many families wrongfully accused of FII. It is guidance for which (among those who agreed to be listed as consultees) 'there is an absence of organisations representing key safeguarding bodies including social work, education, and the police' (Long et al, 2022, p 4) and contains no warnings about the harm to children and their families that can be caused by the misidentification of FII. The English Government's guidance concerning the Safeguarding of Children in Need (HM Government, 2023), considered in Chapter 2, is defective because it fails to adequately address the distinct needs of disabled children and their families. The Information Commissioner's Office (ICO) online guidance (2024) concerning the retention of health and social care records (considered in Chapter 7) is defective because it fails to explain the situations in which records should be erased (such as those that record mistaken or false allegations of FII). The guidance concerning the protection of young people from peer-on-peer abuse (Department for Education, 2018, 2023), considered in Chapter 5, is defective as it fails to explain to schools in practical terms what a school's legal duties are towards a child who makes a disclosure of peer-on-peer sexual abuse.

The origins for all of the material defects in the guidance identified in this book can be traced back to a failure to listen: a failure to take on board the feedback from parents and families as to the consequential adverse impact they are experiencing. In each case, the guidance could be made fit-for-purpose and yet in each case this has not (yet) come to pass.

As we say at the outset of this concluding chapter, one of the most important themes that runs through the accounts in this book is the need for those responsible for the policies and practices that impact on parents to put 'listening to families' at the heart of everything they do: listening, gaining trust and responding positively. In relation to the production of guidance, this requires government departments and Royal Colleges to have the bravery to encourage those individuals who are likely to be impacted by their guidance to be equal partners in its drafting.

One small example of this concerns the need for distinct guidance concerning the process by which the needs of disabled children and their families for social care support are assessed. In 2023, a group of parent carer groups grasped the nettle and prepared a working draft of what fit-for-purpose guidance of this kind should embody (Clements and Aiello, 2023). It is guidance that focuses on needs, not risks. It acknowledges that the consequences of getting it wrong with regard to safeguarding can be horrific, but it draws attention to the lack of consideration given to what happens to families when they are put through inappropriate safeguarding investigations and left without essential support.

When done well, a disability needs assessment and the provision of appropriate services can be transformative, both for the child and the family, and can open doors to other, much-needed services. Yet, for most parent carers, the experience of asking for and receiving a disability needs assessment is overwhelmingly negative – of approaching a system that 'converts the need for help into evidence of risk' (Featherstone et al, 2018, p 7).

Workforce training and new assessment templates

As Baker et al (Chapter 3) note, a typical response when an issue concerning practice failure is identified is to introduce training. They point to the fact that the evidence base for this as an effective strategy (in this field) is limited. Such studies as there are suggest that there is a 'need to be realistic about what training alone is likely to achieve' and that training is unlikely to result in change by itself (McNeish et al, 2017, p 27).

Clements and Aiello (Chapter 2) express the view that many social care practitioners would welcome training and discussion programmes concerning the reform of the process for assessing disabled children. They suggest, however, that any benefits in terms of 'systems change' are likely to be short lived: erased when the practitioners return to their offices, turn on their PCs and start completing template forms that have the effect of embedding all the parent blame assumptions that the training sought to challenge. They refer to an insight gained during their research, that 'if you want to change the system, change the computer programme'.

In this respect, Clements and Aiello discuss the major step taken by the Parent and Carer Alliance (2024) to address this key issue. The Alliance's assessment template requires assessors to make positive and supportive statements to the parent. It encourages practitioners to focus on social care needs rather than risks, and aligns the assessment process, so far as is possible, with the 'needs-led' assessment process that adult social services are required to use.

★★★

The relationship between families and the state is complex and the state obligation to respect family life is central to that relationship. It is a duty enshrined in human rights treaties, in large measure, to refrain states from exploiting the vast power differential that they enjoy. All too often, as the chapters in this book have demonstrated, the state and its privileged institutions have trampled mindlessly on the rights of families; treated the entangled complexity of this vital relationship as simple and linear; and pursued their agendas without listening to the voices of families.

The strong message that emerges from these rich and thoughtful chapters is that there is a need for the Leviathan, for the Behemoth, to tread softly: to listen to families and to react positively when it is apparent that their policies and practices are having unintended and adverse consequences.

References

Blum, L.M. (2015) *Raising Generation Rx: Mothering Kids with Invisible Disabilities in an Age of Inequality*, New York: New York University Press.

Cave, R. (2019) 'I was accused of pretending that my daughter was sick', BBC News, 11 March. Available from: https://www.bbc.com/news/health-47500686 [accessed 20 August 2024].

Chapman, J. (2004) *System Failure: Why Governments Must Learn to Think Differently*, London: Demos.

Clements, L. (2020) *Clustered Injustice and the Level Green*, London: Legal Action.

Clements, L. and Aiello, A.L. (2021) *Institutionalising Parent Carer Blame: The Experiences of Families with Disabled Children in Their Interactions with English Local Authority Children's Services Departments*, Cerebra, University of Leeds.

Clements, L. and Aiello, A.L. (2023) *Draft Guidance: Assessing the Needs of Disabled Children and Their Families*, University of Leeds.

Department for Education (2018) *Keeping Children Safe in Education: Statutory Guidance for Schools and Colleges*.

Department for Education (2023) *Keeping Children Safe in Education: Statutory Guidance for Schools and Colleges*.

Featherstone, B., Gupta, A., Morris, K. and Warner, J. (2018) 'Let's stop feeding the risk monster: towards a social model of "child protection"', *Families, Relationships and Societies*, 7(1): 7–22.

Health and Safety Executive (HSE) (2024) 'Managing risks and risk assessment at work'. Available from: https://www.hse.gov.uk/simple-health-safety/risk/index.htm [accessed 30 July 2024].

HM Government (2023) *Working Together to Safeguard Children 2023: A Guide to Multi-Agency Working to Help, Protect and Promote the Welfare of Children*.

House of Commons Health Committee (2009) *Patient Safety, Sixth Report of Session 2008–09 volume I HC 151-I*, London: Stationery Office.

Information Commissioner's Office (ICO) (2024) 'Right to erasure'. Available from: https://ico.org.uk/for-organisations/uk-gdpr-guidance-and-resources/individual-rights/individual-rights/right-to-erasure/ [accessed 30 July 2024].

Long, C., Eaton, J., Russell, S., Gullon-Scott, F. and Bilson, A. (2022) *Fabricated or Induced Illness and Perplexing Presentations: Abbreviated Practice Guide for Social Work Practitioners*, Birmingham: BASW.

Long, F. (2024) 'Why parents in the child protection system need advocacy', Community Care, 17 July. Available from: https://www.communitycare.co.uk/2024/07/17/the-case-for-parental-advocacy-in-child-protection/ [accessed 15 August 2024].

McNeish, D., Sebba, J., Luke, N. and Rees, A. (2017) *What Have We Learned about Good Social Work Systems and Practice?* Children's Social Care Innovation Programme, Thematic Report 1, Department for Education.

Munro, E. (2011) *The Munro Review of Child Protection: Final Report. A Child-Centred System (Cm 8062)*, Department for Education, London: Stationery Office.

Parent and Carer Alliance (2024) 'Needs assessment'. Available from: https://www.parentandcareralliance.org.uk/projects [accessed 20 August 2024].

Royal College of Paediatrics and Child Health (RCPCH) (2021) *Perplexing Presentations (PP)/Fabricated or Induced Illness (FII) in Children: RCPCH Guidance*, London.

Seddon, J. (2008) *Systems Thinking in the Public Sector*, Axminster: Triarchy Press.

Siret, D. (2019) 'An examination of fabricated and induced illness cases in Gloucestershire: a report from the Parent and Carer Alliance C.I.C', Parent and Carer Alliance. Available from: https://880da30b-c901-4ea4-8227-cbe012681064.filesusr.com/ugd/b664a3_a884eae7d9c24c7390db456561461c77.pdf [accessed 20 August 2024].

Zahawi, N. (2021) Hansard HC Deb 6 December 2021, vol 705, col 47.

Index

References to figures are in *italic* type.
References to notes show both the page number and the note number (121n3).

A

ABC of Child Abuse (Meadow) 77
abuse *see* child abuse; child-on-child sexual abuse
Accessing Public Services Toolkit (Clements) 72
A child like me (Bunny) 147
acts
  Children Act (1948) 7–8
  Children Act (1989) 9–11, 100, 114–15
  Children and Young Persons Act (1963) 8
  Chronically Sick and Disabled Persons Act (1970) 8
  Data Protection Act (DPA) (2018) 103, 108
  Education Act (2002) 70
  Equality Act (2010) 55, 87, 126
  Human Rights Act (HRA) (1998) 1, 12, 55, 56, 66, 67, 70, 109–10, 152n3
  National Assistance Act (1948) 7, 9, 10
  Poor Relief Act (1601) 7
ADHD *see* attention deficit hyperactivity disorder (ADHD)
adults with disabilities *see* autism; disabilities, adults with
advice for families 72–4
Aiello, A.L. 81, 85, 88, 108, 115, 118, 174, 177, 184
the Alliance *see* Parent and Carer Alliance
alliance for parent carers 170–3
ARFID *see* Avoidant Restrictive Food Intake Disorder (ARFID)
Artus, M. 114, 116
assessment processes
  challenges with current 18–19
  'child in need' assessments 10–12
  disabled-children-specific 11, 13, 18, 19
  intrusive practices 14–15
  neurodivergent families, for 132
  one-size-fits-all 16–18
  risks, need for reframing of 177–8
  stories of 7, 13, 14, 16
attendance
  barriers to 38, 39–40, 44–5
  blame for, parent carer 38, 41, 168–9
  factors to consider 46–7
  guidances on 38, 43
  Special Education Needs and Disabilities (SEND) students 38, 40, 41–2, 43, 44
  statistics 37, 45
  stories of challenges 39, 41
attention deficit hyperactivity disorder (ADHD) 130–1
autism
  attention deficit hyperactivity disorder (ADHD) and 130–1
  author's overview of 128–31
  children with, stories of 153–5, 155–6
  diagnoses 126, 129–30
  FII allegations against parents with 123, 125–8, 133–4
  masking 134–5
  neurodivergence 128–9
  parent blame for 123–4
  parents with, stories from 124–5, 130, 133–4, 136–7
  working with people with 131–6
Avoidant Restrictive Food Intake Disorder (ARFID) 155–6, 157–8, 162

B

Baker, P. 175, 178, 182–3
Bass, C. 87
Beardon, L. 129, 135–6
Benson, K.J. 127
Bettelheim, Bruno 123
Bignell, S. 130–1
Bilson, A. 9, 85, 98, 177
blame *see* parent carer blame

C

Caldicott Principles 111
CAMHS *see* Child and Adolescent Mental Health Services (CAMHS)
care plans *see* Education Health and Care Plans (EHCP)
carer blame *see* parent carer blame
The Case for Change *see* Independent Review of Children's Social Care
CBF *see* Challenging Behaviour Foundation (CBF)
Cerebra 6, 72
Cerebra survey 99–100, 102
Challenging Behaviour Foundation (CBF) 29, 33
child abuse
  'child in need' concept 9–10, 11–12, 13, 18, 114–15, 177–8, 181–2
  children's services response to 8–9

Index

parent blame and 17–18
risk factors for 16–17
see also child-on-child sexual abuse
Child and Adolescent Mental Health Services (CAMHS) 44, 155–6, 157–8, 163
child deaths 84
child homicides 8, 9, 10, 11
'child in need' concept
  challenges with 10, 11–12, 13–14, 177–8, 181–2
  Children's Act (1989) on 9–10, 114–15
  impact of 18
  see also safeguarding
child-on-child sexual abuse
  advocacy by families, ongoing 56–8, 59–60, 60–5
  guidances 55–7, 66–7, 69, 71
  legal action 53–5, 66–9
  local authorities' response to 70–2
  Ofsted review of 65–6
  responses to, government 52, 55–6, 62
  statistics 52
  stories of 51–2, 57, 58–9, 60
  training for educators 55–6
  Women and Equalities Committee (WEC) Inquiry 52, 55, 57–8, 62, 64–5
Children Act (1948) 7–8
Children Act (1989) 9–11, 100, 114–15
  see also 'child in need' concept
Children and Young Persons Act (1963) 8
Children's Commissioner
  Department of Education's 70–2
  for England 37–8, 44
children's services authorities
  child protection model 8–9, 15
  duty to investigate 100
  families on 6–7, 101, 103
  IT reform in 19–20
  review of 15–16
  see also assessment processes
children with disabilities *see* disabilities, children with
Chronically Sick and Disabled Persons Act (1970) 8
chronic sorrow 26
Clapton, G. 8
Clark, Sally 78
Clements, L. 81, 85, 88, 108, 115, 118, 174, 177, 183
Colwell, Maria 8
complaints 156–8, 161, 162, 181
complex trauma *see* trauma
Complex Traumatic Stress Disorder (CPTSD) 30
courts *see* family courts
covid-19 pandemic 40, 91

D

data *see* records
Data Protection Act (DPA) (2018) 103, 108
Davies, P. 82–3
Davis, P. 84
deaths *see* child deaths
Define Fine 43–4, 45–6
Department for Education (DfE)
  assessment tools 19
  attendance 43, 45
  Children's Commissioner 70–2
  data collected by 19, 62, 65, 99
  Parent Carer Forum 171
  support expectations of 39
  training for educators, lack of 55–6, 56–7
  see also child-on-child sexual abuse; education system
Department of Health (DH) 78–9
Department of Health and Social Care Report (2021) 15, 108
developmental disability *see* disabilities, adults with; disabilities, children with
DfE *see* Department for Education (DfE)
DH *see* Department of Health (DH)
Diagnostic and Statistical Manual of Mental Disorders (DSM-5) 80, 81, 99, 118, 126, 128
disabilities
  child law, history of 7–8, 9–12
  medical model of 7, 10
  see also 'child in need' concept
disabilities, adults with
  allegations of FII against 123, 125–8
  ongoing care of 26
  as parents 41–2, 124–5
disabilities, children with
  abuse risks of 16–17
  on attendance challenges 39
  discrimination of 12
  fine, children as 38–9, 40, 41–2, 133
  psychological wellbeing of families 26–7
  see also attendance; autism; families
discrimination
  of disabled children 12, 16, 17, 18
  of disabled parents 125–6, 127, 130
  European Convention of Human Rights (ECHR) on 13–14
double empathy problem 132
DPA *see* Data Protection Act (DPA) (2018)
Drayak, Kaydence 142–52, 176
Drayak, Taliah 86–7
DSM-5 *see* Diagnostic and Statistical Manual of Mental Disorders (DSM-5)

E

'Early Help' model 13, 47, 131–2
ECHR *see* European Convention on Human Rights (ECHR)

Education Act (2002) 70
Education Health and Care Plans (EHCP) 28–9, 46, 168
education system
  author's overview of 27–8
  duties of schools 43
  expectations of 39
  families on 42–3
  fine, children as 38–9, 40, 41–2, 133
  local authorities 70–2
  training for educators 43–4, 46–7, 55–6, 56–7
  see also attendance; child-on-child sexual abuse; Department for Education (DfE)
EHCP *see* Education Health and Care Plans (EHCP)
EHRC *see* Equality and Human Rights Commission (EHRC)
EHRs *see* Electronic Health Records (EHRs)
Electronic Health Records (EHRs) 111, 112, 113, 114, 116
End Violence Against Women (EVAW) 55
Engels, L. 179
Equality Act (2010) 55, 87, 126
Equality and Human Rights Commission (EHRC) 53, 54, 55
erasure *see* records
European Convention on Human Rights (ECHR)
  on discrimination (Article 14) 13–14, 56
  on respect for right to privacy (Article 8) 13, 14, 56, 109–10
EVAW *see* End Violence Against Women (EVAW)
'Everyone's Invited' website 65

F

fabricated or induced illness (FII)
  alerting signs 88–9, 91–2
  allegations data on 99–100, 102, 162
  attendance and 38
  autism and, parents with 123, 125–8, 133–4
  Cerebra survey 99–100, 102
  definitions of 76, 79, 92, 98, 99, 123
  as diagnosis 126
  families' stories of 43, 81, 85–6, 87–8, 100, 101, 102–3, 108–9, 127–8, 136–7, 167–70
  harm to families 85–8, 92, 101–2, 116–17, 118
  identification of, challenges with 89–91
  investigations 143–5, 148
  RCPCH guidances on 76, 79–81
  records, health and social care 85, 101, 102–3, 103–5, 106–9, 110–11

risks of 84–5
scholarship on 82–3, 83–4, 85–7, 108
sibling perspectives on 142–52
Facebook groups 170–3
factitious disorder imposed on another (FDIoA) 80, 123, 126
families
  advice for, advocacy 72–4
  alliances of 170–3
  disabilities, with 41–2
  listening to 175–6
  pathological approach to 31–2, *32*
  psychological wellbeing of 26–7
  the system, expectations of 27
  system navigation challenges 25, 27–9, 42–3
  see also stories
family courts 128, 130, 136–7, 146, 149, 180
FDIoA *see* factitious disorder imposed on another (FDIoA)
Feldman, M.D. 86
FII *see* fabricated or induced illness (FII)
Fiightback 108
fine, children as 38–9, 40, 41–2, 133
Firmin, C. 17
Fletcher-Watson, S. 129
Fullard, Lucy 14, 101, 176

G

Gaskin, Graham 110–11
Gaskin v UK (1989) 110–11
gaslighting 50–1, 70, 72–3, 163, 180
GDPR *see* General Data Protection Regulations (GDPR)
General Data Protection Regulations (GDPR) 103–4, 106, 109, 110, 113–14, 158–9
Gibson, J. 114, 116
Glaser, D. 82–3
Green, A. 41
guidances
  for attendance barriers 38, 43
  challenges with 181–2
  for child-on-child sexual abuse 55–7, 66–7, 69, 71
  for 'children in need' 11–12, 13, 115
  for data management/protection 103–5, 106–7, 109–10, 113, 182
  for needs of disabled children/families 10–11, 14, 18
  perplexing presentations (PP) guidance 81, 88–90, 98–9, 101, 108, 109, 124, 160
  'Working Together to Safeguard Children' 13, 16, 100, 131–2
  see also Royal College of Paediatrics and Child Health (RCPCH)
Gullon-Scott, F.J. 87, 108

Index

H
Halliwell, Semina 60
Happé, F. 129
Hardy, Emma 56
HCHC *see* House of Commons Health Committee (HCHC)
Health and Safety Executive (HSE) 177, 179
health system
  author's overview of 27–8
  complex needs, children with 165–6
  see also NHS England; records
homicides *see* child homicides
House of Commons Health Committee (HCHC) 177
HRA *see* Human Rights Act (HRA) (1998)
HSE *see* Health and Safety Executive (HSE)
Human Rights Act (HRA) (1998) 1, 12, 55, 56, 66, 67, 70, 109–10, 152n3

I
iatrogenic harm 85–8, 92
ICO *see* Information Commissioner's Office (ICO)
independence from the system 170–3, 180–1
Independent Review of Children's Social Care 92, 131
Information Commissioner's Office (ICO) 103, 104–5, 105–6, 107, 110, 159, 161, 182
institutions *see* social welfare institutions
Integrated Children's Services (ICS) 20
intellectual and developmental disability (IDD) *see* disabilities, children with
interviewees *see* stories

J
Jata-Hall, D. 127
Jütte, S. 9

K
Kanner, Leo 123–4
KCSIE *see* Keeping Children Safe in Education (KCSIE)
Keeping Children Safe in Education (KCSIE) 55, 66, 68, 69
Khelili v Switzerland (2011) 109

L
Legal Entitlements & Problem-Solving (LEaP) project 6
listening to families 175–6
Local Government and Social Care Ombudsman (LGO) 107
Long, Cathleen 18, 108

Long, F. 180
long covid 91

M
MacAlister, John 15
Maria Colwell Inquiry 8
masking 134–5
McClure, R.J. 90
Meadow, Roy 77–8, 80, 83–4
Meadow's Law 77, 84
medical records *see* records
Milton, D. 132
MSbP *see* Munchausen's Syndrome by Proxy (MSbP)
Munchausen's Syndrome by Proxy (MSbP)
  definitions of 126
  and fabricated or induced illness (FII) 82, 123
  harm caused by (mis)identification 85–7, 92, 148
  history of 77–8
  scholarship on 83–4
  the term *MSbP* 78–9
Munro, E.H. 9, 11
Munro Review 6, 11–12, 174, 176–7, 178

N
National Assistance Act (1948) 7, 9, 10
National Institute for Health and Care Excellence (NICE) 91
neurodivergence
  definitions of 128–9
  parents 127
  see also autism
NHS England
  complaints 156–8, 161, 162
  data management systems 111–16
  parent experiences with 154–6, 156–8
  records 102–3, 106, 107, 110, 158–9, 160–1
NHS Trust 102, 158, 159, 160

O
Ofsted 65–6, 70, 71, 90, 170
Oliver, Michael 7
Olshansky, S. 26
Opie, J.E. 31

P
PALS *see* Patient Advice and Liaison Service (PALS)
Parent and Carer Alliance 170–3, 176, 180, 183
parent carer blame
  fine, children as 38–9, 40, 41–2, 133
  institutionalisation of 8, 12–13
  overview of 6, 174–5
  secret language of 101, 108–9, 160

suggestions for addressing 31–2, 175–9, 181–3
see also attendance; autism; child abuse; 'child in need' concept; fabricated or induced illness (FII); families; records; research (2021) on parent carer blame; stories; trauma
Parent Carer Forums 171
parent carers *see* families; stories
parents *see* families; stories
Parliamentary and Health Service Ombudsman (PHSO) 158, 162
Parton, N. 8
Pathological Demand Avoidance (PDA) 134
Patient Advice and Liaison Service (PALS) 156–7
peer-on-peer sexual abuse *see* child-on-child sexual abuse
perplexing presentations (PP) guidance 81, 88–90, 98–9, 101, 108, 109, 124, 160
personal stories *see* stories
person centred care 27, 178
Phillips, Jess 56, 74
PHSO *see* Parliamentary and Health Service Ombudsman (PHSO)
Pohl, A.L. 129
policies
  on assessments (of needs/people) 10, 131
  challenges with existing 174–5, 178
  disabilities, support for people with 27–8
  on right to respect for privacy and home 14
  trauma informed 179
Poor Relief Act (1601) 7
PP *see* perplexing presentations (PP) guidance
Price, D. 130
professionals *see* training

R

Rand, D.C. 86
RCGP *see* Royal College of General Practitioners (RCGP)
RCPCH *see* Royal College of Paediatrics and Child Health (RCPCH)
records
  accessibility to 158–9, 160
  allegations in, baseless 107–9
  data protection regulation 103
  Electronic Health Records (EHRs) 111, 112, 113, 114, 116
  erasure, right to/duty to 103–4, 105, 106, 109–10, 113–14
  errors in 107
  heath system records 3, 85, 101, 102–3
  partitioning of data 110–11
  'pop ups'/system alerts 109–10, 112, 113–15, 116, 117
  rectification, right to 105–7, 160–1

social care system records 3, 102
special category data 104–5
Summary Care Records (SCRs) 84, 85, 111–12, 113–14
see also General Data Protection Regulations (GDPR)
rectification *see* records
refrigerator mother 123
research *see* scholarship; stories
research (2020) on trauma 29–30
research (2021) on parent carer blame
  author's overview of 6–7, 12–13
  findings from 18–19
  on parent carer blame 6–7
  recommendations from 15
  see also stories
research (2023) on fabricated or induced illness (FII)
  author's overview of 98–100
  survey comments 101, 102–3
risk, reframing of 177–8
Royal College of General Practitioners (RCGP) 113, 115, 117
Royal College of Paediatrics and Child Health (RCPCH)
  alerting signs of FII 88–9, 89–91, 91–2, 117
  challenges with FII guidance 177, 181
  on fabricated and induced illness (FII) 84
  guidance on FII 76, 78–81, 88–9, 98–9, 117–18, 124, 126
  perplexing presentations (PP) guidance 81, 88–90, 98–9, 101, 108, 109, 124, 160
  risk, need for reframing of 177
  scholarship on FII guidance 83
  the term *MSbP* 85
  warning signs of FII 79
Running, A. 127

S

safeguarding
  allegations against parents as 162–3
  autism, and parents with 127
  education system 69, 70, 71–2
  focus on 13, 16
  legal overview of 100
  'pop ups'/system alerts 109–10, 112, 113–15, 116, 117
  records 99–100, 101, 102–3
  risk, need for reframing of 177–8
Saugstad, O.D. 87
scholarship
  on fabricated or induced illness (FII) 82–3, 83–4, 85–7, 108
  on Munchausen's Syndrome by Proxy (MSbP) 83–4
schools *see* attendance; education system

Index

SCRs *see* serious case reviews (SCRs); Summary Care Records (SCRs)
secret language of parent blame 101, 108–9, 160
Seddon, J. 179
SEND *see* Special Education Needs and Disabilities (SEND)
serious case reviews (SCRs) 84, 85
sexual harassment/violence *see* child-on-child sexual abuse
Sheehan, L. 130
SIDS *see* sudden infant death syndrome (SIDS)
Siret, D. 85
social care system
  author's overview of 27–8
  'children in need' 9–10
  reform of 15–16
  rights and 7–8
  see also assessment processes; children's services authorities; records
social welfare institutions 1–2
special category data *see* records
Special Education Needs and Disabilities (SEND) 16, 38, 40, 41–2, 43, 44, 125
Speight, N. 87
Spine 111–12
Stilwell, L. 116
stories
  of assessments 7, 13, 14, 16
  of attendance challenges 39, 41
  of being a parent carer 124–5
  of child-on-child sexual abuse 51–2, 57, 58–9, 60
  of children's services 6–7
  of education system 42–3
  of fabricated or induced illness (FII) 43, 81, 85–6, 87–8, 100, 101, 102–3, 108–9, 127–8, 136–7, 167–70
  of good support 32–3, 44
  of parents with autism 124–5, 130, 133–4, 136–7
  of power imbalances 179–80
  of seeking support 16
  of trauma 29, 30, 33–4, 41–2
  of trust 127, 144, 150, 176
sudden infant death syndrome (SIDS) 77–8
Summary Care Records (SCRs) 111–12, 113–14
Switzerland, Khelili v (2011) 109
the system
  author's overview of 25, 27–8
  challenges with 27–9, 31–2, 178
  changing the, suggestions for 33
  complaints against 156–8, 161, 162, 181
  expectations of, families' 27
  gaslighting by 50–1, 70, 72–3, 163, 180

improving, recommendations for 179
independence from 170–3, 180–1
pathological approach to families 31–2, *32*
policy objectives of 27
risk, need for reframing of 177–8
trauma caused by 29–30
see also education system; health system; social care system

T

Talia, A. 85
training
  on data management systems 112
  educators, for 43–4, 46–7, 55–6, 56–7
  lack of 55–6
  on neurodiversity 132
  professionals, for 31–2, *32*, 43–4, 46–7
  recommendations for 137–8, 183
trauma
  definitions of 29
  fabricated or induced illness (FII) and 81, 85–7, 101–2, 127–8, 165–70, 181–2
  families on 29–30, 33–4, 41–2
  stories of 51–2, 142–52
  trust, lack of 31, 33, 144, 174, 176
  as weapon 50–1
trauma informed policies 174
trust
  importance of 175–6
  lack of 31, 33, 105, 144, 150, 174
  2021 research *see* research (2021) on parent carer blame

U

UK, Gaskin v (1989) 110–11

V

Van Gemert, M.J.C. 86

W

WEC *see* Women and Equalities Committee (WEC) Inquiry
welfare institutions *see* social welfare institutions
White, S. 19, 20
Women and Equalities Committee (WEC) Inquiry 52, 55, 57–8, 62, 64–5
'Working Together to Improve School Attendance' 43
'Working Together to Safeguard Children' 13, 16, 100, 131–2
Wrennall, L. 86

Z

Zahawi, Nadhim 6, 56
Zaremba, Zoe 105

www.ingramcontent.com/pod-product-compliance
Lightning Source LLC
Chambersburg PA
CBHW051547020426
42333CB00016B/2134